THE EGO TRIP

Psychedelic Toads, a Trail of Deaths, and the Guru Who Peddled Transcendence

Kimon de Greef

WHITE RABBIT

Published in the United States in 2026 by Doubleday,
a division of Penguin Random House LLC, New York

First published in Great Britain in 2026 by White Rabbit,
an imprint of The Orion Publishing Group Ltd
Carmelite House, 50 Victoria Embankment
London EC4Y 0DZ

An Hachette UK Company

The authorised representative in the EEA is Hachette Ireland,
8 Castlecourt Centre, Dublin 15, D15 XTP3, Ireland
(email: info@hbgi.ie)

1 3 5 7 9 10 8 6 4 2

Map illustrations by Mapping Specialists, Ltd.

Brief portions of this work appeared in different form
in *New York* magazine and *The New Yorker*.

A CIP catalogue record for this book is
available from the British Library.

ISBN (Hardback) 978 1 3996 1794 9
ISBN (Export Trade Paperback) 978 1 3996 1795 6
ISBN (Ebook) 978 1 3996 1797 0
ISBN (Audio) 978 1 3996 1798 7

Printed and bound in Great Britain by Clays Ltd, Elcograf S.p.A.

FSC www.fsc.org
MIX
Paper | Supporting responsible forestry
FSC® C104740

www.whiterabbitbooks.co.uk
www.orionbooks.co.uk

For Jenny,

with love and admiration

For that is the way of the nonhuman world. The greatest powers of the physical environment slam into the resilient forces of life, and nothing much happens.

—EDWARD O. WILSON, *THE DIVERSITY OF LIFE*

For those people who are graced with the mystical experience—whether induced spontaneously, contemplatively, or chemically—the crucial question is what to do with it.

—ROGER WALSH, "MYSTICISM: CONTEMPLATIVE AND CHEMICAL," IN *ZIG ZAG ZEN: BUDDHISM AND PSYCHEDELICS*

Contents

The Sonoran Desert and the Historic Territory of the Seri Tribe
UNITED STATES
Tohono O'odham Reservation
Tucson
Sasabe
U.S.–Mexico border
Nogales
Caborca
Altar
Hermosillo
Guaymas
MEXICO
Baja California
Gulf of California (Sea of Cortez)
Sonoran Desert
Precolonial Seri territory
Precolonial Seri range
0
100
200 Miles

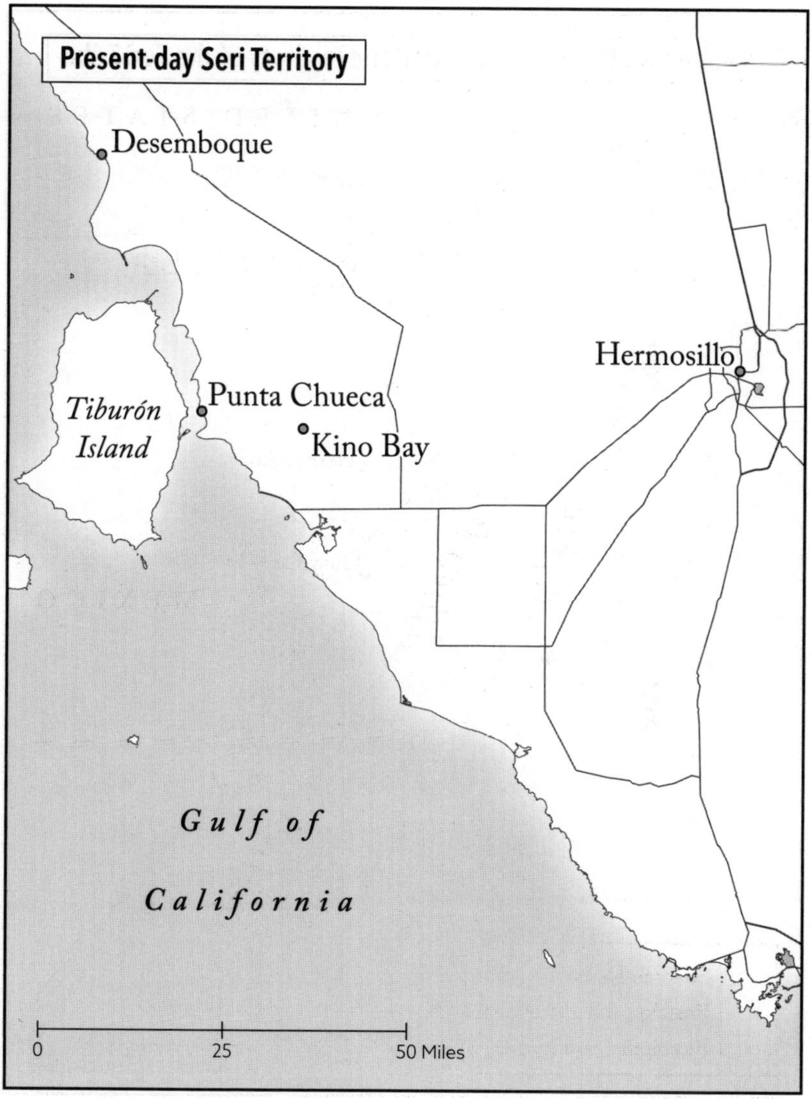
Present-day Seri Territory
Desemboque
Tiburón Island
Punta Chueca
Kino Bay
Hermosillo
Gulf of California
0
25
50 Miles

Author's Note

Substances that alter consciousness go by various names. In this book I have generally used the term "psychedelics," which means "mind-manifesting." I have also used the word "drugs," in the sense that coffee, Prozac, and the God molecule are all drugs.

Prologue

One does not lick toads. Doing so can lead to a painful death. One presses hard on their glands, which discharge explosively, like pimples. The substance that emerges is pale and viscous, hardening into brittle flakes that can be vaporized in glass pipes. This releases a powerful psychoactive compound called 5-MeO-DMT, also known as the God molecule. Its effects come on within seconds and are usually over within twenty minutes, although users frequently lose all sense of time, along with any awareness of themselves. "If most hallucinogens, including LSD, merely distort reality, however bizarrely, 5-MeO-DMT completely dissolves reality as we know it, leaving neither hallucinations nor anyone to watch them," an early adopter attempted to explain in the 1980s. Many people experience ego death—a total, obliterating loss of identity—and a sense of pure awareness familiar to advanced meditators. Others describe mystical encounters or being engulfed by white light.

In the past decade, toad smoking, as the formerly obscure practice is known, has surged toward the mainstream, helped along by a wider renaissance in the use of psychedelics. "It's gone exponential," a clinical psychologist who studies psychedelics told me in 2021. Michael Pollan smoked toad after being warned that it was "the Everest of psychedelics." Hunter Biden credited toad with keeping him clean from cocaine for a year. The former Navy SEAL who claims to have killed Osama bin Laden has spoken about using 5-MeO-DMT as a treatment for post-traumatic stress disorder. Mike Tyson rhapsodized about smoking toad on *The Joe Rogan Experience.* "I've never been the same," Tyson said. "It's almost like dying and being reborn."

The source of these cosmic sensations is the Sonoran Desert toad, a hulking amphibian from the borderlands between Mexico and the United States. Adults can reach nearly eight inches in length, with pale bellies the girth of softballs. They range in color from olive green to mottled brown, bringing to mind all-terrain military vehicles. Their skins are conspicuously smooth for a toad, with bulging glands on their limbs and necks for secreting potent defense chemicals; these are popularly called toad venom but technically classified as a poison, not being injected via a fang or sting. When threatened by predators, the toads tilt their heads downward and their rears upward, as if shielding themselves with their glands. They have been known to hiss aggressively and leap in the direction of prospective attackers. In the 1950s, a pair of biologists tested the effects of the poison by discharging it into the mouth of a puppy. The dog frothed at the mouth, convulsed, and fell over.

All toads produce toxins—one scholar has described them as "veritable chemical factories"—yet the Sonoran Desert toad is singular in producing 5-MeO-DMT. How or why this became so is still not yet fully understood. Evolutionary biology is rich in mysteries, formed slowly and incrementally by life reacting to itself: an uninterrupted sequence of adaptation and chance reaching back more than three billion years. Although dangerous to swallow, the secretions of the Sonoran Desert toad undergo a kind of alchemy when vaporized, becoming a catalyst for breakthrough states of transcendence. That such an otherworldly substance comes from a squat, earthbound creature—its scientific name, *Incilius alvarius,* combines Latin roots for "bog" and "belly"—remains one of nature's more improbable ironies.

The life history of the species is no less extraordinary. The Sonoran Desert is an inhospitable environment for amphibians, receiving about as much rain annually as the Sahara. "It is a gaunt land of splintered peaks, torn valleys, and hot skies," a writer observed in the early twentieth century. Sonoran Desert toads have porous skins that offer little more resistance to evaporation than a glass of water. To escape the heat and aridity, they hunker in subterranean burrows for up to nine months of the year, neither feeding nor moving. In summer, when violent monsoons drench the landscape, they burst from their hideouts to mate and feed gluttonously, like monks abandoning their cloisters for a season of pleasure. Their tadpoles have only a few weeks to hatch and metamorphose before the water dries up; then the toads, along with their offspring, withdraw once more into the earth.

Biologists classify the Sonoran Desert as a pulse ecosystem, with long intervals of stasis punctuated by flashes of activity. When it rains, dry riverbeds flood, swarms of ants take flight, and wildflowers unfurl new blossoms. The roots of the saguaro—the iconic cactus of the desert, with its uplifted humanoid arms—can grow three feet within a day, shooting forth to capture rainfall. It might rain for twenty minutes, and not again for two years. Signaling the turn of the season, the air sharpens with aromatic compounds like petrichor and creosote. Some scientists believe this smell of rain rouses the toads from their dormancy, others that they sense the bass vibrations of thunder. Their blunted snouts pop up through the mud, followed by blinking eyes and stubby legs. As the desert stirs to life, the toads begin to sing.

The mating call of the Sonoran Desert toad, a low, rasping hoot, has been likened to a distant ferryboat whistle. After surfacing, they hop and scramble toward each other, gathering wherever there is water—ephemeral rain pools, river washes, ditches, cattle troughs, ponds, the rocky hollows known as *tinajas.* Males clasp onto females with calloused thumb grips known as nuptial pads, squeezing them around the shoulders or armpits; they have also been known to amorously clutch at cans, bottles, and boots. Overstimulated males often grip other males in error, prompting a distinctive release call that sounds uncannily like clucking chickens. In the 1930s, decades before the psychoactive properties of 5-MeO-DMT were understood, a researcher described catching a large Sonoran Desert toad in Arizona: "How he did protestingly chuckle as we carried him off. His body under my hand was clammy with secretions."

Once the toads have successfully coupled, the females lay glistening ribbons of eggs that can stretch twenty feet or longer. What follows is a merciless race against the sun. As many as four in five pools dry up too quickly, leaving tiny eggs and tadpoles encrusted in the dirt. Those that survive must develop quickly. Toads begin life with gills and tapering bodies; as adults, they breathe air and move about on four limbs. Connecting these disparate morphologies is a passage of extraordinary change: Lungs fill out, mouths widen, tails retract. A tadpole becomes a toad, yet remains the same animal.

In many cultures around the world, toads were invested with powerful symbolic meanings. Toads were associated with witches in medieval Europe. On the Indian subcontinent they were associated with Brahmin high priests. The Bambara people of Mali believed that toads shape-shifted into mice. In Moroccan folklore, toads were said to harbor the spirits known as djinns, or genies. Toads are generally elusive creatures, seldom seen in daylight; they often conduct long seasonal hibernations. Materializing suddenly, active by night, almost supernaturally changing form—little wonder toads became fixtures of folklore and myth. Yet the Sonoran Desert toad, uniquely, would become not only a metaphor but an agent of transformation, bringing on something like psychic death.

George Orwell once described a different variety of toad, following its winter hibernation, as "having a very spiritual look, like a strict Anglo-Catholic towards the end of Lent." Immediately after mating, Sonoran Desert toads begin to eat, fattening themselves for another underground fast. They have no teeth, hunting with raptorial tongues that dart out "with such speed that the victims seem to melt into thin air," a naturalist noted in the nineteenth century. Their diet includes termites, beetles, wasps, centipedes, spiders, snails, rodents, and other toads. One of the toads was once discovered with a bullet casing in its stomach, raising the possibility, however remote, that it was witness to a shooting. Their growth rates are prodigious: A freshly metamorphosed toadlet measuring less than an inch can weigh more than a pound after three brief seasons of consumption. To accommodate their spreading bulk, they must repeatedly shed their skins, which they then swallow. "They're putting on so much biomass," a toad biologist named Brian Sullivan told me wonderingly. "Just growing like pigs."

Faced with the desert's punishing extremes, the toad not only endured but thrived for millennia, a testament to the adaptive force of evolution. But then the pace of change accelerated. The Sonoran Desert was reshaped by cities, farms, freight corridors, border fences, narco-trafficking routes, migrant trails, and myriad other human imprints. Within this altered landscape, the toad assumed a new role, becoming the source of a coveted psychedelic product. Toad collectors extracted its secretions to sell on the black market; tourists flocked to the desert in search of healing rituals; biotech entrepreneurs began developing 5-MeO-DMT into a psychiatric treatment. The Sonoran Desert toad, via the long arc of its evolutionary history, had been transformed into a target of human desire.

The chief instigator of this shift was a charismatic Mexican doctor who styled himself as a twenty-first-century shaman. He chanted Indigenous songs and proclaimed toad smoking to be "the medicine of the future." In just a few years, he catalyzed a modern psychedelic movement, propelling the toad, and himself, into popular consciousness. Yet beneath the astonishing accounts of healing he shared lay a darker and more compromising reality. For all its revelatory promise, the God molecule also held the potential for harm; more than one person I spoke to likened the substance to Tolkien's Ring, too powerful to be wielded without cost. A substance capable of inducing the most profound human experiences also opens the door to exploiting them. Such were the perils of the ego trip.

PART ONE

BREAKTHROUGH

CHAPTER 1

The Rise of the Toad Doctor

Octavio Rettig Hinojosa had a dazzling story, and he told it with messianic conviction. A Mexican physician in his thirties, he had overcome a cocaine addiction by smoking the secretions of Sonoran Desert toads, one of the most powerful psychedelics in the world. Afterward, he introduced toad medicine, as he called it, to an isolated tribe in northern Mexico, where the rise of narco-trafficking had brought on a devastating methamphetamine crisis. While working with addicts in the community, he came to believe that toad smoking was an ancient Mesoamerican ritual—a "unique toadal language," shared by Mayans and Aztecs—that had been stamped out during the colonial era. He obtained letters from the tribe authorizing him as a practitioner of this resurrected tradition, and people began referring to him as *el doctor sapo:* "the toad doctor." He cast himself as the protagonist of a global awakening, making it his mission to share toad smoking with humanity. "Sooner or later, everyone in the world will have this experience," he vowed.

In 2013, his work caught the attention of Klaudia Oliver, a TEDx organizer from Mexico. She had heard about him via a clinic in Baja California that, inspired by Octavio's example, was using toad medicine to treat addiction and PTSD. The field of psychedelic-assisted therapy was in the early stages of a revival, and Oliver, sensing an opportunity, arranged for Octavio to give a talk in her hometown of San Miguel de Allende. She coached him on public speaking and urged him to dress formally. "I don't need a shaman; I need a doctor," she thought.

Octavio was fair-skinned and bearded, with dark hair pulled into a ponytail. He had an athletic build and radiated charisma—"a man with a message," Oliver recalled. In a presentation titled "Rescue of Ancestral Healing Techniques," he spoke passionately about his healing work with toad medicine in a community where all other interventions, from conventional rehab to incarceration, had failed. He had founded a nonprofit named OTAC, which he said was a sacred Indigenous term for the toads. "This comes from the hand of nature," he explained. "From the oldest of cultures." The event was packed, predominantly with university students; at an after-party that night, people queued in long lines to smoke toad with him. Oliver hesitated to join in, unsure if she was ready to try the substance, but Octavio insisted. "He came chasing after me and threw me over his shoulder," she told me. "He was very evangelical about it."

That same month, they traveled together to Burning Man, where Octavio encountered an international audience receptive to his message. Founded in 1986, the annual gathering bills itself as an exercise in temporary community, sustained by gifting and free exchange—an antidote to the materialism and "deep unease" of American society, as the event's creator, Larry Harvey, put it. But over time, Burning Man became trapped by the very forces it sought to escape, morphing into a pop-culture spectacle dominated by the ultrawealthy. Billionaires splashed out on luxury camps with private chefs and champagne bars. Burning Man "*is* Silicon Valley," Elon Musk declared in 2014. Even Harvey expressed ambivalence about the trajectory his utopian experiment had taken. "People are afraid that when things get big, they'll be denatured," he once said. "Because, in a mass society, whenever anything gets big it becomes commodified, right?"

Twenty thirteen was the third consecutive year that tickets sold out, with close to seventy thousand people descending on the desert. Oliver's camp had organized a series of talks, "Paradigm Shift," hosted inside a vast white geodesic dome. "While change is often gradual and invisible, it can also be sudden and shocking," an invitation stated. Hundreds of people were in the audience, sitting shirtless or in bikinis; when the shelter filled to capacity, they spilled outside into the heat. Toward the end of the program, Octavio took the stage in a white linen shirt unbuttoned to the sternum. "This is the shortest way," he announced, "to understand that we are all one." He championed toad medicine as an ancestral form of healing and connection—"the ultimate experience," he called it. English was his second language, but he spoke forcefully, with expansive gestures. "We are distracted by consumerism," he said. "We don't remember where we come from, or who we are in the deepest part of our souls."

Octavio was on the cusp of becoming a "psychedelic superstar," as one clinical psychologist who studies psychedelics told me. But at the time, he was virtually unknown within the broader subculture—as was the practice of smoking toad. Scholars had speculated for decades about the existence of a psychedelic toad tradition in Mesoamerica, based on tantalizing clues from prehistoric sites. This had led, in the 1980s, to a small and secretive group of adherents experimenting with the substance, which they came to revere for its mind-altering properties. In contrast to these more cautious early adopters, Octavio favored an unapologetically maximalist approach to toad smoking, serving large, so-called breakthrough doses—strong enough to overpower any psychological defenses and induce full ego dissolution—to thousands of clients, from addicts to spiritual seekers. Many people described the experience as nothing short of life-altering. "It allows you to have a dialogue with yourself, helping you to see yourself from many different angles," Octavio once wrote, describing the substance as a "teacher medicine."

After his appearance at Burning Man, Octavio began touring the world. "It skyrocketed his popularity," Oliver recalled, describing Octavio as "the Pied Piper of toad." The cultural moment was ripe for a novel psychedelic, and within a few years Octavio had popularized toad smoking to the point where he was practically synonymous with it. He became known by his first name alone, like some pop diva or soccer star, and many of his clients venerated him—"like a god," another toad practitioner said. His influence rippled through such far-flung realms as the Sonoran borderlands, luxury spiritual retreats, and European biotech labs, all constellated around the God molecule. The first time I spoke with Octavio, in 2021, he told me that his work was "the trigger for toad medicine to be spread all over the planet."

. . .

From an early age, Octavio had a gift for persuasion that marked him as a natural leader. In elementary school, he once convinced a group of boys to give him their savings, insisting that he'd cracked how to win the lottery. "He had a very special way of convincing people," his younger brother, David, told me. (The boys lost their money.)

Octavio was born in Ciudad Guzmán, a city in the state of Jalisco, on New Year's Day in 1979. As a child he was an avid reader of science fiction, especially by Jules Verne and Emilio Salgari, an Italian author whose stories valorized pirates, barbarians, and thieves. Octavio's mother owned bookstores, and for years he worked behind the counter. He had a lively imagination and dreamed of traveling into space. His father, Werner, the son of a German immigrant, was an engineer and taught calculus at the local university. In later years, Werner developed an interest in alternative medicine, becoming a successful homeopath who was "good at marketing," David recalled. When the boys were small, Werner divorced their mother and drifted out of their lives. When their father died, in his early fifties, Octavio "was really messed up," David said. Octavio, who bore a striking resemblance to his father, later attributed his addiction troubles to Werner's absence.

The boys were raised by their mother, Bertha, who came from a strict Catholic family. A proud and enterprising woman, she enrolled them in a private school run by Jesuits. Octavio was a star student who seldom needed to study, and his friends were in awe of his intelligence. "I compared myself to other kids and tended to feel that I was more capable," Octavio recalled in a 2016 memoir, *The Toad of Dawn:*

5-MeO-DMT and the Rise of Cosmic Consciousness. "I had a big ego," he added.

When Octavio was thirteen, he spent a week at a seminary, expressing a desire to join the priesthood. "He was really excited about this spiritual life," David told me. But over the next few years, Octavio fell in with a different crowd and began experimenting with drugs. He listened to grunge and wore Doc Martens. He was good at basketball and popular with girls. One afternoon, he got drunk, smoked pot, took cocaine, and swallowed a handful of tranquilizers, waking with no memory of what had happened. Someone had run to fetch David, who found Octavio passed out in a house with "junkies sleeping on the floor, vomit and pills everywhere," he said. Octavio's school friends pulled away, and soon he was hanging out mainly with drug users. His mother was distraught; the atmosphere became so toxic at home that David moved out, going to live with an uncle in Mexico City. "There were so many fights," he told me. "It was hurting us all." Yet Octavio continued using drugs. "I wanted something more," he later wrote. "That was the feeling then: a constant search, an insatiable hunger."

With financial support from his mother, Octavio enrolled to study medicine at the University of Guadalajara in 1996, where, despite his lifestyle, he was able to obtain passable grades. There he befriended a student named Gerardo Sandoval who introduced him, over the next few years, to a prodigious array of psychedelics—including, eventually, toad medicine. During their studies, the two men embarked on a headlong spree of drug experimentation, consuming LSD, mushrooms, peyote, and other substances, often in quick succession or simultaneously. Octavio married a classmate and had a son, but the partying continued. On one acid-soaked vacation with Sandoval he fell for a petite hitchhiker in braids. After less than three years, his first marriage was over.

Like Octavio, Sandoval came from an upper-class Catholic family. He was charming and quick-witted, with sharp eyes and jet-black hair. In his telling, his birth had been accompanied by an air of prophecy:

Two months before he was due, his mother had attended a papal procession in Guadalajara where Pope John Paul II touched her belly and affectionately patted her on the cheek; her contractions began moments later. Sandoval was "raised in high society and educated in the best schools money could buy," he later wrote of his childhood. He boarded for a year at a Christian elementary school in Wisconsin, where he won various awards for academic excellence. By middle school, in addition to Spanish, he could speak English, Italian, and Japanese.

If Octavio stumbled into psychedelics, Sandoval had actively sought them out. When he was thirteen, he read about peyote, a hallucinogenic cactus used by Indigenous peoples in the deserts of central Mexico. Sandoval told his parents that he was spending the weekend at a friend's house and instead rode a twelve-hour bus to Real de Catorce, a former silver-mining settlement on the highland *altiplano* where members of the Huichol tribe had traditionally conducted pilgrimages to harvest the sacrament. Psychedelic tourists began arriving there in the 1970s, inspired by the writings of Carlos Castaneda, whose books had popularized peyote in the West. By the time Sandoval showed up, the town was thronging with seekers, including a Hare Krishna man in flowing robes who led him through his first psychedelic experience.

Back home, Sandoval started listening to the Doors and ambient electronica. He read Castaneda, Aldous Huxley, Timothy Leary, and other writers on mysticism and psychedelics. "All the kids in school thought I was a weirdo, a freak," he wrote. At fifteen, Sandoval left home and moved permanently to Real de Catorce, becoming a guide for psychedelic tourists. Three years later, following a peyote trip in which he saw himself "as a doctor, as a shaman, as a spiritual guide leading the people to the Light," he resolved to study medicine.

Octavio knew him as Gerry. There is a photograph of the two men in hospital scrubs, beaming with their arms around each other's shoulders. "His energy captivated me," Octavio wrote. They became inseparable. Among the drugs they sampled was *Salvia divinorum*, a psychoactive plant in the mint family known for its intense and unpredictable effects. On one of their vacations together, at a beach camp shaded by banana trees, Octavio rolled a salvia joint with the intention of having a good time and getting "really messed up," as he later put it. Instead, he was plunged into a terrifying emptiness and heard a screaming voice that he understood to be God. In a departure from his childhood beliefs, Octavio had been an atheist for several years but now felt himself in the presence of an all-powerful creator. "It was like being in front of the mirror and seeing my values and beliefs shattered," he wrote. He shot toward the center of the universe and heard a voice telling him, he recalled, that "if I wanted to, I had the opportunity to change my destiny and that of humanity." Like Gerry, he believed his path was being guided by divine forces. "This is not something I created with my ego or my mind," he later told me. "I received the call. I heard the voice."

When Octavio related this to his mother, Bertha, her first thought was, "Oh my God, he's lost his mind." Not long afterward, in the early '00s, Octavio and Gerry began using crack together, a period Bertha recalls as "a living death." She had fired several employees for stealing from her bookstores, only to realize that Octavio was the culprit. She acquired a pharmacy in Guadalajara for Octavio to run, but he purloined the inventory to get high and lost the business. He sold his belongings and began peddling drugs to support his habit, shedding more than sixty pounds. At one stage, he says, he was living on the streets. "I was in a rage all the time," Octavio said. "I was never in peace." This continued until 2006, when Sandoval introduced Octavio to his latest foray into psychedelics: toad smoking.

Gerry, too, had become addicted to crack—"the fall into my own abyss," he called it. But everything changed when, on a trip to San José del Pacifico, a mountain town in Oaxaca famed for its mushroom ceremonies, two American hippies served him something he'd never tried before. "I felt an enormous healing power come over my body," Gerry wrote of his first experience. "This was the beginning of my new life." Yet the Americans were secretive about the substance, saying only that it was a variety of DMT, the active ingredient in ayahuasca. Intent on learning the source, Gerry hung around them for months, sharing LSD and a potent harvest of mushrooms from a secret location he took them to. Eventually they divulged that they had been smoking the secretions of Sonoran Desert toads. In a state of obsession, Gerry read everything he could on the species and its use before turning to Octavio.

"He took out a glass bulb and put it in front of my face," Octavio recalled, "and the first thing I thought was, 'Oh no. More garbage. I'm already fucked up enough.'"

"Inhale," Gerry commanded. "Don't be afraid. This will heal you."

He lit the flame and the bulb crackled, producing acrid white smoke. "As soon as I started to inhale, the cravings started to vanish," Octavio told me. "The toad medicine, every single time, brought me back to the same place—inner peace, calmness, love."

The next summer, on a quest to procure their own supply, the two friends drove more than seven hundred miles to the Sonoran Desert. They had almost no money, just a kilogram of mushrooms and some LSD. Along the way they ran out of cash and had to scrape together a loan. They finally reached the town of San Carlos, on the shores of the Sea of Cortez, where they came upon hundreds of the toads hunting insects by moonlight. Drenched in sweat from the heat, they chased after the animals, squeezing their glands onto glass plates and allowing the sticky secretions to dry. Octavio's hitchhiker girlfriend had given birth to a daughter on the day they left; the men picked them up on their way back from the expedition. (Octavio named his daughter Salvia, after the plant that had given him visions of God.) Upon returning to Guadalajara, Octavio locked himself in a room and began smoking toad multiple times a day, sometimes in combination with MDMA, LSD, and other drugs. "I didn't know if I was about to lose my mind, die of a heart attack, or just lose it," he recalled. "But for me there was nothing else to lose. I had reached the bottom." Eighteen months later, he says, he was clean.

Intent on sharing what he'd experienced with others, he began serving toad for free at outdoor raves and among his friends. To be closer to the toads, he relocated to Hermosillo, the capital of Sonora, where he got a job as a general practitioner at a chain pharmacy. He would work there for four years. The store, situated beneath a highway overpass, catered mostly to poorer clients. "I was young, very committed, very open-minded, very honest," Octavio recalled. "And knowing the healing power of nature, I didn't poison people with pharmaceutical drugs." He told his brother he was "doing research" with toad medicine. He would see up to thirty patients at the clinic a day, giving him access to a stream of potential subjects. David recalled how, visiting Octavio's apartment, "you would sit on a couch and a toad would jump out." Octavio's mother, sensing the change in him, consented to try the substance and was so moved by the experience that she invited some of her Catholic friends to join her. "When Octavio met *sapito*," she told me, using the diminutive Spanish term for toads, "that's when he found his mission."

• • •

Octavio liked to portray himself as a pioneer of toad medicine therapy. "This was treated and used as any other psychedelic—a substance for expanding consciousness," he told me on an early phone call. "People ignored that these molecules had healing potential." But decades before him, others had explored the therapeutic uses of 5-MeO-DMT. One of the first was Ralph Metzner, a mild-mannered psychologist from Germany who had long been at the vanguard of psychedelic research. In the 1960s, Metzner had been part of a high-profile Harvard team studying LSD and psilocybin, working alongside Timothy Leary and Richard Alpert, who later became known as the spiritual guru Ram Dass. But when Leary and Alpert's work took on evangelical tones, urging mass psychedelic adoption, the university cut ties with them. Leary became a hero of the psychedelic counterculture—"the most dangerous man in America," Richard Nixon once called him—and coined the phrase "Turn on, tune in, drop out." The war on drugs began, and the entire field of psychedelic research was set back decades.

Metzner followed a different path, withdrawing from the spotlight while continuing to study expanded states of consciousness. He first smoked synthetic 5-MeO-DMT in the early 1980s, when a colleague introduced him to the substance, at the time known only on the margins of the counterculture. (Besides occurring in the wild, the molecule can be produced in laboratories.) Metzner described his first experience with the drug as "a shattering annihilation." He felt himself pulled into the "nucleus of the psyche."

"There were no feelings at all," he later wrote, "other than a kind of impersonal ecstasy. No sense of 'I'—only a sparkling sense of awe-inspiring beauty."

To avoid drawing attention from the authorities, Metzner proceeded with deliberate secrecy, sharing the substance in small, trusted groups. "I felt freed from my usual burden of aches, pains, tensions and fears," one participant wrote afterward, declaring himself "deliciously, effortlessly healed." Another experienced "instantaneous, absolute death of ego." Excited by these outcomes, Metzner began using the molecule in therapeutic settings, traveling around the United States and in Europe. One woman relived her own traumatic birth during a trip and recalled, "An invisible separation wall came down, allowing me to be in contact with life." People were flooded with joy, gratitude, love. They struggled to find words to articulate their deeply mystical encounters: with "the primal current," "the empty space that contains everything," "pure awareness."

Later that decade, after working with synthetic 5-MeO-DMT for a few years, Metzner sought out the toad itself, traveling to Arizona during the rainy season. "My personal attitude towards toads, carried over from childhood ignorance and rumor, had been a mixture of aversion and fear," he recalled. "But by the time of this expedition, my attitude had changed to admiring, even reverential." 5-MeO-DMT had already brought about some of the most revelatory and healing experiences of his life. "You might say I was prepared to worship the Toad Deity that could induce such magical experiences," Metzner wrote.

By flashlight on the outskirts of Tucson, he and two friends set out to milk the animals, which they released unharmed. Holding the creatures in his hands, he was struck by their alien physicality. "The weight and feel of them is like that of a small plucked chicken," Metzner wrote, "except that the body is very soft and yielding, and you don't really feel any bones." Rather than describe his own experience smoking the secretions, he quoted a friend's dispassionate notes: "There was no internal dialogue, ego having been dissolved."

In 2011, the U.S. government listed 5-MeO-DMT as a Schedule I substance, making its possession a crime. Two years later, Metzner published *The Toad and the Jaguar: A Field Report of Underground Research on a Visionary Medicine.* ("Jaguar" had been his code name for the drug.) "Now that 'the cat is out of the bag,'" he wrote in the book's introduction, "and the substance has attained the perverse recognition of prohibition, I feel that the time is ripe for truth-telling." He described his work with the substance and, in measured prose, concluded, "Here is an area of research on healing that if pursued earnestly and carefully could yield results of enormous benefit," including "the alleviation of physical, mental and psychosomatic illnesses and distress."

By the time Metzner's book came out, psychedelic therapy was slowly returning as an academic endeavor. One researcher who eagerly read it was Alan Davis, a clinical psychologist with an interest in addiction studies. Davis (who identifies as nonbinary) grew up in Las Vegas, where they watched friends and family members struggle with compulsive gambling and substance abuse. As a graduate student in 2013, Davis attended a conference where researchers were presenting research on psychedelics. "These are potentially medicines," Davis recalls thinking. Two years later, after reading Metzner's book on 5-MeO-DMT, Davis heard about a Mexican clinic called Crossroads that was using toad secretion for treating military veterans—the same facility that had led Klaudia Oliver to Octavio. Extraordinary reports were emerging, but the science was almost nonexistent. "When I consulted the literature," Davis recalled, "there was barely anything out there."

Anecdotally, the drug was fearsomely potent, with enduring psychological effects. Psychedelic aficionados spoke of it in reverent tones. The psychiatrist Stanislav Grof, who had pioneered the field of psychedelic-assisted therapy in the 1960s and later developed breathwork techniques for accessing altered states without drugs, tried 5-MeO-DMT for the first time and "became Consciousness facing the Absolute," he wrote. "My ordinary identity was shattered and dissolved; I became one with the Source." He believed that he had experienced the "primary clear light" that according to Buddhist teachings accompanies death.

Another prominent voice in the toad's emerging mythology was James Oroc, a barrel-chested New Zealander who had made his name as a paraglider and extreme sports journalist. His first encounter with synthetic 5-MeO-DMT, back in 2003, had shaken the foundations of his worldview. Once a hardened atheist, he emerged from the experience with unwavering faith ("a word that used to make my skin crawl") in a transcendent spiritual reality. Frustrated by the lack of serious scholarship on the substance, Oroc spent months in seclusion, reading volumes on ethnobotany, philosophy, shamanism, and other topics. He proceeded to smoke toad in the Sonoran Desert, writing afterward, "You enter a realm beyond the limitations of any human language." He introduced toad smoking to many of his friends, including at Burning Man, which he attended religiously. He eventually authored *Tryptamine Palace: 5-MeO-DMT and the Sonoran Desert Toad,* a book that helped establish the substance's reputation among psychedelic adventurers. (Prior to its commercial release in 2009, Oroc distributed copies himself, handing them out for free at Burning Man.) He became regarded as an eminence on toad smoking, especially as its popularity exploded in the years that followed, but didn't ignite a revolution the way Octavio later would: That unique combination of messenger and moment had not yet clicked into place. I was hoping to speak to Oroc, but in 2020, soon after I began my reporting, he died in a paragliding crash near the desert where Burning Man is held.

After reviewing these scattered reports on 5-MeO-DMT, Alan Davis and several colleagues set out to collect more rigorous data.

They carried out an online survey of more than five hundred users of toad secretion and the synthetic molecule, publishing a groundbreaking paper in the *Journal of Psychopharmacology* in 2018. The findings reinforced what underground practitioners had long suspected. Nine in ten respondents reported "mystical-type experiences" during their trips; almost as many reported experiencing "something profoundly sacred and holy." Among people who had struggled with substance abuse, nearly 60 percent claimed that their condition had improved—around double the success rate of more conventional therapies.

Davis, wary of overstatement, acknowledged a likely bias in these results: People with negative experiences might have been less inclined to participate. But after conducting a subsequent study at the Crossroads clinic, Davis came away with an even stronger sense of the substance's healing potential. Following a treatment protocol involving both 5-MeO-DMT and ibogaine—a hallucinogen thought to help reduce cravings—participants reported sharp reductions in suicidal thoughts, cognitive impairment, and PTSD symptoms. Most rated their trips as being among the most personally meaningful, spiritually significant, and psychologically insightful experiences of their lives.

The first formal lab study of 5-MeO-DMT in a human subject soon followed, involving a U.S. Air Force veteran who had checked into Crossroads after years of alcoholism. Prior to undergoing treatment, he would drink two liters of hard cider most nights of the week, punctuated by vodka binges ("typically a 750 mL bottle of vodka per incident"). He was also diagnosed with severe PTSD. Several hours after smoking toad, he described feeling "transformed on a cellular level into infinite energy and pure love." The experience, he said, was "deeply spiritual and healing." Three months later, he reported drinking only one or two alcoholic drinks per week.

There are various theories for why psychedelics might help treat addiction and other mental health conditions, none of them yet fully understood. Many studies have identified a correlation between mystical experiences and therapeutic outcomes, and 5-MeO-DMT, as the founder of Crossroads, a doctor named Martin Polanco, put it, is "the most reliably mystical of the psychedelics." The drug also acts unusually rapidly, with a typical trip lasting less than thirty minutes. This means that 5-MeO-DMT, in theory, could be administered at lower cost, and to more patients, than substances such as psilocybin, which remain psychoactive for up to six hours—a seductive promise for the future of psychedelic-assisted therapy, with ready appeal to investors. Even at this research frontier, Octavio's impact could be felt. "I owe my work with toad medicine indirectly to him," said Polanco, who had been introduced to toad smoking by one of Octavio's clients.

. . .

There were more immediate links, too, between Crossroads and Octavio. One of his associates had helped develop the clinic's treatment protocols; some of the toad medicine it used came from the nonprofit he'd established. Called the OTAC Foundation, it was registered in 2012 with sweeping aims: permaculture gardens, rehab centers, a "medicine bank" of toad secretion. At its core was a narrative Octavio was already promoting—that the Seri, a little-known tribe on the Sonoran coast, were the rightful custodians of toad smoking. He had begun working with them the previous year, serving the substance to local addicts, and emerged with a narrative of reviving a lost practice. "He would speak very eloquently about the needs of Indigenous tribes," recalled Ana Ortiz Bernal, a youth counselor who was one of OTAC's founding members, "and how toad medicine had saved his life."

Ortiz had first heard about Octavio in 2012. She was thirty years old at the time, with a psychology degree from Arizona State University, and had recently begun exploring the therapeutic potential of psychedelics. Her family was from Hermosillo, where she remembered hordes of Sonoran Desert toads appearing each summer, gathering in gutters and swimming pools or being flattened on the roads. It had never occurred to her that they were psychoactive until college, when a friend showed her an underground pamphlet describing their effects. When she later learned that a local doctor was using the substance to treat addiction, she felt called to seek him out.

That summer, she drove out to a traditional celebration hosted by the Seri. The tribe lives on the arid shores of the Sea of Cortez, ninety miles west of Hermosillo, and numbered fewer than a thousand people at the time, many living in poverty. When Ortiz arrived at the village of Punta Chueca, a sprawl of dirt roads and cinder-block homes, trash was blowing in the wind. She found Octavio near the shoreline, flanked by an entourage of tourists. He was shirtless and broad shouldered, with a toad tattoo on one arm and a leopard-print cuff on his wrist. His hair was swept back in a colorful headband. Without introductions or ceremony, he led the group toward a *palapa,* a thatched gazebo overlooking the water. Then he packed a glass pipe with dried flakes of secretion. "It happened so quickly," Ortiz recalled. Someone filmed her—just over five feet tall, with straight dark hair and delicate features—as she inhaled deeply, sitting cross-legged. As the drug took hold, she lay back with her arms outstretched, enveloped by a sense of peace she'd never felt before. This marked the beginning of her immersion in Octavio's world. "It was like I'd found my tribe," she told me.

Octavio was beginning to formalize a neo-shamanic approach to toad medicine, one that drew selectively from Seri traditions. Although he didn't speak the language, he memorized sacred Seri chants and would incant these during sessions, keeping time with a wooden shaker. "I could not do toad medicine without the chanting," he once said. Whereas early practitioners often served 5-MeO-DMT in quiet, introspective settings, Octavio favored a more performative style. A friend from that time recalled him "dressed in a red ceremonial Seri shirt and pants, like a Mexican Elvis, shaking his rattle and singing."

As his reputation grew, Octavio started traveling more widely, holding ceremonies for paying clients across Mexico. After a few years of offering the medicine for free, he had begun charging for sessions at the urging of one of his clients. He initially set his prices at around a third of the rate for ayahuasca ceremonies, owing to the comparative speed of a toad trip, "but toad medicine is more effective for many things than ayahuasca," Octavio told me, "so I started to feel that this was not fair for the medicine." He tripled his prices. People kept coming. The commercial appeal was plain; a single group session lasting just a few hours could bring in thousands of dollars. Mexico is home to numerous psychedelic traditions that were violently disrupted by colonial rule, from psilocybin mushrooms to morning glory seeds. Given this history, toad medicine slotted into a recognizable lineage.

In Mexico City, Octavio served toad to artists and intellectuals, earning a following among the urban elite. One early supporter was Roco Pachukote, the front man of Maldita Vecindad (the Damned Neighborhood), an iconic band from the 1980s that fused punk, ska, and traditional Mexican music. "Dr. Sapito was on a unique quest," Pachukote told me. "I wanted to help him spread it." Octavio had begun collecting images of Mesoamerican toad iconography, presenting these as evidence of a lost ceremonial past. He claimed that toad smoking had once been widespread across the region, with the Seri representing a living link to the practice. In 2013, he was introduced to a filmmaker who began shooting a documentary titled *OTAC: The Sacred Ancient Medicine Ceremony*. "The Seri community opened the doors to me," Octavio explains in one scene. "They are the ones enriching—with their ancestral knowledge, with their traditional chants and power songs—the therapy that I had been performing for years."

While Octavio became the face of the movement, others in his circle were working behind the scenes to expand its reach. During the summer monsoons, members of his nonprofit harvested the medicine, amassing a stockpile to support future ceremonies. They gathered at a ranch outside Hermosillo to smoke toad together, strategizing how to share the experience more widely. In 2013, as part of this broader ambition, Ortiz took a job at Crossroads, working to integrate toad medicine into a formal treatment program. Under Ortiz's guidance, the clinic began offering toad sessions as an adjunct therapy to ibogaine—a model that would later draw the attention of researchers like Alan Davis. She took a small container of toad secretion she'd collected; when it ran out, the clinic purchased more from the foundation, which claimed the proceeds would be shared with the Seri community and used to support toad conservation. Demand, Ortiz said, "was almost immediate and exponential." Crossroads featured on major podcasts such as *The Tim Ferriss Show,* drawing not only veterans and addicts but biohackers and wellness enthusiasts. Over time, Ortiz personally administered toad medicine to hundreds of patients.

It helped that Crossroads was located less than two miles from the U.S. border, adjacent to one of Mexico's most prestigious hospitals. The clinic, outfitted with state-of-the-art medical equipment, billed itself as "one of the first ibogaine addiction facilities in the world." Both 5-MeO-DMT and ibogaine were unregulated in Mexico, providing ready access for American patients and researchers. But the same factors that made Mexico a haven for psychedelic innovation—legal ambiguity, weak enforcement—also created opportunities for exploitation. As the clinic flourished, corrupt officials linked with local cartels began demanding protection money, threatening to close it down. One day in 2017, a group of law enforcement officers arrived at the clinic and solicited a payment of $100,000. "It was like a movie," a former executive at the clinic recalled. "They arrested doctors outside the building. They threw a patient into a van." He negotiated the fee down to $10,000 and withdrew the cash in San Diego, driving it back across the border. But the threats became impossible to ignore, and not long afterward Crossroads shut down for good. Not for the last time, the world of toad medicine had run up against Mexico's criminal economy.

• • •

Well before the clinic's closure, Octavio had become a global figure, holding ceremonies in dozens of countries. "I was booked out two years in advance," he recalled. He toured alongside ayahuasca shamans from the Amazon. His business card identified him as a "practitioner of indigenous knowledge for the whole world."

Wherever he went, clients shared ecstatic testimonials. "There couldn't be a better ambassador for *otac,*" a British man posted on Facebook. An Australian journalist smoked toad with Octavio and wrote, "The universe opened up and I drank it in." Many used a Seri word Octavio had taught them: *axatipe,* which means "thank you."

In Octavio's wake came other traveling toad practitioners, including his old friend Gerry, who had first introduced him to the medicine. Within the toad world, the two men's rapid rise to prominence became known as the Mexican Wave.

As Octavio's influence grew, so did his legitimacy. In 2014, he was a guest speaker at the World Ayahuasca Conference in Ibiza, where he served toad outside the venue. The program identified him as a "surgeon with a specialty in addictions" and a spokesman for the Indigenous communities of Sonora. "I was just very popular," Octavio told me. "Everyone was talking about the toad." More conference invitations followed—Mexico City, Zurich, Prague—and researchers began reaching out, looking to study his methods. A Czech PhD candidate named Rita Kočárová smoked toad with Octavio and became his girlfriend, accompanying him on tours and helping out during ceremonies. (By then, Octavio had already been romantically involved with several other clients, including a former beauty queen from Mexico and a New York hairstylist who reinvented herself as a psychedelic practitioner.)

Octavio's star was rising more publicly as well. In 2015, VICE made Octavio the subject of a laudatory documentary, *Getting High with a Hallucinogenic Toad Prophet.* (In keeping with the channel's gonzo ethos, the host smokes toad with Octavio on the beach and narrates being overcome by euphoria.) Octavio starred in at least three other documentaries produced by people he'd introduced to the medicine. He served toad live on Mexican television and was profiled by Spanish lifestyle magazines. In 2018, to promote another psychedelics conference, giant billboards with his brooding portrait went up across Prague. "Wherever you went, you would see him," Kočárová said.

But it was on social media where Octavio cultivated his strongest following, sharing an unending stream of promotional material. His confidence and good looks played well online, and his story—healing himself and the Seri, rediscovering an ancient medicine—proved powerfully resonant with his audience. Toad smoking, in his framing, represented a return to something pure, a rejection of the ills of modernity. Yet it also lent itself neatly to being recorded and shared online. Octavio habitually uploaded footage of his ceremonies to YouTube, where it was possible to watch rhapsodic trips unfold within minutes. Influencers began filming themselves smoking toad or narrating their journeys: "I Tried the Toad and Died," "My Sacred Rebirth," "Smoking the World's Strongest Psychedelic in Mexico." One man, emerging from his trip, maintained the presence of mind to physically point on the screen to where viewers could click through to his next video.

A broader societal shift was taking place around psychedelics, smoothing the path for Octavio's ascent. Terms like "microdosing" and "plant medicine" were poised to enter the cultural lexicon. Michael Pollan was still working on *How to Change Your Mind,* soon to become a keystone text for the psychedelic renaissance. During his research, Pollan smoked toad with one of Octavio's former clients, dubbing her the "Johnny Appleseed of toad." But if anyone deserved that title, it was Octavio himself.

In the absence of institutional gatekeepers, and with the field of psychedelic therapy still taking shape, it was possible for charismatic figures like Octavio to rise quickly. Yet what set him apart was his claim to have revived a forgotten psychedelic practice. The allure of this narrative would prove strong enough to reframe how the world spoke about toad smoking for the next decade and more. Octavio was not only presenting a treatment but insisting that he had restored a key fragment of Mesoamerican history. "If we understand the past, and we connect the past with the present," he said at one of his talks, "then we can go to a better future."

CHAPTER 2

Magical Mystery Toads

In 1935, two chemists at Tokyo's Imperial University synthesized a new molecule and unwittingly launched one of the strangest narratives of the psychedelic age. Toshio Hoshino and Kenya Shimodaira were working on a family of compounds known as the tryptamines, which occur widely in nature and have a range of intriguing biological properties. The neurotransmitter serotonin, which among other things regulates mood, cognition, and social behavior, is a tryptamine. So are many psychoactive drugs, although this would only be discovered later on. The Japanese scientists had recently completed the world's first laboratory synthesis of a molecule called bufotenine, which is produced by toads and certain species of mushrooms. Now, via a sequence of reactions, they engineered a close chemical relative. Diagrams of the two tryptamines looked nearly identical, each represented by two angular rings and a tail, resembling microscopic organisms; the only difference lay in the shape of the head. Such tiny changes in chemical structure "can lead to radically different consequences, like a railroad's

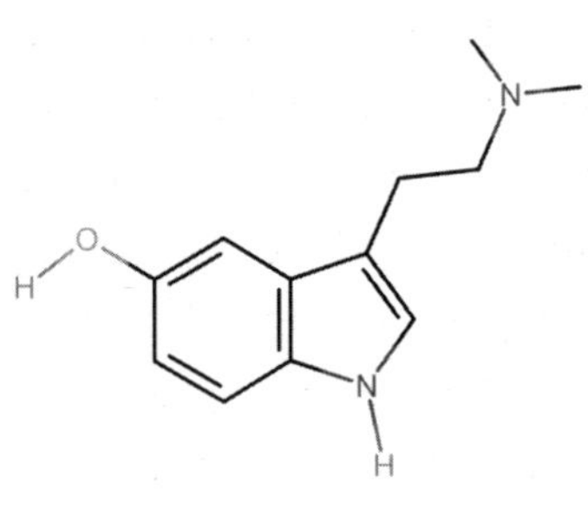

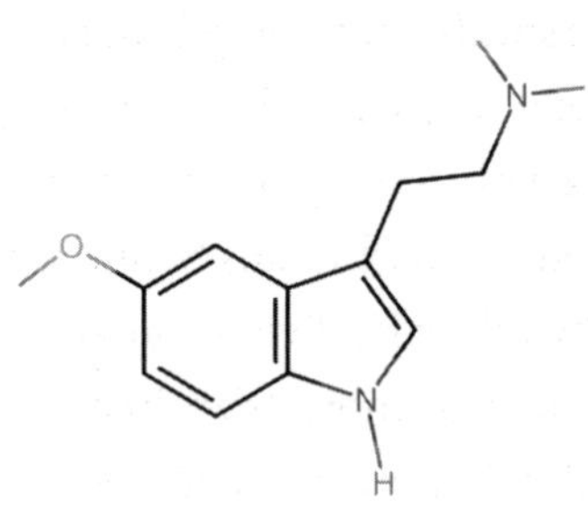

switch points," as the writer and organic chemist Primo Levi once wrote. The new molecule's name, following scientific convention, would be 5-MeO-DMT.

Hoshino and Shimodaira published their findings in the *Bulletin of the Chemical Society of Japan,* leaving no explanation as to why they had conducted these experiments. The early twentieth century was a time of wide-ranging exploration in organic chemistry, with researchers synthesizing new compounds to assess their pharmacological potential or better understand the reactions by which one substance could be transformed into another. Many of these compounds had no evident utility, such as 5-MeO-DMT, which for decades was thought only to be a product of the laboratory.

This changed in 1959, when the molecule was isolated from a shrub native to Brazil. Not long afterward, 5-MeO-DMT was detected in *Anadenanthera peregrina,* a leguminous tree from the Caribbean and South America. For thousands of years, Indigenous communities had been harvesting its slender bean pods to prepare snuffs called *cohoba* or *yopo,* which were typically inhaled using hollow bones or bamboo shoots—the earliest known use of psychedelics in the New World. "With this powder they lose consciousness and become like drunken men," Christopher Columbus observed in the fifteenth century. The Spaniards regarded such practices as demonic and sought to eradicate them as they colonized the region. After witnessing a *yopo* ceremony in the Andes, where the snuff was dispensed from a snail shell with a spoon carved from the bone of a puma, one missionary reported, "They summoned the devil."

The rich biodiversity of the Amazon also yielded other hallucinogenic snuffs containing 5-MeO-DMT. These were prepared from trees in the nutmeg family and were known, in some local communities, as "semen of the sun." In the early 1950s, a distinguished Harvard scholar named Richard Evans Schultes had documented the snuffs being used for "witchcraft, divination and the diagnosis of illness" by the medicine men of more than half a dozen tribes, describing the effects as "virulently potent." Schultes expressed incredulity that such a widely used substance had gone unstudied for so long. "It makes one wonder how many more narcotic plants, up to now obscured by better-known ones, still wait to be discovered," he wrote. These snuffs were only later found to contain 5-MeO-DMT.

A tall, bespectacled man who wore a pith helmet in the jungle, Schultes was considered the father of modern ethnobotany, a field that studies the traditional uses of plants. He was also one of the world's foremost experts on psychedelic rituals in an era before they had captured mainstream attention. In the 1930s, he had uncovered the ceremonial use of psilocybin mushrooms in southern Mexico and identified the source of an ancient Aztec sacrament as the seeds of a native morning glory vine, which contained a chemical cousin of LSD. He went on to live in the Amazon for a decade, documenting thousands of medicinal plant traditions while researching alternative rubber sources for the U.S. military. The only provisions he carried were instant coffee and tins of Boston baked beans.

Even then, Schultes recognized that incursions from the wider world threatened the survival of Indigenous knowledge. "Time is running out," he once warned. "The Indians' botanical knowledge is disappearing even faster than the plants themselves." Yet capturing this knowledge, as an outsider, was a formidable endeavor. In addition to navigating remote and inhospitable regions, ethnobotanists had to draw on scattered records from disparate disciplines—"botany, anthropology, archaeology, plant chemistry, pharmacology, history, geography and sundry other tangential fields of the sciences and arts," as Schultes put it. There was always the risk that in selecting and piecing together this information one might draw false conclusions.

In the 1960s, while Schultes was continuing his ethnobotanical research, 5-MeO-DMT was detected in numerous other plants around the world, including a type of grass that could cause grazing sheep to convulse uncontrollably, a phenomenon known as "staggers." Then, in 1964, the molecule showed up in an animal for the first time, detected in the skins of Sonoran Desert toads, a species that had formerly been of interest only to the occasional herpetologist. This breakthrough was thanks to an Italian chemist named Vittorio Erspamer. Earlier in his career, Erspamer had discovered the neurotransmitter serotonin—a pivotal moment in the field of neuroscience, laying the groundwork for understanding chemical signaling in the brain. His lifelong interest was pharmacognosy, or the study of drugs from natural sources; by the end of his career, he would identify and name more than sixty new compounds, including from octopuses, shellfish, and sea anemones, and twice be nominated for the Nobel Prize. "Land and sea are populated by a miraculous variety of creatures, representing the outcome of the tremendous biosynthetic work carried out by Nature over hundreds of millions of years," he once wrote.

No animals captured his attention like amphibians, which he described as "an inexhaustible mine of active compounds." In his laboratory, which was decorated with pictures of frogs and toads, Erspamer and his assistants minced the skins of different species with scissors and exposed them to a variety of tests: gas and paper chromatography, X-ray fluorescence analysis. Colleagues from around the world sent him samples by airmail, and in the early 1960s he received twenty-one Sonoran Desert toad specimens that had been skinned and dried in Arizona. (At the time, the species was classified as *Bufo alvarius,* a name that remains in widespread use despite being formally changed in 2006.) The findings were striking. All toads produce bufotenine, but this was the only species among some of the most chemically diverse animals in the world that contained 5-MeO-DMT.

Erspamer's study was published in a technical journal in 1965, just as the psychedelic revolution was getting started. At around this time, a small cohort of psychonauts began using synthetic 5-MeO-DMT, alerted by its discovery in South American snuffs, but it would be decades before anyone in this milieu realized that the same molecule could be obtained from a North American toad. Knowledge of psychedelic toads was fractured across niche academic disciplines, and even Erspamer appears not to have been aware that 5-MeO-DMT had hallucinogenic properties. But over the next two decades, something remarkable happened: A misleading narrative about psychedelic toads took hold, involving not only the wrong molecule but the wrong species entirely. Although 5-MeO-DMT can produce experiences of overwhelming intensity, often interpreted as encounters with ultimate truth, the history of toad smoking is riddled with false leads and misinformation.

. . .

In 1956, a psychiatrist named Howard Fabing co-authored a study in *Science,* the prestigious academic journal, about the effects of a purported hallucinogen. Like many others in his field, he had become fascinated by drugs that appeared to evoke states of psychosis, inspired by the discovery, the previous decade, of LSD. People had reported overpowering hallucinations after consuming tiny doses of acid, as the substance would become known in psychedelic culture. "My field of vision fluctuated and swam like an image in a distorted mirror," its creator, a Swiss chemist named Albert Hofmann, recalled of his first trip (during which he somehow wobbled home from work on his bicycle). Accounts like these, Fabing wrote, had "precipitated the whole field of biochemistry into a new look at the brain." Psychoanalysis had long been the dominant paradigm for treating mental illness, but now another possibility was arising. If certain compounds could seemingly induce the symptoms of insanity, then perhaps insanity was a result of faulty brain chemistry—and could thus be treated with psychiatric drugs.

Fabing's interest lay in using psychedelics not as therapeutic agents but as tools for understanding how a healthy mind could malfunction. This was seen as especially urgent in the 1950s, when around half the hospital beds in the developed world were occupied by patients with schizophrenia and other mental disorders. "The stakes are high," Fabing wrote. Scientists had begun revisiting anthropological accounts of hallucinogenic rituals—*iboga* ceremonies in Central Africa, peyote cults in the American Southwest. The term "psychedelics," was not yet in use; instead, such substances were known as psychotomimetics, reflecting an underlying belief that they induced not illumination but madness. Intriguingly, many of them shared a chemical structure with serotonin.

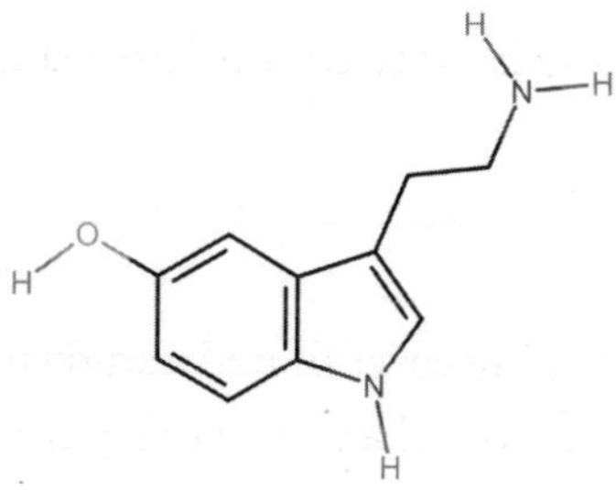

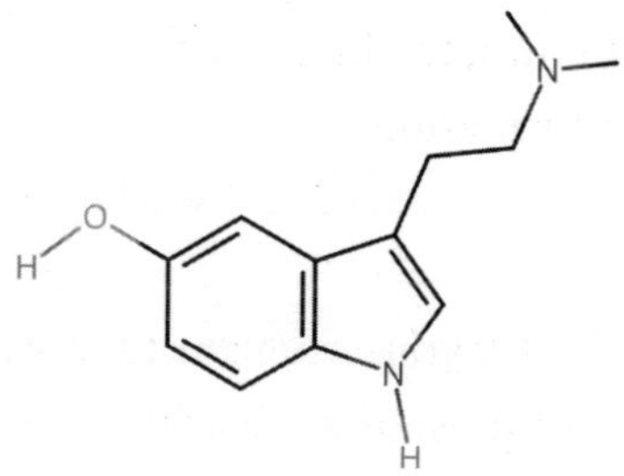

This line of inquiry had led Fabing to bufotenine, the tryptamine relative of 5-MeO-DMT that Hoshino and Shimodaira had originally synthesized. Besides occurring in most toad species, bufotenine was known to occur in fly agaric mushrooms, the iconic red toadstools of fairy tales, and thought to be the origin of the Norse *berserker* legend, involving warriors who reputedly consumed the mushrooms and entered such frenzied states that they were invincible in battle—the root of the phrase "going berserk." Separate accounts from Siberia described nomadic herders using fly agaric in shamanic ceremonies, taking pains to prolong its psychoactive effects. "The urine of persons intoxicated with fly agaric is not wasted," an anthropologist noted in 1901. "The drunkard himself drinks it to prolong his hallucinations, or he offers it to others as a treat."

Fabing hypothesized that schizophrenia might arise from the abnormal production of bufotenine in the brain, possibly instead of serotonin. To explore the compound's effects in more controlled settings, he and a colleague injected subjects with escalating doses and monitored their reactions. One man experienced a bodily numbness that he described as "a pleasant Martini feeling." Another became light-headed and reported visual hallucinations. "I see white straight lines with a black background. I can't trace a pattern," he exclaimed. "Now there are red, green, and yellow dots, very bright, like they were made out of fluorescent cloth, moving like blood cells through capillaries, weaving in and out of the white lines." Based on the results of this experiment, the scientists concluded that bufotenine had hallucinogenic properties similar to LSD.

This finding, published in a reputed journal, would later cross disciplinary lines and be picked up in the rush to solve a major anthropological mystery. Across Mesoamerica, archaeologists had unearthed a preponderance of toad artifacts, including detailed depictions of the parotid glands (located at the top of the neck) in which toads produce their defense toxins. Each of the great civilizations—the Olmecs, the Mayans, the Aztecs—had left behind extensive toad artworks: sculptures, altars, friezes, ceramics. There were middens of toad bones in what appeared to be ritual contexts, sometimes comprising thousands of skeletons. What significance had these ancient societies ascribed to toads?

In the 1970s, amid surging popular interest in psychedelics, a compelling academic theory arose: that toads had been used as ritual intoxicants, much like psilocybin mushrooms or ayahuasca. It was well established that Indigenous cultures across the region had performed healing or shamanic rituals with psychedelics. Of the psychoactive plants identified worldwide, close to 90 percent were native to the Americas, with more than a dozen psychedelic traditions documented in Mexico alone. Fabing's research had suggested that bufotenine, which occurs in many species of toads, was hallucinogenic. The pieces of the puzzle all seemed to connect.

There was also an obvious candidate species: *Bufo marinus*, more commonly known as the cane toad, a lumbering, fleshy creature that can grow up to ten inches in length and weigh as much as six pounds, a little less than a typical newborn baby. Cane toads were native to Central America, dwelling in marshlands and swamps. They corresponded to many of the archaeological depictions of toads, with bulging parotid glands, and their bones were frequently excavated during archaeological digs. It wasn't long before researchers were confidently asserting that there had been a psychedelic cane toad tradition in Mesoamerica. "The Olmecs had a predisposition for consuming toads," one scholar wrote in a book about the region's archaeology. "Consumption of these toads produces hallucinations."

Yet the theory had a glaring weakness. In addition to bufotenine, the cane toad produces an array of other chemicals, several of them acutely toxic. Its glands secrete two classes of compounds, bufogenin and bufotoxin, that can be lethal to humans even in tiny doses. Similar molecules are found in the skins of many toad species around the world and have long been used for preparing poisons. Women in ancient Rome used toad secretions to murder their husbands; sixteenth-century Italian chemists laced salts with toad toxins for poisoning the food of enemies. At English country fairs in the seventeenth and eighteenth centuries, charlatan doctors hawked medicines by feeding live toads to hired assistants, who fainted or became delirious in front of onlookers, only to revive upon swallowing whichever concoction was being advertised. The assistants survived by lining their mouths and stomachs with oil or by consuming large meals in advance. They became known as "toadies," a word that has drifted from being associated with charlatanism to its modern definition: a sycophant or obsequious helper.*

The driving question for proponents of the psychedelic cane toad hypothesis thus became how precolonial Mesoamerican cultures might have isolated bufotenine from these deadlier defense toxins. In the early 1970s, an American graduate student named Timothy Knab went searching the Mexican countryside for a healer, or *curandero*, who could provide an answer. Knab eventually came across an elderly man in the mountains of Veracruz who claimed to remember a potion that had not been used in decades. The man ground the glands of ten cane toads into a paste, added lime water and ash, then boiled the

* The dark art of toad poisoning seemingly made a return in May 2022, when a Russian oligarch whose firm had called for an end to the invasion of Ukraine died from a heart attack after visiting a shaman who served him a "hangover cure" prepared using toads. Three other senior executives at the company have since died in mysterious circumstances, presumptively at the behest of the Russian government, including a former chairman who fell out of a hospital window.

mixture overnight. This was stirred into corn beer, filtered, mixed with cornmeal, and left for several days to ferment before being heated to drive off the remaining moisture. The result was a hardened doughlike substance. The *curandero* refused to consume it and only reluctantly consented to dose Knab, who recorded the experience in dissociative terms. "Profuse sweating is noted along with a sudden increase in heartbeat," he wrote. "The heartbeat becomes continuously harder and stronger. A pronounced chill sets in with twitching of the facial and eye muscles. A pounding headache and delirium shortly follow the onset of twitching." For several hours, he lay in front of a fire, sweating and unable to move.

In a seeming blow to the theory, Knab reported no hallucinations from this experiment. But his account, which he presented at an anthropology conference in Mexico City, stirred the imagination of another young scholar. Alison Kennedy was the heiress of a wealthy Palo Alto family who would later adopt the alter ego Queen Mu and launch an influential cyberculture magazine called *Mondo 2000,* a futuristic mash-up of technology, psychedelics, and arts writing. Before all of this, Kennedy was an anthropology graduate student with an interest in Mesoamerican iconography; this had led her, almost inevitably, to the question of toads. She turned her eye to the artifacts of the Olmecs, who died out around twenty-five hundred years ago and are considered the first major civilization in Mesoamerica. Jaguars featured prominently among their artworks, which many researchers had interpreted as a sign of mythological significance. But Kennedy concluded that this had been a case of mistaken identity. Many of the artworks weren't jaguars, she argued. They were toads.

In support, she presented dozens of illustrations, focusing on what she described as "the attributes of toadiness": downturned mouths, inward-facing forelimbs, glandular swellings. She became drawn, like so many others in her field, to the idea that toads had been used in psychedelic ceremonies.

To account for the toxicity of the toads, Kennedy proposed a solution that reads like science fiction from the magazine she later founded. In addition to toads, the Olmecs had left behind depictions of many other animals, including ducks, which have highly efficient livers. Perhaps ducks had been used as bio-processors, feeding on toads and metabolizing their poisonous compounds so that humans could safely consume them. Kennedy drew attention to Olmec figurines of people wearing what appeared to be duck-billed masks. These masks would have provided protection from "venom spatters" as putative toad shamans "stood at their toad altars lancing the parotid glands," she posited. This relied on the assumption that ducks could eat toads without being poisoned themselves. To investigate further, Kennedy visited a zoo in Texas, where she and the head aviculturist flung some cane toads into a duck pond. The ducks had been reared in captivity and were "toad-naive," as Kennedy wrote, yet they pursued the toads with avidity, juggling their soft bodies before gulping them down. Kennedy described this behavior as "singular and apparently wholly instinctive." Duck bills have neither nerve endings for sensing toad toxins nor blood vessels for absorbing them; the juggling movements were conceivably an adaptation for rinsing poisons into the water. Two of the duck species in the pond happened to be native to Mexico, home of both the Olmec culture and *Bufo marinus.* Here, at least, was proof that ducks had an appetite for the toads.

Now Kennedy took her suppositions even further, reexamining the literature on a famous Olmec site where thousands of toad skeletons had been excavated. The ruins featured an elaborate system of water channels hewn from some three hundred tons of rock, running between a sculpture of a jaguar (or possibly a toad) and an enormous stone receptacle in the shape of a duck. The main channel drained into a series of smaller pools too shallow for human bathing; confounded researchers had guessed that they were for unspecified "ritual use." With a flourish, Kennedy now presented her final claim: That this complex hydraulic system had been designed as an integrated bufo-culture station, including both spawning grounds for toads and a captive population of bio-processing ducks. These bold ideas won her a prize at an anthropology conference in 1979, but there was one problem: No one had taken the obvious next step and tested whether the duck livers were in fact hallucinogenic. For all the scholarly attention it had garnered, the mystery of the psychedelic toad remained unresolved.

. . .

In the early 1980s, after reading about Fabing's bufotenine study, a British artist named Adrian Morgan began a series of personal experiments with toads. These included "licking poison glands, rubbing animals against my forehead, and in one instance collecting venom with blotting paper . . . and then eating the paper," he reported. Disappointingly, Morgan experienced no hallucinations from these tests, which seemed only to aggravate his research subjects. "One specimen of green toad showed its disgust by leaping from an open window into the celery patch below me," he wrote. "It was never seen again."

One spring, Morgan visited a forest outside London and came upon two dead female toads in a pond. He took them home, where he pounded their skins and poison glands in a mortar. Then he snuffed the residue and took notes in an increasingly jagged hand:

> *3:41 P.M. First quantity ingested into right nostril. Within one minute, nostril strongly anesthetized.*
> *3:49 Sneezing violently, profuse sweating of forehead.*
> *4:03 Fleeting pain at temples.*
> *4:05 Salivating strongly.*
> *4:15 Thick saliva at back of throat causing tendency to gag.*
> *4:32 Feeling very tired.*

Midway through, colors briefly appeared richer and moving objects left trails in his vision, like speed blurs. Morgan described these sensations as "only slightly psychedelic" and concluded, "The experience was not pleasant."

Yet the notion of hallucinogenic toads persisted, cropping up in stranger contexts still. While Morgan was pursuing his investigations, stories of psychedelic cane toad use began surfacing in Australia, of all places, where the animals had been introduced in the 1930s to control pests on plantations. The toads had gone rogue, consuming native frogs, birds, insects, small marsupials, even Ping-Pong balls and cigarette butts flicked toward them at pubs—almost everything except the swarms of sugarcane beetles they had been imported to feed on. Australia's plague of beetles had been compounded by a plague of toads.

This was possible in large part because toads are opportunistic and superbly adaptable creatures. They are residents of the gutter, the verge, the ditch. They can hunker down when times are bad and burst to life when conditions favor them. They are capable of producing millions of eggs. In their present form, toads have existed for at least thirty million years, enduring all kinds of planetary upheaval, from ice ages to the rise of humans. Released onto a new continent, the cane toads marauded unstoppably.

In the 1980s, fifty years into the invasion, an Australian filmmaker named Mark Lewis began working on a satirical documentary, *Cane Toads: An Unnatural History,* which Werner Herzog later declared to be his favorite film of all time. Hundreds of millions of the animals had taken up residence across Australia's east coast, expanding their occupied range at a rate of more than fifteen miles annually. Researchers dubbed the toads "an amphibian weed." Streets were slicked with flattened toad carcasses, which emitted a fishy aroma. Bands of vigilantes went after the animals with cricket bats or swerved deliberately to run them over, but the toads continued their relentless spread.

During his research for the film, Lewis picked up on a rumor that people were getting high on the toads. He ended up speaking by phone with a man who claimed to have been in prison, where the inmates "would race to grab a toad if it found its way inside the compound," Lewis told me. His source was unwilling to appear on camera, so Lewis hired an actor to deliver the lines. "You use a little quantity at first, then larger," the man mumbles in the film, which identifies him as a "cane toad drug abuser" from the town of Mullumbimby. He makes a reference to Carlos Castaneda's writings, saying how users of peyote would "see the world through the consciousness of the cactus." With a weak laugh, the man adds, "The toad's the same."

The documentary also features a detective from Queensland who attests that people in "hippie communes" have been tripping on cane toads since at least the 1970s. "When heroin and other drugs weren't freely available, the next best alternative was to go out and get a cane toad," the detective explains. These toads would be boiled down in billycans to produce a sludgy brew, which the hippies purportedly drank. "From what I've been told, they had fantastic color hallucinations," the detective says. "It warped their sense of time."

Australians have a certain reputation for toughness, but even the hardiest among them would likely have been poisoned by the bufotoxins in this recipe. Yet Lewis also heard about a more plausible mode of ingestion. A local narcotics squad was said to possess a jar of confiscated dried cane toad skins that could be "shredded and put into a hookah or a pipe and smoked," apparently causing intense hallucinatory effects. At one point during his research ("to see what all the fuss was about") Lewis rolled a small quantity with tobacco into a joint. "I smoked it, and the only result was that I got a bad headache," he told me. "I would not recommend that kids try this at home."

But in 1988, the year Lewis's film came out, a moral panic began that swept the concept of psychedelic toads into popular culture. "I feel partly responsible," Lewis told me decades later, sounding mystified. This strange sequence began with media reports in the United States of Australian hippies "forsaking traditional drugs for cane toads, which they boil for a slimy, potentially lethal cocktail." Later that year, a doctor at the Haight Ashbury Free Clinic, a San Francisco drug treatment facility established during the Summer of Love, jokingly mentioned the "rare 1960s practice of toad licking" during a lecture. Afterward, the clinic was inundated with calls from reporters around the world, wanting to know about "crazed hippies licking toads in the mountains," as the clinic's director later recalled. Staff assured the journalists that there was no evidence of toads being licked in the United States, but the idea, like some invasive animal, took on a life of its own. At a conference on crack cocaine the following year, the Berkeley police chief announced that toad licking was a "problem that comes up from time to time." An official from the Drug Enforcement Administration was quoted saying that cane toad secretions were "in the same (legal) category as heroin or LSD." Bufotenine had indeed been listed as a Schedule I substance in 1967—even though, at the time, there had been virtually no reports of anybody using it. Citing the DEA, news articles now declared toad licking "the latest way to hallucinate." (One headline: "A Desperation High: Crack? Coke? Croak!") The DEA official later clarified that he had said nothing about toad licking, but the phrase continued spawning fresh rounds of coverage until, as *Scientific American* later put it, "reality imitated fiction."

In 1989, two teenagers were hospitalized in New Mexico after licking toads, which they had read about in the papers. The following year, two men were admitted to an emergency ward in Canada, bewildered and vomiting, after reportedly scraping the back of a pet cane toad and eating its secretions on crackers; the tabloids later claimed that one of the men had committed suicide after being discharged. Dubiously sourced accounts followed of Australians who died after drinking toad tea and a man supposedly being imprisoned in South America on toad-licking charges. Hungry for copy, journalists pressed experts for comment. "It gives them a kick like alcohol," an Australian herpetologist professed, of the toad users. In a foretelling of toad mythmaking to come, it had become difficult to tell fact, conjecture, and fabrication apart. "This is a case of media feeding on media," a reporter who covered the story would later reflect. Psychedelic toads, as a 1993 journal article titled "Misuse and Legend in the 'Toad Licking' Phenomenon" described it, had become an "informational epidemic."

Meanwhile, the television drama *L.A. Law* ran an episode involving a retiree accused of toad licking, and Beavis and Butt-Head licked toads on MTV. ("Tastes like chicken," Beavis remarked.) Psychedelic toads also captured the attention of lawmakers: A state representative in Georgia cautioned his colleagues about "the extreme dangers of toad licking," while a representative in South Carolina proposed sentencing offenders to community service at zoos. The men appear to have been speaking in jest, but Canadian police were serious when, in 1991, they urged officials to ban imports of cane toads and outlaw them as pets, citing "the deaths of several Australian drug users." Before long, Australia also passed laws against psychoactive toad use, listing bufotenine as a controlled substance. Toad licking had become so ingrained in popular consciousness that three decades later, while I was working on this book, people continuously brought it up as a point of reference. Yet the hype about cane toads obscured a crucial detail. As the anthropologist Wade Davis, who became drawn into solving the mystery, would later write, "An animal venom that contained no hallucinogenic agent but that did contain lethal poisons was not likely to inspire a new drug craze." A satirical film had broadcast rumors that snowballed into full-blown hysteria about cane toads, but there was still no evidence that they were psychoactive at all.

. . .

Wade Davis stumbled onto the psychedelic toad story in 1982 while studying zombies in Haiti. In the local vodou religion, it was believed that sorcerers could reanimate the bodies of dead people and control them, a trope that later became a staple of Hollywood horror movies. Davis was a student of Richard Schultes, the Harvard ethnobotanist who had documented early psychedelic rituals. "At any one time he had students flung all across Latin America seeking new fruits from the forest, obscure oil palms from the swamps of the Orinoco, rare tuber crops in the high Andes," Davis wrote of his mentor. His own assignment was to investigate whether there was a scientific basis for the zombie phenomenon—specifically, whether a narcotic powder made from natural ingredients could render victims seemingly dead and vulnerable to control. One morning during his fieldwork, Davis visited a vodou temple where "a macabre assortment of dried animals and plants" hung from a clothesline, reputedly for concocting the drug. Among the ingredients, he noticed, was the flattened carcass of a toad.

Davis returned home with his luggage full of samples—lizards, tarantulas, puffer fish, a live toad hidden in a duffel—and set about analyzing them. The toad was *Bufo marinus*, the cane toad. Davis spent the next few years developing a complex theory of zombies in Haitian society, which he published in *The Serpent and the Rainbow: A Harvard Scientist's Astonishing Journey into the Secret Societies of Haitian Voodoo, Zombis, and Magic.* The book contended, controversially, that there was a pharmacological basis to zombification, with active ingredients derived from pufferfish toxins and a plant known in Haiti as "zombie cucumber." The toxicity of cane toads led him to believe that they played no more than a symbolic role in the formula. But after reviewing the anthropological literature, Davis was struck by the claim, now erupting as tabloid news copy, that cane toads were psychedelic.

From the outset, the purported mind-altering qualities of toads struck Davis as untenable, given the potency of their poison. Yet he knew that the discovery of such a toad would be extraordinary. Of the approximately two hundred natural hallucinogens known to scientists, all were derived from plants and fungi. There had been a few reports of psychedelics from animals—a moth larva from Brazil, a Mexican bird, various fishes—but these fell apart under scrutiny. None had attracted as much interest as the secretions of cane toads, a topic that had generated "an outpouring of academic literature," as Davis and a colleague wrote. But the evidence for psychedelic toad use was vexingly ambiguous. To begin with, the archaeological record was inconclusive at best: Toads in Mesoamerican iconography might have symbolized a wide range of other meanings, from fecundity to seasonal rains, and there similarly might have been other explanations for their skeletons turning up in middens. There were also no colonial accounts of toads being used in rituals, unlike other psychoactive traditions painstakingly documented by the Spanish. Setting these concerns aside, there was still the toxicity of toads to reckon with. "It seems unlikely that the Maya would have been interested in poisoning vast numbers of their priests, who presumably would have been the ones taking the drug,"

Davis pointed out in a paper. He dismissed Kennedy's proposal that ducks had somehow nullified the secretions of cane toads as "sheer fantasy ungrounded in biological reality."

Even worse, the belief that bufotenine was hallucinogenic, which had animated the entire discourse, rested on highly questionable evidence. The psychiatrist Howard Fabing's original study had taken place at an Ohio prison that frequently provided inmates for scientific experiments that would be considered disturbing by modern standards, such as injecting subjects with cancer cells or exposing them to rabbit fever, one of the most virulent pathogens ever discovered. Fabing's own tests involved convicted murderers—"intelligent, co-operative, and quite charming," as he chillingly described them. Upon being injected with bufotenine, some of them turned a deep shade of purple that the scientists likened to "the color of an eggplant." The men complained of prickling faces and tightness in the chest. One retched and vomited. The transient visions they reported—swirling dots, distorted colors—were consistent with the symptoms of poisoning. It was possible, at a time when hallucinogens were poorly understood by scientists, that Fabing had misinterpreted these as signs of psychoactivity.

Other human studies with bufotenine had taken place under even darker circumstances, with similarly equivocal results. In the 1950s, a pharmacologist named Harris Isbell quietly began testing the drug at the United States Narcotic Farm, the nation's first federal addiction treatment clinic—a sprawling facility in Lexington, Kentucky, with high walls and grand art deco buildings. Isbell oversaw a research center where scientists strove to understand addiction from a clinical perspective; in 1962, he received an award from Robert F. Kennedy, then serving as U.S. attorney general, for his work. It was only later that Isbell's troubling research methods became public. Patients were recruited as research subjects in exchange for credit that could be used to purchase heroin and morphine from an on-site dispensary known as the drug bank. "If you wanted it in the vein, you got it there," a former participant recalled. Isbell was also secretly gathering data for the CIA, which became interested in using psychedelics as mind-control drugs during the Cold War. For nearly a decade, under a project known as MKUltra, the agency had been covertly sponsoring psychedelic research at more than thirty institutions—including the Narcotic Farm, where Isbell had access to a captive population of subjects.

In one experiment, Isbell kept seven men on LSD for nearly three months straight, which he described as "the most amazing demonstration of drug tolerance I have ever seen." In another, he had inmates injected with psilocybin and recorded various invasive measurements, including rectal temperatures, as the drug took effect. Isbell also ran studies with more obscure substances, including bufotenine. "I will write you a letter as soon as I can get the stuff into a man or two," he informed a contact at the CIA.

Yet Isbell could find no evidence that bufotenine was hallucinogenic, noting in a letter to a colleague that the drug's only symptoms were "a feeling of fear," flushing of the face, tachycardia, quickened breathing, and lacrimation, a medical term for crying. These studies were never published, only obliquely mentioned in other papers on bufotenine, and the full extent of Isbell's work with the substance may never be known. In 1973, following the Watergate scandal, the director of the CIA ordered the destruction of all records from MKUltra, and only a small fraction of the files survived.

There would be just one more experiment with bufotenine in the 1950s, at a Long Island psychiatric hospital—the second largest in the United States—with a railway platform where patients arrived on carriages with barred windows. In this study, schizophrenic subjects were dosed with bufotenine, in some cases after being sedated with electroshock therapy. One patient flushed reddish blue and became unresponsive, salivating so profusely that she almost drowned. Afterward, she spoke of a repressed memory from the age of three, when she had witnessed her mother dying of a hemorrhage. The researchers dismissed this episode, incredibly, as having "no therapeutic consequence" and concluded that bufotenine had no hallucinogenic properties. The study was terminated when three patients nearly died and had to be resuscitated.

Perhaps because of their appalling ethical standards, these were the last formal studies with bufotenine for several decades. Many scientists concluded that the substance was little more than a cardiovascular and respiratory toxin, regarding any hallucinations as incidental. Yet the myth of psychedelic bufotenine, obtained from cane toads, had somehow endured. In 1988, after reviewing this perplexing literature, Davis published a paper arguing that cane toads "could not have been used as a ritual narcotic, let alone serving as the basis for a state religion." He believed that to be the end of it, but two years later a reporter called him from Toronto, where another man had just been hospitalized for toad licking. The media panic about toads was reaching a fever pitch. In frustration, Davis eventually turned to an old colleague who he thought might be able to make sense of the situation, mailing him a copy of his recent paper. It was at this moment, when the myth of psychedelic toads seemed to finally run aground, that things took an unexpected turn. "I keep hearing about all these freaks around here going into the desert and smoking toad," his friend, the medical doctor Andrew T. Weil, replied. "I know this guy who does it all the time."

. . .

In 1988, Andrew Weil was not yet famous across America as a celebrity doctor with a vigorous beard, two *Time* magazine covers, and bestselling books like *Spontaneous Healing*, a treatise on the body's natural ability to heal itself. At the time Davis contacted him, he was practicing integrative medicine, (a field he'd founded) in Tucson while privately consuming various psychedelics. Weil had a polarizing reputation when it came to drugs. As a Harvard student in the 1960s, he had been rejected from Timothy Leary's psilocybin trials for being too young, only to retaliate with an exposé that led to Leary's firing. This hadn't made Weil popular in psychedelic circles, but it had given him a national platform. After medical school, he went on to conduct some of the world's first clinical trials with cannabis, publishing in prestigious journals that the drug was only a mild intoxicant. This had made him a target for drug prohibitionists under Richard Nixon, whose war on drugs was just beginning. While still in his twenties, Weil quit his medical research job and, in a stoned burst of productivity, authored *The Natural Mind: A New Way of Looking at Drugs and the Higher Consciousness,* a manifesto arguing that the urge to alter consciousness was innate and should be studied, not criminalized. It positioned him as an early dissenter from mainstream drug policy and the psychiatric status quo.

The backlash was immediate. Critics accused Weil of legitimizing drug use, and his book drew fire from medical authorities and moral crusaders alike. But *The Natural Mind* also became a foundational text in the emerging discourse around psychedelics, posing questions that would resurface decades later: "What do these drugs tell us about the relationship between mind and body? Are they legitimate tools (in any sense) for changing the mind in a direction of greater awareness? How can a society come to terms with the individual urge to alter awareness?"

In 1971, Weil returned to Harvard and joined the research staff of the Botanical Museum, where he and Davis would later become colleagues, both mentored by Richard Schultes. Weil also began appearing as an expert witness in criminal trials involving drugs, where he observed a policy of never speaking about their effects without being under the influence himself. He once testified in a case against a man who had been charged with selling LSD to an undercover agent. On the first morning of the trial, in a packed New Orleans courtroom, one of the defendant's supporters came over to Weil and said, in a suggestive voice, "Close your eyes and open your mouth." He felt a small tab being placed on his tongue and embarked on an acid trip that lasted all day. After testifying positively about the drug and emerging unscathed from a hostile cross-examination—the prosecuting attorney finally threw up his hands and exclaimed, "I give up!"—Weil asked the judge for permission to address the court. "I mean this with no disrespect," he said, "but you should know that for the entire time that I have been in the witness stand, I have been under the influence of LSD."

Among the substances Weil experimented with was synthetic

5-MeO-DMT, which had made its way onto the fringes of the recreational drug scene in the 1960s without gaining widespread popularity. This had come about through the discovery of 5-MeO-DMT in Amazonian snuffs, which alerted psychedelic enthusiasts to its psychoactive properties. In 1967, at a symposium on drugs in California, some Swedish chemists had presented research on the molecule, predicting that 5-MeO-DMT would become "an important tool in psychopharmacological studies." (How right they were would only become clear more than half a century later, when 5-MeO-DMT became a leading drug candidate for treating depression and other mental disorders.) Weil had attended that symposium, soon becoming an early adopter of 5-MeO-DMT himself.

At the time, people typically smoked small pinches of the drug—a white odorless powder—on a base of dried parsley or mint leaves. Others, including the psychiatrist Ralph Metzner, would later experiment with snorting it, which slowed the onset of the high and prolonged its duration. But when the U.S. government began cracking down on psychoactive substances, banning LSD and other drugs in 1971, users of 5-MeO-DMT became extremely guarded, ushering in an era of deliberate secrecy. A religious organization called the Church of the Tree of Life listed 5-MeO-DMT as a sacrament and quietly made it available to members. The church was founded to protect the use of psychedelics that had not yet been scheduled by the authorities, exploiting federal religious exemptions granted for peyote consumption by Native Americans. "I and most other Church members enjoy employing this sacrament on occasion, but not frequently," one member wrote of 5-MeO-DMT. The molecule also remained legally available from a number of research chemical supply companies, although private sales were officially prohibited. "It will be necessary to give the impression that you are a professional researcher," one written guide advised prospective buyers. "It may be helpful if you have a letterhead printed for your research group. Make your inquiries simply, soberly, and discreetly. Good luck."

With his medical credentials, Weil was able to obtain a supply without difficulty and set about "turning a lot of people onto 5-MeO-DMT," he told me in 2024. "I found it really interesting," he added. He has described the experience, memorably, as a "rocket ship into the void." On one occasion, he and a friend smoked 5-MeO-DMT in a canyon in Arizona and experienced "a period of shared consciousness—we were just in each other's minds," he said. Many people he introduced to the molecule had blissful experiences, but others thrashed around or struggled to breathe. Weil resolved to discontinue these sessions after an especially large man became violent during a trip and attempted to throttle him. "It was too powerful," Weil said.

But he remained fascinated by 5-MeO-DMT, which could induce states of consciousness that reminded him of intense meditation—a quieting of the mind and absorption into the present, culminating in a kind of spiritual ecstasy. Weil continued using the synthetic molecule, off and on, until the mid-1980s, when he was astonished to learn that the same high could be attained from a local species of toad. He had been living on the outskirts of Tucson and, during the summer rains, would commonly encounter large groups of the toads on his property, hunting insects ("they were eating machines") or depositing long strings of eggs in his swimming pool. A toad had once hopped onto his chest while he was lazing, stoned, in the hot tub. "The idea that they might be psychedelic," Weil told me in his rich Philadelphia accent, "just seemed so off the wall."

• • •

The first person in modern times to assemble all the clues and determine that Sonoran Desert toads were psychedelic was a reclusive resident of Denton, Texas, named Ken Nelson. In the early 1980s, as a young man serving in the military, Nelson had read a magazine article about toad skeletons being unearthed at an archaeological dig in North Carolina, which a scholar had speculatively ascribed to hallucinogenic use by the Cherokee—yet another manifestation of the belief that psychedelic toad rituals had once been commonplace in the Americas. Afterward, Nelson had searched for more information in a university library, where he came across Erspamer's laboratory analysis of Sonoran Desert toads from the 1960s, which reported "enormous amounts" of 5-MeO-DMT in their glands. The molecule's psychoactivity had since been established. Drawing this information together, Nelson resolved to conduct a daring experiment.

In 1983, he set off for Arizona during the summer rains, accompanied by his girlfriend, Pat, and a collie called Quanah, named after a Native American chief who had advocated for the religious use of peyote. Quanah spotted the first toad, which Nelson captured and squeezed onto the windshield of his Chevy Sport. Once the liquid had dried, he scraped it off and smoked a small amount. A combination of rigorous science and unfounded speculation had led, eventually, to the discovery of the world's only known psychedelic animal.

Back in Denton, Nelson enrolled in a technical writing course and began working on an instructional pamphlet that meticulously explained how to extract and use 5-MeO-DMT from Sonoran Desert toads. Self-published under the pseudonym Albert Most, it described how the substance could induce "almost overwhelming psychedelic effects" within thirty seconds of inhalation. "Relax, breathe regularly, and flow with the experience," the text advised. "You will be completely absorbed in a complex chemical event characterized by an overload of thoughts and perception, brief collapse of the EGO, and loss of the space-time continuum."

His identity would remain a secret for more than thirty years, until, in 2017, the VICE show *Hamilton's Pharmacopeia* misidentified the pamphlet's author as Alfred Savinelli, an herbalist and entrepreneur from New Mexico. After it aired, Nelson contacted the producers with evidence that he'd authored the pamphlet, leading them to shoot an entirely new episode; by the time it came out, in 2021, Nelson had died of Parkinson's. (It was Savinelli, as it happens, who introduced me to the world of toad smoking, when I contacted him for a story about the poaching of white sage—a native California herb, increasingly threatened by overharvesting, that his company advertised in wholesale volumes. When I got him on the phone, in 2020, he volunteered that he had pioneered the practice of toad smoking. This was to be the first of many deceptions I encountered in my reporting.)

In the 1980s, as Nelson's work circulated in the psychedelic underground, more people were turned on to toad smoking. One of them was a fixture of the Tucson counterculture who went by the name of White Dog. "As soon as you smoke this stuff you will ditch your ego. It's gonna scare the shit out of you," a friend advised him in the 1980s. White Dog stood nearly six feet four, with dreadlocks down to his waist and a beard just as long. "He was like an Ent," one of his acquaintances recalled, referring to the taciturn yet formidably powerful tree giants from *The Lord of the Rings.* After spending his childhood in Minnesota, White Dog had joined the Peyote Way Church of God, a syncretic movement that made use of religious freedom laws to permit the consumption of peyote by non–Native Americans. At some point, he had worked in the merchant marines, where his colleagues knew him as Roger. To avoid a shift one day, he smashed his knee with a hammer, resulting in a permanent limp. White Dog later renounced formal employment altogether, sustaining himself as a seasonal fruit picker and by selling various natural drugs. He grew his own poppies and produced low-grade opium. He hitched rides to southern Texas and harvested gunnysacks of peyote. He supplied mushrooms and cannabis to Havasupai Indians from the Grand Canyon, with whom he shared an enthusiasm for reggae music.

In Tucson, White Dog enjoyed hanging out at a house with a large swimming pool where guests took psychedelics and swam in the nude. Many of them were "into Native American stuff," a white man who went by the moniker Smiling Eagle told me. They performed approximations of Hopi dances and wore leather moccasins. They were partial to LSD, mushrooms, and peyote. But when White Dog introduced toad smoking to this circle, most people regarded it as "too far out." The substance, obtained from an animal widely regarded as poisonous, was said to bring on unnervingly extreme trips. "It didn't catch on," Smiling Eagle recalled. "There were so many better ways to get high."

Weil smoked toad with White Dog on a few occasions, finding the effects to be incredible. The 5-MeO-DMT experience was elevated, for him, by the knowledge that it derived from a living animal. And so when Davis contacted him in 1990, confounded by the academic controversy about cane toads, Weil immediately invited him to Tucson. A few days later, they paid a visit to White Dog, who lived outside the city in a ramshackle compound surrounded by cacti and mesquite trees. They found him at sunset, dressed in red sweatpants and a lilac shirt, tending a fire heaped with stones for heating a sweat lodge off to one side. The men stripped and crawled inside, where White Dog told them what he knew about toad smoking. He described the toad secretion as an "astral propellant" and claimed to have smoked it "maybe a hundred times."

In this Arizona sweat lodge, the story of the psychedelic toad, which had origins in a Tokyo laboratory and wound through such diverse fields as anthropology and biochemistry, found a kind of conclusion. Fittingly, it was two protégés of Richard Schultes's who had pulled it together. Soon afterward, they published two papers revealing the identity of the psychedelic toad, including personal descriptions of smoking the secretions. Davis reported "a sense of wonder and well-being," including "an insect-cicada sound that ran across my mind and seemed to link my body to the earth." Weil wrote, more clinically, "This is a powerful psychoactive drug, one that I think would appeal to most people who like the effects of hallucinogens." But instead of arousing interest in the toads, their self-experimentation ignited a storm of controversy, including coverage in major newspapers and journals. An academic reviewer disparaged their research as "little more than an endorsement for abuse of a hallucinogenic material with potentially deadly side effects." Popular attitudes toward psychedelics had not yet begun to loosen, and the story was mostly dismissed as a curiosity. More publicity in this vein followed in 1994, when a California teacher was detained—with his wife and four pet Sonoran Desert toads named Hans, Franz, Peter, and Brian—on drug charges. The teacher was from Calaveras County, which happened to be celebrating its sixty-fifth annual Jumping Frog Jubilee, inspired by a Mark Twain yarn about a scam involving frogs. The teacher's crime, somewhat absurdly, was the possession of bufotenine, which remained a Schedule I substance even though no one was known to be using it. (The teacher had confessed to smoking his toads' secretions, but 5-MeO-DMT was not yet a scheduled substance.)

Fewer people paid attention to a provocative anthropological argument Davis and Weil had raised: that Sonoran Desert toad secretions might once have been used in rituals across Mesoamerica, perhaps forming part of pre-Hispanic spiritual practices. During their research, they had come across an obscure paper from 1972 that speculated whether the Olmecs, Mayans, and Aztecs had known about the psychedelic properties of the species. Many scholars believed that these societies traced their origins to the Sonoran Desert, which made it conceivable that such knowledge had traveled with them. The author, an anthropologist named Peter Furst, had read about the discovery of 5-MeO-DMT in Sonoran Desert toads and inferred, as Ken Nelson would independently verify, that it signaled possible psychoactivity. "Was it the shamans of the pre-agricultural desert cultures who discovered the potent psychotomimetic effects of toad poison?" Furst wrote.

Davis and Weil were careful to note that this was purely hypothetical. But given the widespread use of hallucinogens in the Americas, it was difficult to rule out. "It is an axiom of long-distance commerce that the ideal trade item is one that is highly esteemed, easy to transport, durable, readily available at the source, and difficult or impossible to find at the point of exchange," they wrote. "*Bufo alvarius* venom meets all requirements." One could certainly imagine desert people becoming curious about a toad that appeared, as if by magic, at certain times of the year. They would have known that the toad was toxic, and perhaps that toxicity could be an indicator of visionary properties. Or perhaps they ate the toads as a survival food, carefully avoiding their poison glands, and noticed an unusual smell while cooking them. It would not have been a great leap to experiment with various modes of ingestion. "If the Mayans knew how to build pyramids," a psychologist who works with 5-MeO-DMT told me, "they could figure out how to smoke toad secretions in a pipe."

And yet nobody knew if this had actually happened, or if this was merely another compelling toad story. Who had made use of the substance, and where? In the meantime, few people were smoking toad, and for another twenty years these questions remained something of an academic curiosity. Then Octavio showed up with an answer.

CHAPTER 3

People of the Desert and Sea

In 2011, after following the toads to Sonora, Octavio was working night shifts at his pharmacy job. On the side, he was smoking toad most days and sharing it free of charge, although it would be some time before he became known as *el doctor sapo.* He had the medicine but no origin myth, no narrative of ancestral use and rediscovery. But on 11/11/11, a date Octavio later interpreted as cosmically significant, he served toad to a bohemian couple from Hermosillo. They led him to what others had been seeking for decades: a link between psychedelic toads and Indigenous tradition.

Odily Fuentes, a self-described hippie of around thirty, had dark hair and a figure she showed off in bikini poses on Facebook. Her husband, Luis "Xixi" Ogarrio, was an artist fifteen years her senior, with a piercing at the base of his nose through which he sometimes threaded smooth pieces of bone. They ran a swimming school for infants and frequently consumed psychedelics. "We were always interested in Indigenous people," Fuentes told me, "looking for that original connection." Octavio served them toad in Kino Bay, a resort town on the Gulf of California, less than ninety minutes' drive from Hermosillo. When he recounted his recovery from using crack, they told him about the plight of the Seri.

The tribe, also known as the Comcaac, lived in two tiny fishing villages in the coastal desert north of Kino. Their territory fell within a corridor used by powerful cartels for smuggling drugs toward the U.S., which had spilled over and driven an alarming rise in addiction among the Seri. "Even the kids were smoking crack," Octavio recalled. The tribe was isolated and impoverished, with a reputation for being hostile to visitors, but Xixi's family had forged a relationship with a prominent local clan. One of his brothers was an amateur ethnographer who, twenty years earlier, had befriended a Seri elder named Chapo Barnett. Chapo was an authority on the tribe's traditional chants and dances, which were at risk of dying out; younger generations were likelier to listen to *narcocorridos,* the songs glorifying Mexican cartels. To many outsiders, Chapo's appearance was arresting: diminutive and alert, with arched cheekbones and deeply etched wrinkles. He was also, as one writer observed, "especially successful in understanding the behavior of gringos." Xixi's brother, Carlos Ogarrio, saw Chapo as the embodiment of a vanishing shamanistic legacy. He set about recording his chants, becoming a valuable ally to the Barnetts.

Seri people liked to joke that if you threw a stone, you would hit a Barnett. Their family, also known as the Wolf Clan, was highly regarded within the community for their knowledge of spiritual traditions—a reputation that would soon anchor a new chapter in the story of toad medicine. Prominent in their lineage was Chapo's father, a gaunt and regal patriarch named Miguel who had resisted efforts to convert the tribe to Christianity in the 1950s. Miguel was known to sing and dance furiously in public, one of his grandsons recalled, because "religion was already getting into people." Miguel sang as a form of protest. Born in the early twentieth century, near the end of a brutal sequence of wars that had nearly killed off the Seri, he grew up in the last remnants of a hunter-gatherer culture that had endured for millennia. He wore his hair long and disdained to speak Spanish. Like many Seri of his generation, he lived in a world enlivened by spirits, which often visited him in his dreams: shark-finned deer that lived beneath the sea, a moon with a flower for a mouth. When he was a young man, a visiting anthropologist once invited him to draw these visions, and Miguel, who had never used pencils or paper, unhesitatingly produced a series of vivid and detailed artworks.

Just one generation later, Chapo came of age in a radically transformed society, increasingly organized around the church and commercial fishing. Like his father, Chapo was a custodian of Seri culture, particularly a hypnotic dance known as the pascola. But in his early thirties, one of his young daughters died of an illness, and Chapo fell into a crippling depression. His daughter had been admitted to a clinic in Hermosillo and passed away overnight; the next morning, Chapo was seen gently closing her eyelids. He came to believe that her death had been his punishment for defying evangelical ministers in the community, who preached that God abhorred Seri customs. He cut his long hair short and renounced singing and dancing, withdrawing from social life and wandering the desert alone. For years, he lived in this self-imposed exile, shunning the traditions he had once championed. But slowly he returned to his old ways, resuming fishing and carving ironwood sculptures to sell. Eventually he began singing and dancing once more. Championed by Carlos Ogarrio, he became a celebrated figure outside the community, performing at conferences and Indigenous gatherings around the world. In 2017, he was awarded Mexico's national arts prize for his knowledge of Seri culture.

Chapo's own sons, on the other hand, showed little interest in these family traditions. "Their predilections lie more in the direction of cars and drugs," a writer familiar with the tribe observed in the 1980s. The social geography of Sonora was shifting as drug cartels established lucrative trade routes into the United States. The remoteness of Seri territory, the poverty of its people, and the system under which it was governed all presented strategic opportunities for narcotraffickers. The tribe had sovereign control over an *ejido,* or communal land area, covering some 350 square miles of the mainland, protected by a loosely organized traditional guard. The police and military seldom entered, and as Mexico's cartels gained power, the entire region became a haven for lawlessness. Unlicensed cars known colloquially as chocolates, brought across the border illegally and often used for other criminal activity, ended up in the hands of Seri residents, who were able to purchase them cheaply. (Elsewhere, presumably, the cars would have drawn too much scrutiny.) "Seri towns probably have the highest number of cars per capita of any indigenous village in Mexico," a researcher would later write. In the early 1980s, one of Chapo's sons acquired a luxurious 1968 Mercury sedan and would hurtle along the unpaved streets of the village, lifting billowing clouds of dust. More recently, a broken-down Hummer stood rusting outside one home with chickens scratching for food on the seats.

The cartels focused on smuggling marijuana at first, but it was cocaine, sourced from South America, that later gave them their unassailable power. In the early '00s, building on this foundation, they established facilities in Sinaloa and neighboring states for producing industrial volumes of crystal meth. Each of these drugs spilled over and found a market among the Seri. But it was meth, or *cristal*—cheap, fearsomely addictive—that became most problematic. Fishermen used the stimulant to cut their hunger on long days at sea. Divers who harvested shellfish used it to fortify themselves against the cold. They became hooked, as did women and the elderly. "It was a pandemic of addiction," one anthropologist told me. Whole families were afflicted, including the Barnetts.

Shortly after Octavio heard this story, one of Chapo Barnett's sons, Raymundo, turned up in Hermosillo, looking for a way out. He turned to Ogarrio's family for help, and they took him to Octavio. Raymundo was in his early forties and hadn't eaten or slept properly in months. He was rail thin, his clothes in tatters. "His face was full of sadness," Octavio later wrote. He served Raymundo toad three times that night while the recorded chants of his late grandfather, Miguel, played on a speaker. When the session was over, Raymundo broke into a joyous smile and declared that for the first time in years he felt relief from his cravings.

The following week, Octavio made his first visit to Seri territory. The nearest village, Punta Chueca, lay at the end of a rutted fifteen-mile dirt track that took ninety minutes to navigate. The road wound northward from Kino Bay, past rugged mountains with weathered ocher cliffs and plains of towering cacti. The sea came into view, with

Mexico's largest island, Isla Tiburón, looming across the strait. Punta Chueca lay on a curving sandspit at the edge of the water. "When I told people I was going to work with the Seris," Octavio recalled, "they were like, 'Doc, don't go there! These people are bad, they are dangerous, they are murderers, they are kidnappers, they smuggle drugs.'" Octavio unselfconsciously described driving into the settlement to me as "like a Western movie—just looking for the Indians." He added, "It was pretty savage. Pretty raw."

The village was undeniably desolate. Prefabricated concrete houses, some of them on the verge of collapse, stood on dusty lots littered with trash. Feral dogs roamed the streets, and rusting hulks of cars lay at the roadside. There were overturned fishing boats and groups of men who eyed the new arrivals suspiciously. The few designated public spaces—a forlorn sports ground, a school for traditional dances that was never completed—had been taken over by meth users.

Octavio had come to Punta Chueca, accompanied by his new friends Odily and Xixi, to treat more members of the tribe with toad medicine. Four of Chapo's children were addicted to meth, as well as three of his nephews. One nephew was named Miguel, after Chapo's father. At nearly six feet tall, he weighed just 130 pounds—"like a zombie," he would later recall. The first time Miguel smoked toad, Octavio wrote, "the coloring of his skin went from pale to green, then purple. He stopped breathing for about two seconds, then began to vomit a brown, gelatinous material. He was squirming and screaming so violently, his body contorting." Within half an hour, after the effects subsided, Miguel had palpably transformed. His eyes were shining. He reached into his shoe and pulled out a hypodermic syringe and a plastic-wrapped dose of heroin, which he tossed away. Then he smoked toad again.

In all, Octavio served the medicine to four Seri people on that trip, using a broken lightbulb in place of a pipe; a few others declined to be dosed, he told me, "when they saw the intensity of the process." The sessions took place on a secluded beach outside the village, beside the lapping wavelets of the gulf. Octavio's friends smoked toad as well.

Xixi was wearing a bright Bob Marley T-shirt. The group haphazardly chanted oms. That same day, Raymundo took them to a sacred cave on the hill above Punta Chueca, looking out toward the island. "It was as if we had gone back to prehistoric times," Octavio wrote. The same group smoked toad as Raymundo sang some Seri chants, which he had formerly shown little interest in learning from his elders. Octavio would later describe this moment as the "return of ancestral healing to its true home."

He had begun to sense the outlines of a larger story. Years earlier, escaping the strife caused by Octavio's addiction, his brother David had moved in with one of their uncles, an archaeologist. The two of them shared a fascination with Mesoamerican history, and when they heard about Octavio's encounters with the Seri, they began sending him thousands of images from sites across Mexico. Octavio saw a pattern emerging, piecing together what would become his defining theory: that the Seri were the last custodians of a sacred practice that had once stretched across the region. If he was correct, this encounter was truly momentous: A tribe that had been cut off from its past by punishing incursions from outsiders was now, thanks to him, reconnecting with a bygone spiritual lineage.

Soon after his first visit, Octavio obtained a letter from the head of the tribe's council of elders, an aging fisherman named Antonio Robles, inviting him back to the community to treat more meth users—"my experiment with the toad," as Octavio called it. Several of Robles's own sons were addicted. "He seemed to be carrying all the pain of his family and community on his back," Octavio wrote. Robles, who spoke little Spanish, would later issue more documents authorizing Octavio as a practitioner of the ancestral Seri tradition of toad smoking. "Dr. Rettig has worked with our community and the members of our tribe, reintroducing the use of this medicine that had been forgotten," one of these letters stated. "This has greatly benefited the health of our people."

In early 2012, Octavio quit his job at the pharmacy and moved to Punta Chueca. (Once again, his mother thought he was crazy.) Over the next few months, while living in a small room at Raymundo Barnett's house, he administered toad to a procession of patients. A few elders also tried the substance, including Chapo, the dancer. During the peak of his first toad experience, when most people have no control over their bodies, he stood up, opened his eyes, and wandered off. "It's very beautiful up there with the spirits, but it's not for strolling around or meandering about," he said, as Octavio later recounted in his memoir. "People want to stay there looking around and getting to know the place. We are *from* there, and we will return."

As these sessions went on, Octavio became increasingly convinced that he had rediscovered something ancient—"the missing link of pre-Columbian ethnopharmacology," as he later called it. The idea that such a transcendent ritual had been forgotten might have seemed unlikely, but the Seri had barely survived a genocide, reduced to fewer than two hundred people by the early twentieth century, and entire strands of memory had been severed. One of Chapo's brothers, a tall and angular man named Pancho, told me that he had encountered Seri gods during his sessions with Octavio. "When I had the toad," he said, "I remembered the history."

• • •

Long before Spanish settlers arrived in Sonora, the Seri were desert nomads, roaming in loose bands across the blazing landscape. Their historic range was among the most inhospitable in the Americas, encompassing craggy peaks and hard-baked plains that received less than five inches of rain in a typical year. This rain was highly variable, arriving in summer bursts that washed in sheets across the earth and flooded the arroyos, churning up sand and rock. There were also gentler winter storms, although these were just as undependable. An area that was wet one year might be parched the next. Portions of Seriland, as the territory became known, would sometimes receive no rain for twelve months or longer.

The Seri organized their lives around the availability of water, moving opportunistically and over great distances, camping at dry lakes that filled after heavy rains or at bedrock pools that collected runoff. Often it was only a matter of weeks before they had to move on. Prevented from gathering in large numbers, the Seri retained a fiercely independent streak, with little need for political organization beyond war captains in times of conflict. Their society revolved around the extended family, with more than sixty distinct terms of kinship. "There is no people to be found under the sun which distinguishes the degrees of friendship and relationship with more names," a Spanish missionary wrote of the Seri in the seventeenth century—a claim borne out by modern linguists, who consider the Seri kinship system among the most elaborate ever documented. There were strict speaking rules within Seri families, such as never directly addressing one's parents-in-law. "Such behavior undoubtedly reduced the chance of friction," a book on the tribe drily noted.

Accustomed to constant itinerancy, the Seri kept few material possessions. They fashioned temporary shelters with poles and brush that disintegrated once abandoned, vanishing virtually without trace. They wore skirts made with skins from the pelicans that glided up and down the coast. They painted their bodies and faces with bright pigments—gypsum, pollen, tree sap. They frequently went barefoot, walking with a swift and graceful gait. Boys were known to chase down jackrabbits on foot. Elders who got too old to keep up with the tribe were left behind to die with some water and a dog for company. For carrying water, the Seri fired some of the thinnest eggshell pottery in the world, scraping clay with clamshells to around a tenth of an inch thick. Men would haul large clay vessels known as ollas for miles, suspended from wooden yokes with cords of mesquite fiber or human hair. Sometimes they stumbled after long journeys, shattering the vessels; trails to major water holes were scattered with shards.

For food, the Seri hunted deer, bighorn sheep, jackrabbits, rodents, and reptiles. They dug open and robbed the nests of pack rats, collecting seeds, fruits, and mesquite beans. They harvested nectar and pollen from carpenter bees. They consumed more than seventy-five species of plants—mesquite, amaranth, agave—and had names for more than four hundred. As extensive as this desert knowledge was, most of the tribe's sustenance was derived from the coast. The channel between Tiburón Island and the mainland was beset by such treacherous currents that Spanish explorers later named it Infiernillo—Little Hell. For centuries, the Seri navigated these waters in lightweight reed boats known as balsas. "It breasts gales and rides breakers and stems tide rips that would crash a canoe, swamp a skiff, or capsize a yawl," a nineteenth-century anthropologist wrote admiringly. While riding these vessels, Seri boatmen harpooned fish and sea turtles, which left glimmering trails of phosphorescence as they swam on summer nights.

The Seri also harvested crabs, mussels, oysters, lobsters, and the eggs of seabirds. They harvested floating mats of seagrass, drying and grinding its seeds into a nutritious flour—the only culture in the world known to do this, despite its ubiquitous distribution globally. Reflecting the richness and diversity of their diet, they were regarded as a tall and powerful race by writers steeped in racial prejudice. "The tribe abounds in models of physical perfection," a scholar observed in the nineteenth century. "The Spanish ladies in Hermosillo view with envy the slender shapes and the comely hands and feet of the young maidens," another wrote.

Their speech was wholly unlike that of other tribes in Sonora, more closely related to the languages of Indigenous groups from Baja California, which was visible on clear days across the water from Seriland. Oral tradition indicated that the Seri had once made journeys back and forth across the gulf on their balsas, paddling from island to island, a journey totaling some fifty miles each way. One of these islands, San Esteban, had a sheer sea cliff where Seri men were known to play a dangerous game of chicken, sliding on upturned turtle shells down a gravel slope and daring one another to bail out last. "Sometimes a man went too far," one scholarly description notes, and "it was said that as he was heading for doom, the first man to yell 'your wife is mine' could take her as a second spouse." The site is also a painful reminder of the Seri's long history of violence. In the 1860s, the entire San Esteban community was massacred by the Mexican military, and only their dogs survived. The site became known as Ensenada del Perro Triste—Cove of the Grieving Dog.

• • •

In the sixteenth century, lured by the prospect of gold, Spanish explorers began arriving in Sonora. They generally steered clear of the coastal desert, and at first there were only scattered accounts of contact with the Seri. "They are excessively wild," a Jesuit priest remarked. The Jesuits were establishing missions across Sonora for converting the Indigenous population to Christianity, but the Seri were unlike any other tribe they encountered, practicing no traditional agriculture and speaking an unrelated tongue that, with its guttural consonants, reminded one friar of German. "They roam like gypsies from one place to another," he wrote. "They live like cattle, without God, without law, without faith, without princes and without houses."

This meant that the Seri, as the historian Tom Sheridan has argued, were culturally polar opposites to the Spaniards, who lived in a rigidly hierarchical society and "subdued the earth through agriculture and metallurgy." These irreconcilable worldviews would drive centuries of conflict. The first documented skirmish between the two groups took place in 1662, when as many as three hundred Seri men and women fought to the death with a group of colonists. The surviving children were taken and raised in the mission pueblos near modern-day Hermosillo, forcibly removed from their families and culture. Afterward, some Seri settled at the missions, but seldom permanently. They "are more inclined to hunt than to plow fields," one missionary complained. To entice them to stay, the Jesuits provided them with corn and strove to teach them agriculture, but many Seri came and went as it suited them; others stayed away entirely. As Spanish settlement encroached farther into Seri territory, there was a sharp rise in horse and cattle raiding, with the animals often killed and butchered on the spot. "Life in the desert and on the sea had turned the Seris into opportunists who took advantage of many different resources," Sheridan writes. "Spanish livestock must have been irresistible targets—big but relatively slow 'deer' who fed many Seri families."

By the early eighteenth century, a grim pattern of stock theft followed by reprisals had become entrenched, driving cycles of violence. On one occasion, after Seri raiders made off with animals belonging to a rancher named Salvador de la Huerta, horsemen thundered after them and killed three men. Two weeks later, during a party at de la Huerta's hacienda, some fifty Seri surrounded the house. The rancher came out with his musket drawn but was felled by an arrow. The Seri fired arrows through the windows, set the roof alight, and attacked guests as they fled, shouting in Spanish, "Look at how we are eating your fat calves!" Twenty-one people died in the assault, more than half of them children. In the retaliation that ensued, nine Seri men were killed and some thirty women and children imprisoned.

These confrontations spilled into all-out war in 1748, when Spanish military forces seized mission lands where a few hundred Seri had taken up farming. "They are whipped, beaten, and forced to work as though they were evildoers," wrote a priest who visited the area. At another mission settlement, he reported, "fifty families, not counting children, work every day from sunup to sundown and are underfed and quite badly mistreated, even the pregnant women." The priest added, imploringly, "These are Christian Indians, not rebels." When the mission Seri protested, eighty families were arrested and the women deported as far away as Guatemala, to the far south of Mexico. The army made no distinction between different Seri bands, some of whom had been living peacefully alongside the settlers. "Their goal is to extinguish and annihilate the Seri nation once and for all," the priest wrote of the military operation.

Within a year, the entire Seri nation was in open rebellion against the Spaniards, launching attacks on settlements across the frontier. "Havoc and ruin" ensued, in the words of another missionary: ranches set alight, inhabitants killed, livestock slaughtered. "In the past they have stolen the cattle and horses they needed while setting the rest free," a government communiqué stated. "Now, after supplying themselves with meat, the Seris kill and leave to rot whatever they encounter, in order to destroy the settlers or force them into retreat." At one mining town, Seri warriors killed more than three hundred head of livestock; at another, they killed more than forty people. "They burned the houses after looting them," a priest wrote, "desecrated the church, poured out the holy oils, and with infernal fury lanced the painting of Our Great Mother and Lady of Guadalupe nine times." In a subsequent battle, a single Seri warrior was said to have wounded seventeen Spanish soldiers; afterward, the decapitated heads of dead Seri were paraded as a warning in several pueblos, where Indians from other tribes were ordered to dance with them.

Facing an adversary with greater firepower, the Seri—who neither rode horses nor carried firearms—became unsparing guerrilla fighters, staging raids and withdrawing back into the desert. Those who pursued them faced extreme heat and long spells without water. The Seri poisoned water holes with rotting animal carcasses and ambushed soldiers at night. If they were outnumbered, they took refuge in the mountains or on Tiburón Island, paddling back and forth on their balsas. The island, as a chronicle of one failed Spanish expedition lamented, "was like a military garrison from which bands of warriors emerged at times to attack our territories."

In 1750, the governor of Sonora ordered a military campaign to Tiburón "to expel and dislodge the inhabitants." His plans included the deportation of all Seri over the age of ten to the islands of the Caribbean, with younger children to be distributed among settler families on the frontier. This amounted, as Sheridan writes, to a "campaign of cultural genocide." The authorities had already sent Seri rebels to work in tobacco factories near Mexico City, some twelve hundred miles away, but the men had escaped and made their way back to Sonora, resuming hostilities against the Spaniards. A group of missionaries who had preached to the Seri, and formerly opposed attempts to subdue the tribe by military force, supported this deportation scheme, giving up on a seventy-year effort to mold the tribe into agrarian Catholics.

"The removal of the Seris," they concluded, "is not only necessary but requisite and urgent."

But the Tiburón campaign was a humiliating failure. An invading force of more than seven hundred men killed thirteen Seri and took fewer than thirty prisoners. Driven to desperation by thirst, the troops came close to mutiny. Dressed in heavy leather armor during some of the hottest months of the year, they trekked through valleys and over steep slopes, frequently being ambushed while sleeping. The few water holes they came across had been fouled with carcasses and were writhing with maggots. They reported some gruesome victories: A Seri archer was scalped and had his ears cut off, and a Seri boy of around five years old was baptized out of fears that he would die from the blows he had sustained while being captured. (The baptismal water was saved for drinking; it is unclear whether the boy survived.) But after two weeks on the island, sapped of morale, the army withdrew. "It seems unlikely that all members of the Seri nation were driven completely and finally from Tiburón," a captain euphemistically testified. "To the extent this seed is allowed to flourish, further hostilities will be born."

The following decade, a Jesuit missionary listed more than a hundred colonial settlements that had been attacked by Seris and rebels from other Sonoran tribes. Dozens of settlements—towns, missions, gold mines—were abandoned, reduced to ruins in the desert. Hundreds of Spaniards were killed; thousands of cattle and horses were slaughtered. As before, the Seri were able to evade capture by retreating to Tiburón or mountainous hideouts on the mainland, becoming feared and hated in equal measure.

In 1760, a new governor of Sonora led more than a hundred troops into one such refuge, a rugged formation of peaks outside Hermosillo known as the Cerro Prieto. An earlier expedition had left Seri fighters "dead and eaten by animals, dead and partly buried in the earth, dead lying in caves, and dead in the water-pockets of the sierra," according to historical records, but the skirmishes had continued. Now the governor's men encountered a small band of Seri, who held them off for several hours despite being outnumbered five to one. The battle ended when the Seri leader was mortally wounded. As he lay dying, he rose to transfix the governor with an arrow; the two men died beside each other.

No matter how dogged their resistance, the Seri were up against the might of the Spanish empire, which had already conquered most of central and southern Mexico. A few years on, the authorities ordered the largest military mobilization in the history of colonial Sonora, dispatching more than a thousand soldiers into the Cerro Prieto. In place of pitched battles, the army adopted guerrilla tactics of its own, with small, mobile units of soldiers hunting down fugitive members of the tribe. Hundreds of families were killed. An elderly Seri man explained to his Spanish captors that "tranquility was not possible among his own people because they lived in constant tribulation," according to an account of the operation. "If a stone rolled in the hills at night or if a bird moved among the branches, they became frightened and fled."

An interval of relative calm followed in Sonora, with the surviving members of the tribe driven back onto Tiburón or deep into the desert. But the Mexican War of Independence, which began in 1810, weakened government authority along the frontier, leading to a resumption in stock raiding by the Seri. In 1844, a burly, square-jawed rancher named Pascual Encinas established a farm on the edge of their territory, clearing mesquite forests and fencing off pastures for livestock. The settlement grew to more than twenty families, with neat adobe houses and thousands of horses, burros, and cattle. Like the missionaries before him, Encinas believed that the Seri could be peacefully inducted as colonial subjects. He introduced stamped copper tokens as payment for Seri labor—until some Seri obtained sheet metal and systematically began counterfeiting the tokens, exchanging them for supplies at the rancho store. When his livestock began disappearing, Encinas issued an extremist threat: a Seri head for each animal taken.

Two days later, when another of his horses was killed, Encinas ordered his cowboys to shoot the first Seri person they encountered. War broke out once more. The Sonoran government began offering bounties for dead Seri men (150 pesos) and women (50 pesos). Encinas's cowboys rode in groups, an anthropologist wrote, "and the Seri were picked off one by one." A single ambush left more than seventy Seri people dead. Bleached Seri skulls lay across the desert landscape. "The Seri were hunted from the plain," one account from the period notes, "as precisely as were the stealthy jaguar and sneaking coyote." Within a decade, Encinas estimated to a researcher many years later, the tribe's population had been reduced by half. After more than two centuries of violent conflict, their resistance was broken.

By the 1920s, only a small number of Seri remained, hiding out at the edges of their former territory. Stock raiding had largely ceased. That decade, the development of commercial fishing at Kino Bay—then a rough-hewn camp, exposed to the elements—slowly drew the tribe into the modern economy. Mexican and Seri fishers caught sharks, turtles, and a giant species of sea bass known as the totoaba. Totoaba swim bladders, prized as a delicacy in China, were dried and exported; with no market for the flesh, six-foot carcasses piled up on the beach, picked over by vultures and coyotes. There is a photograph of Miguel Barnett, the Seri patriarch, standing barefoot on the shore in 1935, surrounded by gutted fish; birds are wheeling overhead, scavenging discards from the cleaning tables. Mexican fish buyers often paid the Seri with marijuana or bootleg mescal, spurring alcoholism and brawls. In winter, when the totoaba were shoaling, around two-thirds of the tribe camped in dunes on the outskirts of Kino, living in shelters of brushwood and scrap metal. This camp became more permanent after 1926, when an American businessman opened a fishing club that brought streams of tourists to the area. "The North Americans amused themselves by giving out clothing, food, money and knickknacks," the historian Edward Spicer wrote, describing the Seri as "an almost completely dependent, poverty-stricken people."

. . .

From its humble origins as a fishing camp, Kino Bay has developed into a gaudy vacation town, with a strip of hotels and private villas stretching down the beach. The buildings extend right up to the sand, with high walls and few access paths to the shore. There are seafood restaurants with thatched roofs where buskers in cowboy hats serenade the tables and, at the roadside, vendors selling shrimp cocktails inside coconuts. The convenience stores have blasting air conditioners and fridges of ice-cold beer. The streets are lined with planted palms; people zip around on quad bikes. Kino became a popular destination in the 1960s for "snowbirds" from the United States—retirees with RVs who drove down for the mild winters—but their numbers have thinned since Sonora became more violent. Now Kino functions mainly as a coastal escape for residents of Hermosillo. Some of the largest homes, bristling with security cameras, are said to be owned by narcos; others belong to hoteliers, lawyers, and the executive of a Sonoran pork farming conglomerate. The grandest mansion of all occupies an entire residential block but was abandoned prior to completion when its owner was arrested; its amenities include the skeleton of an indoor swimming pool flanked by giant Roman-style columns and a fortified basement with an evacuation tunnel running off the property. I was told that the owner was a former leader of the Sinaloa cartel whose wife had been seduced by a rival and then killed, with her head delivered to him in a refrigerated box. But the more likely story in circulation is that the property belonged to a billionaire cocaine smuggler who mysteriously died while undergoing surgical procedures to alter his appearance; two of his surgeons were later brutally murdered. Both episodes are indeed true but nobody could confirm if either man had owned the mansion. Truth and rumor run side by side in Sonora, with the border between them not always distinct.

I arrived in Kino in the summer of 2021 with an arrangement to meet Octavio, who was the focus of a feature I was reporting for *The New Yorker*. We had spoken by phone, and he had invited me to observe his toad sessions, but his communication style was haphazard and I was unsure whether he would show up. Our plan was to drive to Punta Chueca for the Seri New Year celebrations, which traditionally take place at the end of June, marking the onset of the summer monsoons. The event had been promoted by several government agencies, with Octavio featuring in a broadcast from the Mexico Tourism Bureau. "Toad medicine has become a global icon for the rescue of traditional medicine," he said on camera. The Seri tribe had allowed him, "as a doctor and a pioneer," he added, to share their Indigenous knowledge with the world.

Yet now there was no sign of him. Octavio wasn't answering his phone. My driver and I waited at one of the Kino restaurants for two hours, sweating over fish tacos, until an abrupt message from Octavio instructed us to meet him at a nearby gas station. He pulled up there in a white Ford truck sporting a stylized decal of a toad and bumper stickers of the Seri flag. He wore a trucker cap with a hand-painted toad on it—a gift from a Mexico City policeman who had recently smoked toad with him. "How are you, bro, how are you?" Octavio said, clasping my hand. He was shorter than I had expected from seeing him in photographs and videos, with sinuous forearms and tousled hair falling over his shoulders. He had dark sunglasses on and was vibrating with energy. Accompanying him in the truck were his teenage daughter and some Mexican television journalists who were shooting a segment about toad medicine. I climbed into the back seat and he drove a short distance to the beachfront, pulling in to a compound of opulent white houses where, without a word to me or any of his passengers, Octavio hopped out and strode through an ornately carved wooden door.

Assuming that this would be a brief stop, I waited outside with Octavio's entourage. Other cars had pulled up, some of them decorated like his, and people were milling around in the parking lot. I got talking to a Mexican couple named Saskia and Gerardo, who were there with their eighteen-month-old daughter. Saskia was serene and maternal in a loose tie-dyed dress; Gerardo was wearing quick-dry shorts and had a more nervous manner. He was an engineer, I learned, and had until recently been an alcoholic. Saskia had threatened to leave him unless he smoked toad with Octavio, which she herself had done a year earlier. "When I got the medicine," Gerardo told me, "all my emptiness was full again."

They were there as volunteer assistants for Octavio, they explained. A friend had accompanied them—a machine tool dealer who was coming to terms with sex addiction and a divorce. When I asked where they were all planning to spend the night, he shrugged and said, "We don't know; we're just following Octavio."

Everyone was speaking with unusual openness, which seemed at odds with the ambiently chaotic mood of the gathering: less healing retreat than improvised road trip. There was still no sign of Octavio, so I crossed through the elaborate doors into a villa with a wide stone patio overlooking the water. Down-tempo electronic music was playing, and a dozen or so people had their phones out, capturing the view. I found Octavio rolling a thick joint in the kitchen, a tastefully designed space with orange walls and blue tiles. The villa belonged, he said, to some people he knew: a pair of prominent judges who argued cases before Mexico's Supreme Court. The people on the patio were there to smoke toad with him and, at some point, attend Seri New Year. It became evident that we would be staying for a while. As Octavio lit the joint and began telling me his story about uncovering the Seri's lost tradition of toad smoking, I was reminded of how another 5-MeO-DMT practitioner had once described him: "He gives the impression of someone who is used to explaining himself, his mission and his motivations. He's probably said this all hundreds of times. Once he launches into a talk, there's really no stopping him. It's not so much a conversation as it is an avalanche of Octavio's passion and intensity."

Coughing occasionally from the smoke, Octavio settled into a steady cadence. "As a Mexican, I had heard about mushrooms and peyote for many years, but no one was talking about the toad," he said. "And so it was amazing to discover that this substance, which had saved my life, was something that people in the past were using for healing. I consider myself a rescuer of some of these methods, maybe a pioneer. But for sure this is not something new for humans. It belongs to our ancient memory."

He spoke like this—discursively, emphatically—for nearly an hour, while the rest of the group hung around, seemingly in no hurry to leave. Then Octavio changed into a traditional blue Seri jacket and sat for a television interview on the patio with everyone watching him. He seemed completely at ease as the center of attention. Toad medicine "is an anti-hallucinogen—something that will remove the madness from your mind," he told the interviewer. "Everything that pulls you away from the here and now, everything that is not real."

It struck me as potentially freighted that Octavio had donned Indigenous garb for this appearance, yet he was insistent about being a spokesperson for the tribe. "He knows more Seri songs than some Seris," one of his followers told me. "He brought the toad to the Seri people." Many in the group, I noticed, had adopted an aesthetic vaguely suggestive of indigeneity: chunky beads, geometric patterns, tattoos of sacred symbols. They seemed sincerely moved by the story Octavio told, viewing the Seri as spiritual authorities and him as their emissary.

The interview concluded and Octavio flung himself into an armchair. Saskia was breastfeeding her daughter. The sunlight shimmered on the sea. The torpid mood was offset only by the bustling movements of a Sri Lankan photographer who, without pause, was taking pictures of everyone. His name was Brian, and he told me that he had been a lifelong spiritual seeker, including spells as a Buddhist monk, a mystic Sufi, and a devout follower of Osho, the Indian guru who inspired a cult movement. Brian explained that, unlike his earlier paths, smoking toad afforded him direct contact with the divine: "There's no guru, no teacher." Despite this assertion, Brian appeared to have attached himself to Octavio: He had recently quit his job, sold his house, and purchased two expensive cameras for documenting toad ceremonies.

Sitting nearby, keeping apart from the group, was a compact, muscular man with "Death Before Dishonor" tattooed across his back.

His name was Oscar, and he had recently arrived from Houston for treatment with Octavio, having already been in rehab eleven times. The son of Mexican immigrants, Oscar had formerly been a drug dealer, playing the kingpin in limousines and VIP nightclubs; his drink of choice was a bright green Hennessy cocktail called the Incredible Hulk. He had been involved with gangs since childhood and bore the scars of knife and bullet wounds. "I was living in a war zone," he recalled. "Everyone was driving around with machine guns." The night before he left for Sonora, he was awakened by gang rivals shooting at his home, but the past few months had been such a blur of drug use—heroin, crystal meth, cocaine—that he felt too numb to retaliate. No longer caring if he survived, he rolled over and went back to sleep. Now, a week later, he pronounced himself a changed man. "I got my spirit back," he told me. "I know what it is to have a heart again."

The temperature began to cool, and gray pelicans soared by on the breeze. People were lounging on couches, some of them taking pinches of *rapé,* an aggressive tobacco snuff from the Amazon. Octavio, holding another enormous joint, was deep in conversation; then he abruptly stood and announced that we were leaving for Seri New Year. The response was immediate. Phones and bags were gathered. We filed out and drove in convoy toward the mountains, which were glowing in the afternoon light. The road to Punta Chueca, a treacherous gravel track when Octavio first traveled it in 2011, had since been paved, a development he attributed to his work with toad medicine. "Before, nobody was coming here," he announced from behind the wheel. "I opened the door."

. . .

By the late 1930s, Kino Bay posed an existential threat to Seri culture. The tribe's numbers were dwindling. Their traditional way of life was unraveling. Alcoholism ran rampant in the rapidly developing settlement, where Mexicans outnumbered the Seri eight to one. Young men from the tribe were cutting their hair and forsaking traditional dress for Western clothing. Prostitution introduced waves of venereal disease, while measles and influenza spread unchecked. The tribe had experienced epidemics as early as the eighteenth century, when more than fifty Seri at a mission settlement died of measles, yet avoided the extreme death tolls experienced by more sedentary New World communities. Within just two years in Kino, measles outbreaks cut the Seri population from "perhaps 350 to about 160," an anthropologist wrote. The trauma from these episodes would linger. In the early 1970s, when a Seri boy in Punta Chueca developed a skin rash feared to be measles, the village erupted in panic. "The news spread like wildfire and within minutes all the Seris except the stricken boy's family were packing and fleeing," a researcher who witnessed the scene recalled. "There was terror in the air and in less than twenty minutes every Seri boat and pickup truck had left."

The Seri had long been displaced and hunted by Sonora's rulers, but now the state took an interest in preserving their culture, albeit on its own terms. This shift formed part of a broader nationalist movement known as *indigenismo,* which sought to integrate Indigenous groups into Mexico's economy while retaining aspects of their cultural identity. In a bitter twist, the Seri were seen no longer as a threat but as a people to be saved.

In 1938, a well-connected Mexican fish buyer named Jesús Solórzano was appointed to organize a Seri fishing cooperative. The Mexican Revolution (1910–20) had ushered in a wave of reforms, with cooperatives becoming a favored tool of the new regime—part social experiment, part economic engine—intended to empower the rural poor. Solórzano was not Seri himself, but he gained the trust of the tribe and proposed relocating them to an old fishing settlement called Desemboque, nearly seventy miles up the coast. This was framed as a protective measure, shielding the Seri from Kino's corrupting influences, but was also motivated by economic interests, isolating the tribe from rival fish buyers. Desemboque was forbiddingly remote, located on a windswept plain near the mouth of a dry riverbed, nearly a day's drive over rough terrain from the nearest town. Long before the arrival of settlers, Seri nomads had camped there during seasonal migrations, fishing and gathering mollusks. They knew it as Haxöl Iihom—Place of the Clams. Now Solórzano persuaded most of the tribe to move to Desemboque, transporting them by truck. With government support, he built an icehouse and helped establish an elementary school. He ran a small but well-appointed store. For a time, Desemboque was upheld as a model "Indian community." Alcohol and marijuana were banned, and fishing provided a reliable livelihood. But the cooperative's existence was fragile from the outset, dependent on forces beyond the Seri's control. Disputes with buyers and Sonoran officials led to its collapse within a decade, while the old social problems returned. In one fight between Mexican and Seri fishers, men barricaded themselves behind houses and fired rifles at each other while women and children ducked for cover. "One of the Seris may die as he appears to have a fractured skull as the result of being hit by the butt of a Mexican rifle," a visiting anthropologist wrote. The cooperative had been intended as a supportive measure, but life for the Seri remained deeply precarious.

At the time, the region's dominant commercial fishery centered on shark livers, used for producing vitamin supplements in the United States. The waters surrounding Tiburón Island—Spanish for "shark"—teemed with makos and hammerheads. Pascual Encinas, the militant rancher who warred with the Seri, had once led a mule across the channel, towing it behind his canoe. The mule hobbled ashore on three legs, the fourth having been torn off. A century later, the Seri, whose ancestors had navigated the gulf in reed balsas, reinvented themselves as shark fishers. But the market promptly collapsed due to the advent of synthetic vitamins, slashing Seri fishing incomes by half. Stocks of other key species, such as the totoaba, plummeted due to overfishing. The Seri adapted once more, shifting their focus to sea turtles, long a cornerstone of their diet. But they were no longer harvesting for subsistence, nor in accordance with their traditions. "The process of acculturation attempted by the soldiers and missionaries is being accomplished by the peso and the dollar," a scholarly volume on the Seri later noted. Dynamite fishing, which had been practiced in Kino for years, became even more widespread as competition for dwindling resources intensified. The explosions could be wildly dangerous for Seri fishers, who were sometimes killed or maimed in the process. One Desemboque man had both hands blown off and his jaw broken, leaving him permanently deafened and unable to support his wife and three small children.

The oceanographer Jacques Cousteau once called the Gulf of California "the Aquarium of the World." In its natural state, it was one of the most productive and diverse seas on earth, sustaining thousands of species. Many were found nowhere else, such as the vaquita, a small variety of porpoise. But by the mid-twentieth century, as the Seri were becoming increasingly dependent on marine resources for income, industrial fleets had begun to strip the gulf of its riches. In 1940, John Steinbeck observed Japanese shrimp trawlers "scraping the bottom clean," as he later recounted in *The Log from the Sea of Cortez.* (This was an older name for the gulf, commemorating a Spanish conquistador who led the colonization of Mexico and was responsible for millions of deaths.) Steinbeck boarded one of the vessels, where he watched the heaving nets being hauled in. "The big scraper closed like a sack as it came up, and finally it deposited many tons of animals on the deck," he wrote—a roiling mass of fish, sharks, rays, and other organisms, including bright corals and anemones dislodged from the seabed. "Fish were thrown overboard immediately, and only the shrimps kept. The sea was littered with dead fish, and the gulls swarmed about eating them."

Yet even as economic pressures on the Seri mounted, many of their traditions endured, deeply rooted in the tribe's understanding of nature and their environment. A crucial part of this heritage was the vision quest, which took young Seri into the desert for days of fasting and solitude. Some returned as shamans with *hacáatol cöicóos,* or "songs of spiritual power"—lyrical verses describing desert winds, seabirds in flight, the shifting tides—that had appeared to them during trancelike states. (There is no record of the tribe using hallucinogens, even though datura, a psychoactive plant consumed by other Indigenous groups in the Americas, grew in their territory.) Supplicants often reported seeing visions of jagged light and bright dots, which the Seri depicted in distinctive face-paint designs. Not all who sought to become shamans succeeded: The Seri were particularly amused by the story of one man who embarked on a vision quest but took his lunch with him.

Song was equally central to the Seri origin myth, which tells of a primordial figure named Hant Caai who sang the world into existence, creating a race of giants. These giants were later trapped by a great flood and transformed into boojums, a tree native to Sonora that resembles an upside-down parsnip studded with toothpicks. (An American botanist named it after a nonsense word in a Lewis Carroll poem.) According to Seri oral tradition, a second figure, Hant Hasooma, then appeared: a short, rotund male who wore a wide-brimmed hat. While rubbing his legs on Tiburón Island, he dislodged clumps of earth that tumbled to the ground and turned into people, giving rise to the Seri.

In 1944, an American ethnomusicologist named Henrietta Yurchenco, who would later give a young Bob Dylan one of his first radio interviews, recorded shamanic Seri songs during a trip to Desemboque. The ban on vices was no longer in effect, and participants expected her to pay them with alcohol and marijuana. Yurchenco had to wait seven weeks for her recording equipment to arrive and lost twelve pounds due to the scarcity of food in the village. To prevent her acetate discs from melting, she stored them in the community's icehouse.

Just a few years later, the songs she had documented began fading from use as another outside influence took hold in Desemboque. Evangelical missionaries from the Mexican Apostolic Church began proselytizing in the village, which they did more effectively than the Catholics centuries before them. Traditional songs, along with drinking and marijuana, were soon forbidden. "Seri culture, once concerned with living in the present and thoroughly optimistic as to the future, has now become chiefly concerned with conforming to virtually impossible Protestant Fundamentalist taboos," an anthropologist who had spent time with the tribe wrote furiously the next decade. His name was William Smith, and he had been visiting the Seri since 1944, when signs of their changing culture were already evident: store-bought clothing in place of animal skins, tins for carrying water. He went on to spend months at a time in Desemboque and on Tiburón, becoming a paternalistic figure who "came to regard the Seris as his own personal tribe," a colleague observed. (In around 1967, Smith was expelled from Mexico after a confrontation with a high-ranking government official over Seri rights; he never returned.) The church services he abhorred took place most evenings and largely comprised hymns, with congregants known as "the Singing Ones"—a galling irony, given the traditional role of song in Seri life. By the mid-1950s, in response to rising Christian influence, around a third of the tribe had departed for another fishing camp, which became the village of Punta Chueca; among those who moved was a young Chapo Barnett, the acclaimed Seri dancer.

By then, to his displeasure, Smith had been joined in Desemboque by a pair of American linguists, Edward and Mary Beck Moser, who moved to the village in 1952. The Mosers were non-proselytizing Bible translators who built themselves an adobe house and began the first formal study of the Seri language. Smith accused them of undermining Seri culture, but few others would do more to document the tribe's traditions. One of their early visitors was a young botanist named Richard Felger who, as a child, had grown orchids on his bathroom wall and reared alligators in his bathtub. Felger had manners that struck some people as abrasive. His first words, on walking into the Mosers' house, were "Where can I press my plants?" Nevertheless, his passion for botany was infectious. He and Mary Moser spent the next thirty years studying Seri ecological knowledge, producing a tome, *People of the Desert and Sea,* that is considered a classic of ethnobotany.

For all the disruptions wrought by outsiders, the Seri had preserved a rich and detailed set of traditions, from the medicinal uses of desert plants to vision quests and music. "It did not take long to realize that there was a vast unrecorded knowledge about to vanish," Felger later recalled. "The kids were interested in pickup trucks and pop culture like teenagers anywhere and there was a truncation of knowledge." He and Moser described how Seri girls had once played with dolls made from eelgrass; how women prepared face paint with pigments from cactus fruits, honeycomb, and agave; how basket weavers coiled desert scrub into intricate designs; how hunters lured deer by emulating crying fawns; how pack rat nests were raided for their stores of seeds. "Very few edible plants were overlooked," they wrote. Felger, especially, was amazed by what he learned. "The elders knew a lot about plants that no botanists knew," he wrote.

Like many ethnobotanists of the era, his icon was Richard Schultes, the Harvard scholar who had shaped the entire discipline. Felger became obsessed with impressing Schultes, hoping to study under him, but failed to become part of his clique. In a further blow, Felger's girlfriend left him for another Schultes acolyte—Andrew Weil, the integrative medicine doctor who would later help solve the toad mystery in Tucson. "Richard was crushed," one of Felger's former colleagues told me. "He had this chip on his shoulder, this sense that nobody respected his work." Felger eventually got Schultes to visit Seriland; there is a photo of the elder scholar on Tiburón Island in a white buttoned-up shirt and spectacles, kneeling in a circle of stones used for vision quests. If anything might have earned Felger the recognition he craved, it would have been the discovery of a psychoactive toad tradition. But for all his exhaustive documentation of Seri lore, Felger never encountered anything like it. *People of the Desert and Sea,* in fact, makes no mention of the subject, noting only that amphibians were "inconsequential in Seri culture."

. . .

As Octavio drove us into Punta Chueca, we were greeted by a hand-painted sign advertising ancestral Seri medicine. He had kept up a monologue the entire way, sometimes waving his hands so animatedly that he let go of the wheel; at one point, he took a selfie with both hands and nearly swerved off the road. We headed through the village toward the beach, where a few hundred people had gathered in a dusty public square. An elderly Seri woman was chanting into a microphone. There were stands selling handcrafts—beaded necklaces, ironwood carvings, woven baskets—and groups of women who, for a fee, would paint your face with traditional Seri markings. On one wall nearby was a giant unfinished mural of psychedelic toads, one of several in the village. I met a Mexican tour guide with a sunburned nose who told me that five buses, each carrying around fifty visitors, had arrived for the celebrations. "Tourism to Punta Chueca has really taken off," he said. "It has a lot to do with the toad."

Filmed by two cameramen, Octavio moved through the crowd with an entourage of more than a dozen people, his toad cap pulled backward over his long hair. He was greeted by people in every direction, like a film star walking into a premiere. He paused for a Seri woman to daub geometric blue lines and red dots on his cheeks and whispered something to her in Spanish that made her blush. "It's an honor for me to have the Seri paintings on my face," he told me afterward, placing his hand on his heart in a rare moment of stillness. Then he was off again. A stiff breeze was blowing and festive streamers rippled in the air. "My dad's always a big center of attention here," his teenage daughter, Salvia, told me, with the hint of an eye roll. "He's just really well loved."

We had arrived just in time for a ceremony with the Seri flag: vertical bands of red, white, and blue, with a deer's head suspended at the center. Six young women solemnly carried the flag toward the chief of the elders' council, Enrique Robles, whose father had written the original letters authorizing Octavio's work with the tribe. To my surprise, one of the women—blond, fair-skinned—wasn't Seri. Sensitivities over cultural misappropriation seemed milder than in the United States or my home country of South Africa. Tourists posed for selfies in Seri attire, many with their faces painted. There were women in bikini tops and older men with Seri necklaces who looked like fans at a Grateful Dead reunion. "Toads!" a group chorused, when I asked why they were there.

After the flag ceremony, four members of the Seri traditional guard stepped up in boots and camouflage pants, shouldering assault rifles. As people pressed around them, taking photos, they fired live rounds over the sea. I noticed a Mexican man in a bulletproof vest standing farther back, holding an even larger gun. I pointed him out to my driver, who grew up in Sonora and is knowledgeable about the cartels. "Sicario," he said without hesitation, using the local word for assassin.

Later that night, there would be a sweat lodge ceremony on the beach, followed by toad sessions hosted by Octavio and some of his former Seri patients. This would all be taking place in narco country. The juxtaposition was startling.

That evening, as the setting sun lit the clouds orange, I watched three young men approach Octavio in the parking lot. He proceeded to blow *rapé* up their noses with a curved wooden pipe. The youngest recipient, who was fourteen, immediately began throwing up. He bent forward with his hands on his knees and collapsed on the dirt. Before long, the two older youths, both in their early twenties, were also emptying their stomachs, and a pack of dogs gathered to lap up the vomit. A middle-aged woman came over with rolls of toilet paper; two of the young men were her sons, she told me, wiping their mouths. The entire family had traveled nearly a thousand miles from the city of León, in central Mexico, to participate in toad ceremonies with Octavio; the snuff was necessary for purging toxins, she said. Her husband, a heavyset lawyer with Seri face paint and a wide-brimmed hat, was standing nearby. He began telling me how much he admired the toad doctor when Octavio came over and flung an arm around his shoulder. "Man, I love this guy," Octavio said to me, his eyes streaming from a hit of *rapé*. "He just got me free on a homicide charge."

CHAPTER 4

Backlash

Araceli Ramírez Hidalgo, a sociable housewife in her forties, had a history of losing money in pyramid schemes. This troubled her husband, Jorge Villalpando Medel, a broad-shouldered lawyer who saw it as his duty to protect her. One year she got caught up selling dietary supplements, another year cosmetics. "They abuse people," Villalpando said of the companies, "but also offer them a sense of purpose and relief."

The couple had met in their teens and been married for two decades, raising two sons, when, in 2015, Ramírez fell into a prolonged depression following the death of her mother. At a friend's suggestion, she turned to alternative therapies: energetic massage, sweat lodges, psychedelics. Villalpando was skeptical but sometimes joined her, as did their children. Until then, their family life had been more conventional—Catholic, middle class, fiercely supportive of their local soccer team—but a cultural shift was under way, even in their hometown of León, a manufacturing hub with a provincial reputation. The wellness industry was expanding, traditional taboos around psychedelics had softened, and practices once seen as fringe were reaching new audiences. "We wanted to heal," Villalpando recalled, "so we started experimenting." They attended an ayahuasca ceremony, sipping the bitter liquid beside a roaring bonfire; afterward, Ramírez reported seeing visions of her dead mother. A psychedelic practitioner later told the couple about toad medicine: "Just one puff, you're going to experience ten years of therapy." They smoked toad with him, together with their sons, on several occasions. But Ramírez wanted to go even deeper. When she heard that Octavio would be in town—"the eminence for supplying this substance," as Villalpando called him—she was eager to attend a session. Octavio would be serving two hundred or more people over a weekend, charging around $150 a head. Ramírez reserved a spot, promising her husband that this would be her final experiment with psychedelics.

On October 5, 2018, she went early to the venue, a remote property set amid warehouses and factories on the outskirts of León. The location hadn't been publicly advertised; participants received the address only a few days in advance. Ramírez arrived at the gates of a nondescript recreational facility with a soccer field, a small hall, and a shaded *palapa.* A man she recognized from previous ceremonies was at the entrance, checking names off a list. He greeted her and handed her a liability waiver. Ramírez was planning to spend the day there and have an Aztec-style massage; Villalpando was set to join her after work, and Octavio would serve toad that evening. But at around noon, Villalpando received a frantic call. Ramírez had smoked toad and stopped breathing.

As a subsequent investigation would uncover, Octavio had begun the ceremony that morning while people were still arriving. He spent a few minutes with each person—administering toad, chanting Seri songs—before moving on, leaving them in the care of his assistants. Clients sprawled on the lawn in various states of dissolution. Some moaned or screamed, while others looked blissful. This was how Octavio routinely worked: rapid, high-dose sessions, featuring large groups and minimal preparation or aftercare. For years, other practitioners had warned that this approach was reckless, but Octavio dismissed them, insisting that the medicine, and his practices, were safe. The psychedelic underground was entirely unregulated, with a secrecy that lingered from the war on drugs; even many people who sought Octavio out weren't aware of the fallout from his work. The hype surrounding him and toad smoking had ensured that even as criticism of Octavio grew louder, new clients continued seeking him out.

As her turn approached, Ramírez hugged a friend. "I'm nervous," she said. Octavio handed her the pipe and counted slowly as she inhaled. Then, in full view of the other clients, Ramírez went limp and started convulsing. Chaos followed. Octavio forced water into her nose and gripped her around the waist. When she didn't respond, he blew *rapé* up her nostrils. Other participants, in the midst of their trips, were screaming and crying; one onlooker was so distressed that she locked herself in a bathroom, trying to calm herself with breathing exercises. When she came out, she saw Ramírez lying motionless on the grass while Octavio, seemingly unperturbed, continued serving toad to more people. Then one of the organizers cried out that Ramírez had stopped breathing. Octavio rushed back and began CPR, assisted by another participant, a medical doctor who later recalled that Octavio seemed to be panicking. He pounded Ramírez's chest and blew air into her lungs. Ramírez involuntarily defecated. Someone called an ambulance. Multiple witnesses heard Octavio yelling, "She died! She died!"

By the time Villalpando got there, around half an hour later, medics were placing his wife on a gurney. Her lips were swollen, her skin dark purple. Around forty people, looking frightened, were huddled beneath the *palapa.* An ambulance took Ramírez to the hospital, where she was admitted to a resuscitation bay. Octavio's defense lawyer showed up in the waiting area; according to Villalpando, he offered to cover the medical expenses on Octavio's behalf. "Tell that sonofabitch I'm going to put him in jail!" Villalpando shouted. Not long afterward, a doctor called Villalpando into the ward, where Ramírez was hooked up to a monitor showing no vital signs. Ramírez was pronounced dead that afternoon.

I met Villalpando at his office, a cluttered set of rooms in a run-down neighborhood of León, in the summer of 2021, a few weeks after attending Seri New Year. Villalpando wore a pin-striped shirt and had his dark hair in a topknot. As we spoke, he showed me a photo of his wife from before her turn toward alternative healing. Ramírez looks unhappy in the picture, her hair dyed auburn and cut into bangs, her eyebrows severely sculpted. She is wearing a pearl necklace and a demure white blouse. It is difficult to picture her at an ayahuasca ceremony. "She wanted to become a better mother, daughter, wife," Villalpando said.

Over the next two days, he told me about his efforts to bring Octavio to justice, sharing documents from a thick folder of evidence he'd accumulated. He spoke with controlled fury, though he broke down several times, his deep voice cracking. At one point his youngest son showed up after soccer practice; he had been twelve when Ramírez died, Villalpando explained, and taken her death the hardest: "She used to drive him to school, feed him, help style his hair." Villalpando described Octavio as "a populist demagogue, offering easy solutions to difficult problems." The chief protagonist of the global toad-smoking movement had left a trail of harm while evangelizing the transcendent effects of the God molecule, embodying a wider reckoning with the risks and ethics of psychedelic healing. "If I didn't stop Octavio," Villalpando said, "he was going to keep hurting people."

. . .

Whispers of reckless facilitation had followed Octavio since the start of his career as a traveling toad doctor, forming a pattern that would repeat across continents. The complaints were always the same—rushed ceremonies, clients left in highly vulnerable states—but went unheeded for years, overshadowed by the revelatory promise of healing. These traced back to Octavio's very first international tour, in early 2013, when he flew to Salt Spring, a small Canadian island near Vancouver.

With a population of around ten thousand, Salt Spring had long been a refuge for countercultural seekers: draft dodgers, back-to-the-landers, artists drawn to its natural beauty. The island was home to wilderness schools, New Age therapists, and organic farmers cultivating more than five hundred varieties of apple. Psychedelics formed part of the local ethos. It was fertile terrain for introducing toad smoking.

Octavio's host was a spry, impish woman in her sixties known as Tofu Deb. She ran a thriving tofu business and grew some of the strongest weed on the island. Her home had long been a hub for psychedelic experimentation, whether with MDMA or Orange Sunshine, a notoriously potent variety of LSD. She had invited Octavio to Salt Spring at the urging of a friend who, a few months prior, had smoked toad with him in Tulum. "There's this shaman going around with the most powerful medicine," Deb recalls her friend saying. She impulsively booked Octavio flights and put him up in her home.

Over the next few days, as word spread on the island, people started showing up for toad sessions. Among the first was a woman in her forties I'll call Sarah. She and her partner had been taking psychedelics together since they were teenagers and knew Deb's place well: a cozy wooden house with an unkempt garden and vats of bean curd fermenting outside. The front door opened onto a brightly painted kitchen filled with Hindu, Buddhist, and Native American art. Night had fallen by the time Sarah arrived, and more than a dozen people were wandering around in what she described as a "field of shifting energies." Octavio was smoking a joint and had a supremely confident manner. Every now and then, small groups would go outside to receive the medicine, then drift back indoors with dazed expressions.

Sarah's partner had a history of traumatic experiences with psychedelics and, before his turn came, asked Octavio what to expect from the trip. Octavio seemed impatient to be done for the night and was eyeing an attractive young woman who had smoked toad with him earlier. "Put on a fucking diaper and go outside!" he commanded. "Don't be such a baby!" Sarah was taken aback by this outburst, especially in the context of a psychedelic ritual, but found herself following him onto the lawn. Octavio "had this very directive quality," she later told me. Her partner received the medicine first, making it through without apparent difficulty. Sarah went next. As the effects came on, Octavio chanted for a bit and then abruptly returned to the house, leaving her unsupervised on the lawn. Lying on her back, Sarah gazed up at the sky. It felt as if silver threads of starlight were passing through her eyes and into her brain—"like cosmic acupuncture," she said, "setting everything right."

In the weeks that followed, hundreds more clients showed up, some arriving by ferry from the mainland. Octavio presided over the sessions in cavalier fashion. He performed no health screenings of his clients and offered little to no preparation before their trips—no discussions of safety, intention setting, or other tools commonly used by psychedelic practitioners for helping cultivate a conducive internal state, or "set," for the coming experience. "There was often a bit of a party vibe," Sarah said. "The lines between ceremony and recreation were very blurred."

Octavio delighted in the potency of the island's weed, consuming more cannabis oil than local growers believed was humanly possible. He also helped himself to MDMA, which was of rare quality and in generous supply. One night, Deb, his host, had taken MDMA with a friend when Octavio strode in and handed her a toad pipe. "I was gone for at least forty-five minutes," she recalled. "I almost died on my kitchen floor." She experienced a disembodied, dreamlike state and saw a Mayan face appear before her, asking, "Have you seen enough?" Years later, she recognized the face on a magazine cover and stuck it on her wall, believing it had saved her life.

As Octavio continued serving toad, the intensity only escalated. At a beach party one night, with beers and joints circulating, he confronted a man who had been drinking heavily. The man had a history of alcoholism. "You need to turn your life around," Octavio said, preparing a heavy dose. Believing that he was dying, the man attacked Octavio during his trip. Octavio's practices were beginning to frighten those around him, and someone suggested that Deb draft a basic indemnity waiver. Another time, at her house, a man smoked toad five times in succession, screaming so loudly that people feared he had been possessed by demons. Clients tore off their clothes in the garden, alarming the neighbors. When this became too much for Deb, Octavio went to stay with Sarah and her partner for several weeks.

Sarah would later distance herself from Octavio and quietly warn others not to attend his sessions, but at the time, like many others, she was captivated by his presence. "I couldn't distinguish Octavio from the medicine," she told me, describing her first toad experiences as "devotional in nature." She cooked for him, did his laundry, and provided him with weed. Some nights, she would drive forty minutes into town and back to buy him cheeseburgers. ("The shaman needs a burger," she recalls thinking.) When Octavio fell out with one of his assistants, Sarah began helping out during sessions, where she observed women of all ages becoming "orgasmically aroused" under the influence of toad medicine. The drug is known to unleash powerful sexual urges in some people, often without any conscious awareness or memory. "They were just throwing themselves at him," Sarah told me. Octavio usually rejected these advances, but he also began sexual relationships with several of his clients. One woman who became his lover around that time recalls opening her eyes after a trip: "Octavio's face was close to mine, and we locked eyes." Around the men on Salt Spring, Octavio boasted about how many women he'd slept with. He was keeping score, he said, as part of a competition with an old friend—a toad practitioner known as Dr. Gerry.

As Octavio's visit went on, Sarah learned that some doctors from a local health-care practice were writing a public letter advising people not to attend his sessions. Octavio was accused of performing untrained chiropractic adjustments on his clients, vigorously cracking their backs and necks while they were under the influence; a number said that they came away with painful injuries. Octavio later denied this to me, even though video footage on his own YouTube account shows him twisting the necks of at least two people during ceremonies on Salt Spring. (He conceded that people's reactions were at times "severe" and "without preparation," noting that some were likely left with "bruises and scratches.") The letter was scheduled for publication in a community newspaper, with a staff reporter preparing an accompanying article, until Sarah persuaded the editor to kill both pieces. "I don't know why I was so invested in protecting him," Sarah told me, "and whether, had those stories been published, they could have prevented future harms."

At the end of our interview, Sarah mentioned a disturbing story that Octavio had shared with her one night while smoking weed in a hot tub. A few months earlier, he and a young woman whom he referred to as his soulmate had spent the night, accompanied by several others, at a property near Tulum. Octavio described how they had smoked toad together near a cenote, a kind of underground cave filled with water. The woman went missing afterward, and police divers later pulled her body from the cenote.

. . .

The Maya of the Yucatán Peninsula believed that cenotes were portals to the underworld. At Chichén Itzá, one of their grandest cities, hundreds of sacrificial victims were cast into the waters of one cenote as an offering to the rain god Chaac. Spanish conquistadors seized the city in the sixteenth century and renamed it Ciudad Real. Chichén Itzá became a cattle ranch, and the civilization of the Maya, after more than three thousand years in existence, soon lay in ruins.

The monumental pyramids and rich cultural artifacts they left behind captivated researchers for centuries. One of the foremost Mayanists, as these scholars became known, was a prolific Yale archaeologist named Michael D. Coe. In the 1960s, Coe excavated toad skeletons in southern Mexico, prompting early speculation among researchers about the animals' psychoactive uses. The following decade, he published a book exploring the Maya belief in cyclical time, observing that one such cycle was said to repeat every five thousand years—an idea later seized upon and distorted by New Age writers, who, drawing on mystical and esoteric traditions, reimagined it as a divine warning. The "Mayan prophecy" spread through popular culture, fueling a global obsession with the idea that the world would either end or ascend to a higher plane on December 21, 2012.

As the date drew near, doomsday parties were organized around the world. Among the most extravagant was a two-day electronic music festival on the beach in Tulum, within sight of a ruined Maya city. "If the world were to end tomorrow, what would you do today?" *DJ*

Magazine wrote in a preview. "You'd want to go raving, right?" The lineup featured international psytrance acts—a driving, high-tempo genre of electronic music associated with psychedelic festival culture—with names like Hallucinogen, Zen Mechanics, and Shpongle. Artists painted psychedelic artworks live onstage. More than eight thousand people flocked from around the world to attend.

That December, Octavio and some friends set off on a two-thousand-mile road trip from Hermosillo to Tulum, stopping along the way to offer toad ceremonies. In Cancún, he met up with a tall, dark-haired woman in her twenties named Ana Patricia Arredondo. A former beauty queen, she had taken a long-distance bus to join Octavio, whom she had met online after searching for depression therapies and smoked toad with a number of times in the past. She introduced herself to the group as his girlfriend and, over breakfast at the hotel, talked loudly about how she had been sexually abused in her youth, a member of the traveling party, Carmina Borja, told me. Yet Arredondo's relationship with Octavio seemed strangely unequal. As she spoke about her traumatic upbringing that morning, Borja recalled, he stood up and left the table, and over the following days he often ignored her altogether, treating her no differently than anyone else, although they went to bed together every night. Odily Fuentes—the friend who had first introduced Octavio to the Seri—was also on the trip, and likewise described Arredondo to me as Octavio's girlfriend. Octavio called her Paty.

The group stayed at a private estate near Tulum with access to several cenotes. Octavio planned to use one of these for a toad ceremony commemorating the Mayan apocalypse. Two dozen people had booked to attend, mostly wealthy tourists who frequented the area—"the Tuluminati," as Fuentes described them to me. She and her husband chose to attend the festival instead, leaving the property on December 20. Later that day, Octavio called her. The ceremony had been canceled. Arredondo was missing.

When Fuentes returned, Octavio took her to a cenote where he said he and Arredondo had smoked toad together. As he showed her the site, Fuentes thought that he seemed strangely calm. "Before that day, he had clear eyes," she told me. "Afterwards, they were dark." For nearly a week, they searched for Arredondo all over the property—"a nightmare," Fuentes said. On December 26, Arredondo's body was recovered "in a complete state of putrefaction," as one news report noted; it had become stuck among stalactites in a submerged section of the cave and had to be carefully dislodged before divers could return it to the surface.

Fuentes believes that Arredondo might have died in an accident but that Octavio was withholding details of what happened that day. He was on the verge of becoming famous. "He was afraid to lose popularity or credibility," Fuentes said. When I asked Octavio about the episode, he denied that Arredondo had been his girlfriend, contradicting several sources close to him as well as news coverage from the time. Later, when I asked how he would characterize his relationship with her, he wrote, "I don't think I will speak about it." But during a conference presentation in 2018, he showed a picture of them together at a Mayan pyramid. "I didn't see her drown," he told the audience. "No one saw her drown." With emotion in his voice, he said, "When people were waiting for the world to end, my world was *really* ending." He stretched his arms out wide, closed his eyes, and drew a deep breath. "I am here, free, because I am innocent."

In later years, as concerns grew about Octavio's approach to serving the medicine, Arredondo's death became a flash point in the toad community. That he had shared the substance in such an unsafe setting seemed, at minimum, to indicate a severe lack of caution. "It is astonishing to us that this death, occurring back in 2012, appears not to in any way have persuaded Octavio to take a precautionary principle," a group of his critics wrote a few years later. Others interpreted the incident in more ominous ways. Fuentes found herself wondering if, on the eve of a fateful date, Arredondo had somehow become an offering to the Mayan gods, echoing the cenote sacrifices of the distant past. I could find no evidence to support this claim, and Octavio has angrily dismissed any suggestion that Arredondo died in such a manner. A few weeks after her death, Fuentes said that Arredondo appeared to her in a dream, asking a haunting question: "When is Octavio going to change?"

. . .

Consuming psychedelics makes people inherently vulnerable, subjecting their minds to destabilizing forces. A radical promise is that this experience can be liberating, but with this freedom comes the potential for harm. A skilled guide can help mitigate such risks. Yet with these substances long driven underground, nearly anyone can assume the role, with few barriers to entry and little meaningful oversight. With psychedelics gaining mainstream acceptance, a loose and sprawling economy of facilitators has taken shape, including seasoned healers but also more opportunistic and even delusional figures. A friend in Cape Town attended a mushroom ceremony not long ago led by a man who, during the trip, announced that he was a descendant of Jesus and that his "true name" was Lucifer. He had consumed a dose along with his clients and spent the next few hours strumming a guitar. Afterward, my friend went looking for a more structured experience, ending up with a woman who determined his dose—an enormous one—with the assistance of a pendulum. "That was an even worse experience," my friend said, summoning a weary laugh.

The relationship between practitioner and client is charged with an asymmetry in power. The roles are archetypal: guru and student. The incapacitating qualities of psychedelics only heighten these dynamics further. Sexual abuse is so prevalent in ayahuasca circles that a leading psychedelic research institute has issued explicit safety guidelines. ("It is not necessary for healers to touch intimate parts of your body.") These same vulnerabilities have led to violations in other psychedelic settings. In the 1980s, before MDMA was banned in the United States, two psychiatrists working with the substance were found guilty of sexually assaulting their clients. Afterward, to guard against such misconduct, researchers adopted a new protocol for psychedelic therapy: Two therapists, one man and one woman, would be present for each session.

This became the standard when clinical trials with MDMA resumed in the 1990s. But in 2018, a participant in a study in Canada accused her therapist of repeatedly sexually assaulting her with the knowledge of the second therapist (who happened to be his wife). Videos showed the couple pinning the woman down and embracing her during sessions, whispering, "It's okay. You're safe here." While she was still enrolled in the trial, she went to live at their home, where she and the husband began a sexual relationship. In a civil claim brought to court later that year, the male therapist, who has since been barred from practicing, claimed that their relationship had been consensual and called the woman "a skilled manipulator." (Canadian police had recommended criminal charges, but the prosecutors did not approve them.) The case was settled out of court on undisclosed terms, and the therapist's wife, a psychiatrist, gave up her medical license after receiving a formal reprimand from healthcare regulators in British Columbia.

The harms surrounding psychedelics extend beyond violated sexual boundaries. Participants in ceremonies have experienced psychosis and physical injury. People have died or committed suicide, although the absence of formal reporting systems makes it impossible to know how many. Considerably more research has focused on the therapeutic benefits of psychedelics than on their risks, resulting in an unduly rosy portrayal of the field. "In the wake of two decades of resurgent psychedelic research, and largely positive media coverage, many people may expect psychedelics to yield only benefits," a 2023 study on adverse psychedelic experiences noted. Participants in the study reported a wide range of symptoms—anxiety and fear, social disconnection, a diminished sense of self—that sometimes lasted for months or years. "Many of our respondents reported that their difficulties were exacerbated by a lack of information about what was happening to them, which increased their anxiety, feelings of social isolation, and existential confusion," the authors wrote.

These risks are only amplified when it comes to toad smoking, due to both its intensity and its lack of cultural grounding. Unlike substances such as ayahuasca or mushrooms, there is no intact tradition of use, no established framework for making sense of its effects. Joël Brierre, a practitioner who runs 5-MeO-DMT retreats and trains other facilitators, told me that toad medicine was "particularly susceptible" to misuse. Online dealers have made toad secretion easy to obtain globally; administering it is relatively straightforward, requiring only a lighter and a pipe; there is no formal tutelage, no mandatory system of apprenticeship. Brierre estimated that nine in ten people serving toad were doing so without sufficient responsibility and care. Nevertheless, many of their clients were likely to have sublime experiences. "Practitioners are taking credit for the potency of the molecule," Brierre said, warning that this could lead to "the scariest of ego trips."

In Salt Spring, back in 2013, Sarah learned that Octavio's next destination would be Ireland. Hoping to prevent further fallout, she organized several meetings with his supporters to discuss how Octavio's hosts could "set up better systems of support," she told me. But nothing came of these discussions, and Octavio was soon on his way. Before leaving Canada, he held several ceremonies in Vancouver, where his clients included the renowned trauma therapist Gabor Maté. Maté was shaken by the experience, describing Octavio to me in an email as "charm, charisma, talent, and loads of trouble." (He declined to elaborate, writing, "I have no desire to speak more about this.")

A combustible template was forming for Octavio's travels, marked by curiosity, awe, and disorder. In Ireland, a strapping former rugby player named Ronan was in the midst of an existential crisis when a friend invited him to a toad ceremony. "There's this guy coming, he's a doctor, and he's got something like ayahuasca," the friend said. Ronan had little experience with drugs beyond the occasional joint, but something about the idea pulled at him. He drove into the mountains of Wicklow, a rugged stretch south of Dublin, where he briefly met Octavio and was reassured by his medical credentials. There was no discussion of what was to come, no effort to prepare him for what he was about to experience. Soon, he was in a room with strangers, hearing people "roaring and shouting outside." Then it was his turn.

He stepped through the door, and Octavio handed him a pipe. "It was just like, 'Here we go!'" Ronan recalled. As he began inhaling, he felt the life being sucked out of him. A thought suddenly formed: *If I'm going to die, I'm going to take him with me.* He went for Octavio's throat, and the two men grappled with each other. He dimly heard Octavio coaxing him, "Let go, let go." As the effects of the medicine grew stronger, Ronan collapsed to his knees while Octavio chanted, shaking his rattle. "And then I just got it," Ronan said. He felt a deep energetic purge and "stood up in this bliss of ecstatic wonder." The stars were dancing in the sky. As he recounted the memory to me, Ronan's eyes shot wider: "I was connected to something."

This epiphany was cut short moments later, when Octavio sent him back inside to call the next person. "He didn't come in or ask how people were," Ronan said, describing Octavio as a "swashbuckling, let-the-chips-fall-where-they-may kind of guy." Even without any integration support—the next time he spoke to Octavio was six months later, at another toad ceremony in Ireland—Ronan would look back at the experience as the most profound of his life. He later visited Sonora and apprenticed himself to Octavio for several weeks, chasing toads and smoking ample quantities of their secretions. During one impromptu group session, he ended up pressed against another visitor's back, who had his own tongue pressed against Octavio's forehead; they were interrupted from this "spontaneous energy exchange" by a mechanic arriving to inspect Octavio's truck, which had broken down the previous night. Later in the trip, they camped in Seri territory, where, after a long night of smoking toad and taking mescaline, Octavio proffered a pipe and asked, "Who wants toad for breakfast?"

Ronan aspired to partner with Octavio and become a toad practitioner himself, but he soon became wary of the "spiritual egoism" surrounding the medicine. "The experience is imprinted with him," Ronan explained. "Head-of-the-cult kind of thing." He likened the medicine to Tolkien's Ring, a source of intoxicating power that could corrupt whoever wielded it. (Ronan became a breathwork facilitator instead.)

As his stature grew, Octavio was also securing institutional support, boosting his influence even further. In 2014, he was endorsed as a "carrier of traditional indigenous medicine" by the United Nations Association of Venezuela. The organization's vice president had smoked toad with Octavio, describing the experience in a promotional video as "heavenly and transcendental." Afterward, she issued Octavio official-looking letters for passing through border inspections with toad secretion; this was necessary, she emphasized, for Octavio to "continue his work of healing in the world." Octavio stuck UN stickers on his car, obscuring the distinction between a small nonprofit and the global body it evoked, and was introduced in several podcasts and articles as a UN-supported doctor. Over the next five years, he traveled to more than thirty countries, presenting himself as an internationally recognized healer. Promotional materials for these tours featured a lightly edited version of the UN logo, its familiar blue globe adorned with a leaf and a feather so that it resembled a dream catcher.

One of Octavio's first such trips, early in 2015, was to Australia. His sessions were advertised on Facebook pages for retreats, music festivals, and followers of Osho, the cultish Indian spiritual leader. Octavio traversed the country from Perth to Byron Bay, three thousand miles to the east. One of his clients was Dean Jefferys, a ponytailed filmmaker in his sixties who had produced an early documentary on ayahuasca. During his first session with Octavio, Jefferys had visions of smoking toad on "sacred stone temples," as if in a past life. For more than a week afterward, in the hours before dawn, Jefferys had flashbacks to "toad reality," as he called it. Then, one night, he felt a dark energy in the bedroom—something "more than a nightmare," he wrote on Facebook. Octavio had left town, and there was nowhere to turn for help. "He's too busy serving thousands of patients to take a phone call," recalled Jefferys, who founded a support group on Facebook to deal with what he called "the trail of destruction left behind by Octavio."

It wasn't long before people began sharing disturbing testimonies. "I haven't slept six nights now," a woman in Dublin posted. "I lay awake all night trying to accept the flashbacks but can't. My situation is now serious." Another woman, from Melbourne, recounted how her husband was left unattended on the ground, struggling to breathe, as Octavio continued serving patients. She recommended several ways to make toad sessions safer, such as limiting the number of participants, weighing doses, having trained people at hand to assist in emergencies ("I would suggest a first aid kit"), and providing rituals to help with preparation and integration. Octavio replied that her post was "judgmental and unfair," adding that nobody could be held responsible for patients' responses to psychedelic substances.

Things took an even darker turn in 2016, when footage began circulating of Octavio being aggressive with his clients. In one video, he kicks and slaps a visibly terrified man on a beach in Venezuela while forcing him to take no fewer than six hits of toad. "Don't make me beat you up," Octavio shouts, thrusting a finger in the man's face. At one point, after receiving yet another dose, the man falls back with his arms spread-eagled, slamming his head on the compacted sand. He tries to run away, sobbing, "Octavio, no!" Octavio told me that the man had not been inhaling properly "because he was afraid—afraid of facing his own mind, his ignorance, his inexperience." He added, "I am open to acknowledge that some of my actions might be disturbing for most audiences, but this is a very deep therapeutic work." In another video from around that time, filmed in an orchard of citrus trees, Octavio repeatedly pours water down the throat of a comatose client; you can hear the man choke, his windpipe gurgling, for more than five minutes. Octavio defended the practice, saying he used water to "provoke a breathing response" for people who seized up while experiencing the medicine. His critics likened it to waterboarding.

Octavio believed that psychological resistance was something to be broken through, by force if necessary. When clients refused more toad, he sometimes administered small electric shocks with a device resembling a Taser. "One of the biggest fears of people is electricity, so as soon they just hear the buzz—*bzzt!*—everyone is paying attention," he once explained at a psychedelics conference. "And that's what I'm trying to do. A real *mindfuck* for people."

A clip had recently emerged online showing Octavio, in a T-shirt with Hindu motifs, serving toad to a man on a verdant mountain slope. After dribbling water into the man's mouth and blowing *rapé* into his nose, Octavio zaps him on the buttocks and orders him to stand up. The man swears at Octavio and vomits. Octavio, spliff in hand, whoops with jubilation. He had adopted this technique, he told his conference audience, after running into trouble with "an almost two-meter guy who was a crackhead." The man's parents had brought him in for treatment. "And after his first intake of the medicine, he didn't want to go again," Octavio said. He described fighting with the man—screaming, wrestling—to force him into accepting a full breakthrough dose. "Then I just had this bright idea," Octavio continued, in colorfully inflected English. "I said to his father, 'Next time you bring me your kid, do you know one of those little artifacts that people use to "pinch" the cattle when they are going to the slaughterhouse? Bring me one of those.'"

"Can I make just a little request?" another practitioner, who was participating in the discussion, asked. "Can I request that you just not do that again?"

"No," Octavio said. "This is not out of my suitcase yet, because it's really effective. It's not harmful."

. . .

Even as outrage grew over Octavio's methods, he retained the loyalty of many former patients. Some of Octavio's most ardent defenders were people he had physically overpowered, including the man from the Venezuela beach, who later appeared in a video denouncing the "blasphemies" of Octavio's critics. Suffering can be a necessary trial on the path to growth, but this belief can also provide cover for abuse, binding people more tightly to those who harm them. What looks like trauma to one person might represent healing to another, the distinction often murky and open to interpretation.

Before long, the toad community was "split right down the middle," as Hope Latimer, a moderator on another Facebook support group,

"Beware of the Bufo Gangsters," told me. Her first encounter with Octavio had been at the 2014 World Ayahuasca Conference, in Ibiza. It was the rainy season, and Octavio, an invited speaker, was serving toad on a rocky hillside. Latimer recalled that participants were wandering about, "halfdressed and unsure of their surroundings." Several people lay unconscious as Octavio splashed water in their faces. One woman, left unsupervised during her trip, crawled away and was discovered beneath a tree, bleeding and covered in mud after rolling in the dirt. Octavio's reaction was to push her into a swimming pool with his foot.

Believing that Octavio had good intentions for sharing the medicine, Latimer reached out to him privately. In person, she found him receptive and engaging, and she thought he might rein in some of his more irresponsible practices. But Octavio carried on much as before, seemingly immune to feedback. When challenged, he would point to thousands of positive testimonials about his work, including near-miraculous accounts of healing. "But imagine you wanted to go skydiving," Latimer said, "and they threw fifty people out of the plane at once. Let's say thirty-five of them land safely. What happens to the rest?" Laughing bitterly, she added, "Oh, and the next day, the skydiving school has left town."

Many psychedelic practitioners were horrified by Octavio's methods. But as the most prominent figure in the toad world, Octavio had come largely to define the practice, and many aspiring facilitators emulated him. "It created a certain set of expectations," one therapist told me. Octavio wasn't alone in establishing this paradigm, with another toad practitioner becoming almost as influential: his old friend from medical school, now widely known as Dr. Gerry.

Gerry cast a long shadow in the toad-smoking world. He was the one who had introduced Octavio to the medicine, and he sometimes referred to Octavio as "my protégé." Yet as the practice became more popular, it was Octavio who claimed the spotlight, fueling acrimony between the two men. "He was jealous of Octavio doing ceremonies," Gerry's wife, who became his lover after smoking toad with him, told me. After Octavio starred in a VICE documentary, Gerry starred in a

VICE documentary. After Octavio published a book, so did Gerry—with the same publisher. When Octavio formed a nonprofit foundation, Gerry did as well. The men bad-mouthed each other to their clients and attempted to sabotage one another's ceremonies. In a public Facebook post, Octavio once called Gerry "the most disgusting being on the planet."

Latimer met Gerry in 2015 and briefly worked as his assistant, helping run ceremonies in California. "I've never seen more dangerous overdosing in my life," she recalled. One man gagged and began foaming at the mouth. A young woman blacked out after repeatedly hitting herself in the face. "Gerry was completely ambivalent," Latimer said. Sometimes, when clients "with a strong spirit" showed up, she added, Gerry intentionally served them extra-large doses and laughed at their reactions. ("Hope did this without any evidence and because she was outraged that I rejected her as an assistant," Gerry wrote in a public statement. "She is not a medical doctor and does not have a background in pharmacology or psychology. She is not qualified to give opinions regarding the dosage of 5-MeO-DMT.")

As the psychedelic renaissance gathered momentum, a demographic shift was taking place among people seeking treatment, making these practices seem even more ill-advised. One 5-MeO-DMT practitioner told me that the bulk of his clients had formerly been "psychonauts, spiritual seekers, and healthy young people." In just a few years, this switched to people needing "potent intervention in their lives," whether for addiction or chronic depression. "Most people coming to this medicine *already* have mental health issues and trauma," Latimer said. "To be further harmed really spins them out of control."

Latimer began spending more time on the Facebook support groups, where she noticed that people who posted about challenging experiences with the medicine were often attacked in the comments. A man in the Netherlands who described himself as autistic shared a testimonial of smoking toad with Octavio and spending ten weeks afterward in a psychiatric hospital, experiencing terrifying flashbacks while being medicated with various antipsychotics. "You didn't allow your ego to vanish and be who you really are," one of Octavio's supporters replied. "You keep blaming others about your incapacity to work on your problems, and I sense that this situation repeats in other areas of your life." Another wrote, coldly, "I don't know what you want with all this drama."

For some, it was easier to blame the victim than to question the movement they felt part of. This enforced a kind of spiritual meritocracy: If you didn't experience the full breakthrough, the fault was likely your own. Latimer identified an insidious line of thinking that she characterized using a #MeToo analogy: "He didn't rape *me,* so he isn't a rapist." For devotees of Octavio and Gerry, she went on, "it's impossible that they might have harmed people, because this is the God molecule—and so these men are like gods." The experience was so earth-shattering that facilitators could become figures of almost mythic power, mediating access to the divine. "If I get in your line of sight while you're taking the medicine, and you're in the God consciousness, I become God," Latimer explained. A pervasive New Age ethos of radical nonjudgment further insulated toad facilitators from criticism, reinforced by the culture's roots in prohibition—an oppositional, underground mindset that fostered a sense of collective loyalty. This attitude was on full display on Facebook, where one supporter wrote, "I best serve the Sacred Medicine and myself by not adding to the infectious negativity and Ego on display by condemning or judging Dr. Octavio Rettig." In light of this permissiveness, Octavio was able to solicit positive reviews effortlessly, once posting a single word—"Testimonios"—and receiving more than a thousand replies.

Acting as a volunteer psychedelic integration coach, Latimer reached out to people who were suicidal or debilitated by anxiety. Some had experienced flashbacks while driving; others felt ashamed after orgasming during trips. None of them had been screened prior to smoking toad with Octavio or Gerry, even clients with bipolar disorder or other psychiatric conditions. "They weren't being given answers about what had happened to them," Latimer said. "They were feeling mocked or neglected, and completely abandoned." Octavio told me that "sexual releases or orgasmic responses are very common," explaining that this was why he served toad in groups. ("So there is nothing to hide.") He conceded that "more than one person might feel exposed after this." He also said that "people with psychiatric disorders or other medications are not candidates to do bufo," contradicting statements in previous interviews with me where he claimed he'd treated a wide range of psychiatric conditions. Dr. Gerry has broadly denied such allegations in the past. According to Latimer, the people she spoke with were often told that the medicine had merely highlighted unresolved issues in their lives—a mindset she described as gaslighting. Yet this attitude was ubiquitous in the toad community. "What I've learned from this medicine is that there are no good or bad practitioners," one prominent facilitator asserted at a psychedelics conference. "When you have a practitioner who is bullying you, or pampering you, it's fine. Maybe that's what you need, and your spirit chose it previously."

Despite the growing controversy, people continued flocking to Octavio and Gerry for treatment. Practitioners who worked more cautiously with toad medicine tended to have lower profiles and were harder to find. "Who gets famous in this world?" Latimer said. "The self-promotors, the narcissists." A feedback loop among clients further distorted the field: People who had positive experiences were quick to share them with others, while people who didn't tended to withdraw from view. "People are harmed a lot more than you hear about," Brierre, the practitioner trainer, told me. "We see the fallout. It's terrifying." He attributed this to "the rise of the rock-star shaman."

• • •

Like many other psychedelics, 5-MeO-DMT is understood to be non-addictive and low in toxicity. This does not mean that the substance is inherently safe. At high doses, users become oblivious to their surroundings, leaving them at the mercy of physical hazards: stumbling, burns from ritual fires, head injuries from thrashing. The terror some people experience can also provoke violent fight-or-flight responses. A psychotherapist who smoked the synthetic molecule in the 1990s seized up "as if in rigor mortis" and turned purple while feeling trapped in "a horizonless horror," he later wrote. "I was completely disconnected somatically, unable to locate or feel my body. . . . What remained of me was but a ghostly speck of awareness, an entombed locus of ricocheting attention in a completely unfamiliar locale, pervaded with a sickening despairing intuition that the 'waking state' me was in grave danger, perhaps already dead." He survived only thanks to an onlooker performing CPR.

Members of psychedelic web forums have shared similarly unnerving accounts. "I thought I was really dying," one 5-MeO-DMT user wrote. "I began to try to rip my hair out. I was terrified out of my mind." Another, in a post titled "The Road to Hell and Back," declared, "I felt nothing but hatred for this drug and stupidity for trying it. If you want a near death experience, just take a heroin overdose." A young man recalled running around in sheer panic ("biting at my t-shirt and angrily yelling 'NO! NO! NO!'") and almost being run over by a car.

In spite of these nightmarish experiences, there have been few public reports of deaths associated with 5-MeO-DMT. In the early '00s, a young man was found dead on a camping trip in the United States with elevated levels of the substance in his body. In 2017, an artist from Wyoming snorted synthetic 5-MeO-DMT with friends after a night of heavy drinking; he fell off his chair, threw up, and asphyxiated. In 2019, the Spanish porn star Nacho Vidal, formerly best known for selling candles made from a mold of his penis, allegedly presided over a toad ceremony in Spain at which a participant died; Vidal was charged with culpable homicide, but the case was later dismissed.

There is also an undated account, documented by the psychiatrist Ralph Metzner, of "a chiropractor with a history of inappropriate sexual advances toward clients" consuming 5-MeO-DMT with his fiancée and another woman beside a hot tub. "They had also been experimenting with prolonged breath-holding underwater," Metzner writes. The fiancée submerged herself while the others reclined at the poolside. In a grim foreshadowing of Octavio's tragedy at the cenote, the chiropractor suddenly realized that she was floating face down and hauled her out, but she had drowned.

In 2013, less than a year after Arredondo's death, Octavio served toad to an elderly man in Ibiza. After inhaling from the pipe, the man opened his eyes and flashed an eerie smile. "And when I see this smile I say, *Please, please, please don't die on me!*" Octavio recounted during a talk. "And he died there. He went completely from pink to pale in a few seconds." He added, with an exculpatory note, "I think this person had a beautiful opportunity to transcend in love and in light."

At another conference, Octavio spoke about a different death in his care: an alcoholic in his forties who attended a ceremony in Teotihuacán, an ancient Mexican city with towering stone pyramids, in 2016. The man stopped breathing after smoking toad, and a postmortem determined he had died from a blood clot in the lung, possibly triggered by the acute physiological stress of the experience. "I tried to resuscitate him, but it was in vain," Octavio said. He was briefly taken into custody but released without charges. (The Mexican justice system is notoriously opaque, and I was unable to find records of this. In 2021, Octavio told me that he'd been arrested twice on homicide charges, but when I asked him for details, he said, "Do your fuckin' job, bro.") He told the audience that the man's unhealthy lifestyle was to blame and implied it was the only death he had witnessed, omitting the earlier incident in Ibiza. "This was an accident," Octavio said. "And this accident might happen again." Such risks, he argued, were unavoidable: "Because we are sick and living in a sick society, and we need to take desperate actions." He cast toad medicine as a "way out from the madness we create" and warned, "Just like in war, just like in sports, there will be casualties."

As he spoke, his tone grew more defiant. "One day I will be judged for my actions in this world, but none of you can do that," he said. "Only God will do that." Until then, unshakable in his self-belief, he would continue serving toad medicine. "I know that this is good for people, it's good for society, and I also think that it was good for this guy"—he invoked the man's death—"because it was a blessing for him."

Octavio was similarly unrepentant when called out for his facilitation practices. "People had problems with themselves and the process of the medicine, not with me. They project on me their own darkness," he contended, with no apparent irony, in a 2018 interview with Dean Jefferys, the founder of the Facebook support group. On another occasion, Octavio said, "There is no way, right or wrong, to work with this medicine, because there is no tradition. Right now we are in some kind of wild, wild west, and anyone is doing whatever they want."

In 2018, as stories of death and recklessness continued to mount, a group of organizers announced the first global gathering of the psychedelic toad community, the World Bufo Alvarius Congress, to be held in Mexico City that July. This was an opportunity, they wrote, "to finally come together and meet one another face to face, as brothers and sisters in this work." Yet there was an underlying note of tension. "The diversity and approaches to toad medicine have caused division and concern," they added. There was going to be a confrontation with Octavio.

• • •

The Bufo Congress unfolded over three days at a hotel in Mexico City's historic downtown district. In the hallways, vendors sold Seri crafts, singing bowls, jade figurines, "I ♥ Bufo" T-shirts, and myriad toad medicine pipes. Around three hundred people had assembled from around the world. They wore shawls, loose clothes, chunky jewelry, feathers. Octavio brought his mother with him—a sensibly dressed woman in her sixties with short, neatly styled hair—and took her skydiving, something she would never have dreamed of prior to smoking toad. (She had transformed into one of Octavio's staunchest defenders, lashing out at his critics on Facebook. "I have suffered with him from a distance; I have seen him cry," read one late-night post a few months earlier. "As a mother, it hurts me greatly to see such ingratitude.") The congress featured presentations on psychedelic science, Sonoran Desert toad biology, and Mesoamerican archaeology; outside the venue, facilitators offered breathwork, qigong, and yoga. The official schedule had set aside an additional day for private toad ceremonies, and some of these took place at Teotihuacán, the ancient city, as hordes of tourists streamed by, photographing the pyramids.

One afternoon session focused on divergent approaches to working with toad medicine. In the aftermath of Octavio and Gerry's ascent, quiet efforts were under way to make the practice safer. Two months prior, an anonymous collective that called itself the Conclave (like the Catholic cardinals who meet secretively to elect a new pope) had published a best-practices guide for serving 5-MeO-DMT. The Conclave was made up of practitioners and experts from the United States, Mexico, Canada, and Australia. Owing to the molecule being banned in some of these countries, the group operated with extreme caution; I spoke with one source who described its work in intimate terms, only to deny being a member, as if observing the first rule of Fight Club. The best-practices guidelines amounted to an implicit rejection of Octavio's methods, advising practitioners not to "mechanically bludgeon an ego into submission" with large doses of medicine. "No one—NO ONE—should ever be galvanized to move by any external device that removes their consent," stressed another section, obliquely referencing Octavio's electric zapper.

The final panel discussion of the day was titled "Facilitators' Ethics and Code of Conduct." Without Octavio's knowledge, it had been arranged as an intervention. "There was a hidden agenda," one of the participants, an Argentinean woman named Flor Bollini, told me. Bollini was known for serving toad to tech CEOs and billionaires; *Forbes* would later dub her "the Corporate Shaman." She had previously witnessed Octavio serving toad "in a brutal way," she said. Sometimes he would clamp his hand over people's mouths to prevent them from exhaling. "It was devastating to watch," Bollini recalled. Practitioners like Octavio and Dr. Gerry had created a machismo culture around toad smoking, she told me. "The most powerful molecule going around had been left in the hands of these basic Latin men. And Latin men in general serve from their ego. They serve toad as a punch in the face."

Octavio took the stage in a white shirt and black tie. Bollini, lithe and diminutive, sat to his left. Other speakers included James Oroc, the skydiving New Zealander who had written a book about 5-MeO-DMT, and at least one member of the Conclave. Dr. Gerry was supposed to be there but, just weeks earlier, had been disinvited from the congress; the organizers had received information about his conduct that, if true, amounted to "grievous criminal acts," they wrote in a statement. He had been accused, it soon came out, of fraud and sexual assault. Gerry has denied this, and I was unable to find evidence that he was ever charged. The panel started off cordially, but grew heated when Octavio was questioned about his methods. He had made a "star entrance" to the congress, an audience member later wrote, "greeted ecstatically by many appreciative acolytes." At one point, a show of hands revealed that he had served toad to at least a quarter of the people present. But in response to criticism he began "shouting angrily, charging around the room, and lashing out at those who raised objections." Octavio demanded to know if anyone in the audience had been traumatized by his ceremonies and, when a man raised his hand, began remonstrating with him: "You insisted, you asked for the medicine!" Things became so heated that one of his supporters, an elderly European woman, "let out a primal scream of objection."

The pressure had been building for some time. Two months earlier, at a psychedelics conference in Oregon, Octavio had given a talk in which he played footage of himself being violent on the beach in Venezuela. (In a further sign of how untroubled he was by the videos, he had uploaded them to his personal YouTube account.) He asserted that consent from clients was only necessary to a certain point and that changing one's mind during a ceremony was cowardice. After his talk, the event organizer, a religious studies professor at Southern Oregon University named Martin Ball, leaped up before anyone could ask questions. Before the event, several people had asked to address Octavio publicly about the malpractice allegations, but Ball had refused. He now began furiously defending Octavio, gesticulating around the room and yelling, "Fuck you! Fuck you!" He described how he had recently posted a photo to Facebook of Octavio wearing a Lakota headdress, which had belonged to Ball's grandfather, a white man who had lived with the tribe and "was initiated into their medicine ceremonies." In a wounded tone, Ball went on, "And the amount of FUCKING ASSHOLES out there who feel like, '*How dare* you put a picture of Octavio, someone who's so *evil,* and then put a headdress on him?'" Some people got up and left, including parents who had brought young children to the event. "If all that you can do is fucking insult people on Facebook," Ball shouted, to whistling and applause from some of the remaining audience, "go and FUCK yourself!"

A trim, intense man with a sharp nose and a goatee, Ball credited himself with coining the phrase "the God molecule." He once began a talk about 5-MeO-DMT with a jaunty solo on a wooden flute, then removed his shoes and asked, "How many of you out there know—with full confidence, humility, pride—that you are God?" He was a prominent toad practitioner himself, although his approach to serving the substance struck many people as unsettling. In 2016, while addressing a psychedelics society in Los Angeles, he breezily described some of his methods: vomiting on his clients during sessions, sticking his thumbs "way down people's throats" until they gagged, and "touching people on their genitals because that's what they need." He recalled lying on top of a woman who had stopped breathing and pushing his tongue into her mouth. These interventions, he explained, were intended to help people move through "energetic blockages." (Notwithstanding these admissions—which were first reported on by the psychedelic nonprofit Psymposia—Ball, a prolific writer, subsequently self-published a book titled *Facilitating 5-MeO-DMT: An Anthology of Approaches to Serving the God Molecule.*)

A month after the uproar in Oregon, Octavio traveled to a conference in Prague, where he clashed with a panel moderator when she challenged him on his safety record. This encounter was especially charged, given that the woman was Rita Kočárová, the psychologist who had been his girlfriend for the past two years. Octavio had introduced her to toad smoking in 2016, an experience Kočárová later described to me as "traumatic." After being given no information about the substance, she was left alone in a suburban garden, trapped in one of the most harrowing trips of her life. When she confronted him about this afterward, he apologized and invited her to another ceremony. "And I was just crazy enough," Kočárová said. They became lovers. Kočárová later posted a photograph of herself slack-jawed during one of her toad sessions with Octavio, who was shirtless and gripping her around the waist.

But as the furor around Octavio escalated, Kočárová found their relationship increasingly untenable. She had begun a research project on the therapeutic potential of toad secretion with the Czech National Institute of Mental Health but was urged to abandon it. "Everyone was talking about Octavio," Kočárová said. She was a founder of the Czech Psychedelic Society and had helped organize the conference where their confrontation took place. As criticism of Octavio intensified—some of it directed at her by association—she faced growing pressure to take a stand.

Onstage, she tentatively asked the panel if they would be open to sharing personal stories of malpractice or times when psychedelic interventions "went a bit wrong." Octavio sat twirling his mustache and scowling at her. When his turn came, he spoke about the two men who had died in sessions with him, once again vehemently absolving himself of any responsibility. "I've seen people going blue on the medicine," Octavio divulged, "but none of the people who were blue has died. The people who died"—he broke into a strange smile, as if delivering a joke—"they didn't announce it." He said that the deaths had been traumatic for him, but framed them as the "greatest blessing" in his life. By way of explanation, he shared a damning insight. "I know after *that,*" he declared, "that the medicine, it's safe. Humans—we are dangerous."

The week after the Bufo Congress, Octavio traveled to Europe for another round of ceremonies. During one session, he administered multiple doses of toad to a cocaine addict, followed by *rapé* and large quantities of water. According to firsthand accounts, the man became unresponsive and stopped breathing. Octavio began to panic, shaking the man and exclaiming, "He's gone! He's gone!" A bystander with medical training performed CPR while someone else called an ambulance. When notified that the police had been called, Octavio allegedly left to hide the toad medicine, although he has denied doing this. The man was placed in an induced coma in the hospital, where doctors reportedly had to clean his lungs of what they described as "mud"—a mixture of *rapé* and vomit. (He survived and reportedly quit using cocaine.) In the days that followed, Octavio continued using water and *rapé* liberally in his ceremonies. Kočárová recalls warning him that unless he took safety more seriously, another of his clients would soon be dead.

Octavio left Europe shortly after the incident, returning to Mexico in late September 2018. The following week, in nearly identical circumstances, Araceli Ramírez died in León. News of her death spread quickly through the toad community, bringing long-simmering tensions to a head. Signaling a shift in sentiment, the World Bufo Alvarius Congress issued a statement distancing themselves from Octavio, writing, "A line needs to be drawn in the sand for the safety of the community at large."

In early 2019, a group of anonymous toad practitioners and users published a public letter online. Coordinated in part by Kočárová, it outlined "reckless, unethical and potentially criminal behavior" by both Octavio and Gerry, detailing consequences ranging from injuries and death to psychological trauma and a "shell-shocked and divided" psychedelic community. It described Octavio's approach as "high-volume, high-dose, haphazard, dose-them-and-then-leave," and included reports of him "manhandling people while they are in the medicine." Four deaths were documented—Ramírez, Octavio's girlfriend, and two men—along with "rumors of more."

The section on Gerry was even more sinister, with multiple accounts of "not accidental, but intentional harm to others." One of his former girlfriends, a woman from Slovenia, alleged that he had raped her in the summer of 2016 after drugging her with an unknown substance, possibly LSD. An American woman recounted losing consciousness during a toad session and waking to find Gerry's penis near her face. Another former girlfriend said that he had coerced her into sex and threatened to kill her if she had an abortion; she added that Gerry had once confiscated her U.S. passport and traveled overseas for two weeks, keeping her locked up—"alone, sick, and with no food"—at a property in Mexico. There were also reports of Gerry embezzling donations of up to $50,000 for a nonprofit he had founded, promising clients that 30 percent of their fees would go toward the organization. In reality, according to a former partner who had registered the nonprofit in Washington State under his Social Security number, it never received any funds at all.

Following the publication of the letter, Gerry dismissed the range of allegations as "foolish," claiming they were nothing more than attempts to "twist my personal life with lies." He ascribed negative perceptions of his work to "people who lack spiritual intelligence or people who are not entirely prepared for this degree of experience," insisting that such individuals "fall into the hands of their own ignorance"—a breathtakingly contemptuous dismissal of his former clients and romantic partners. "I vehemently deny all claims of malpractice including of rape, fraud, and drugging participants," Gerry wrote in a statement, blaming the accusations of sexual assault on "ex-girlfriends who severely misrepresented situations." The authors of the public letter, he added, had been motivated by jealousy: "They take my work and discredit it in the name of their ego." In a 2023 documentary interview, he cast himself as a martyr: "They crucified Jesus Christ back in the day." I was unable to find any evidence of criminal or civil charges against Gerry being pursued.

Gerry declined to speak to me unless I paid him a "medical consultation fee" of $250 per hour, but his American wife at the time, Kate, with whom he has a son, ardently defended him when we spoke. A recovering opioid addict, Kate is in her thirties and blond, with piercing blue eyes. "Legally Gerry has never gotten in trouble," she told me. "Nothing has even been filed or reported on any crime." On a tense and sometimes bewildering call, she described the women who had accused Gerry of sexual assault as "nightmares of people who are incapable of being unbiased." The woman in Ciudad Juárez hadn't been locked up, Kate clarified: Someone had let her out daily to eat. The Slovenian woman who claimed to have been drugged had been in a "complicated relationship" with Gerry. "I think he was trying to help her," Kate told me. "He would want me to say it was an accident." She trailed off. "Knowing the guy, though—I've had similar experiences." For example, she said, if Gerry believed someone needed a larger dose of mushrooms, he would give it to them without asking. Every New Year, without necessarily informing them, he would send friends candy laced with LSD. Kate later insisted that these candies were "always labeled." She told me that in the past Gerry had surreptitiously given her "ten hits of acid" in a single dose, although she didn't seem to find this problematic. Then she said, abruptly, "I think we should talk about something else."

I spoke with Octavio in Hermosillo after reviewing the allegations. When I asked him about Gerry, he didn't hold back. "He's very charismatic, he's very smart, he has this strength and this powerful energy," Octavio said, "but he is, I think, just too obsessed with himself. There's a lot of talk about narcissistic Messiah complex around this kind of thing—myself, other people. I think Gerry hasn't gone through some personal work." Octavio was waiting for new clients to arrive. "Nobody is saying that I'm a bad guy," he went on, "but some people are saying that Gerry has this kind of *evil* energy. I think he's not the best person to be carrying a message of peace, honor, truth, and healing."

Moments later, Octavio's phone rang. To my disbelief, it was a video call from Gerry—their first conversation in years. Octavio pivoted from disparaging Gerry to greeting him like a long-lost brother, and they bantered amicably for several minutes. He turned the screen toward me and I waved. Afterward, they met up in Sonora and posed for selfies together, causing alarm on the Facebook support groups. Kate told me that my reporting had "brought them back together."

This was not quite the journalistic impact I'd been aiming for, although it seemed to reveal something deeper about the toad world: how easily misconduct could be brushed aside, as if it had never happened.

. . .

In the aftermath of Ramírez's death, the Mexican authorities opened an investigation. Agents went to the property where the sessions had taken place to collect evidence, but it was "clean," Villalpando said—no pipes, no toad medicine. Octavio did not specifically deny removing these from the site, saying only, "I didn't hide, escape, or run away." For three weeks, numbed by grief, Villalpando stayed at home with his sons. He eventually visited the prosecutor in charge of the case for an update, identifying himself as a lawyer. But the case file had "nothing in it," not even statements from the medics. The prosecutor implied that Ramírez and Villalpando were responsible for what had happened: She had attended voluntarily, with Villalpando's permission. While this wasn't untrue, it felt painfully beside the point. Villalpando described the experience as "revictimization."

An autopsy had determined the official cause of Ramírez's death as an "anaphylactic reaction to an unknown substance." To Villalpando, there was no question that the toad medicine had killed her. Suspects with money almost never faced prosecution in Mexico, he said. He mistrusted the authorities to handle the case. It was easy to bribe officials or hire lawyers who could make legal problems disappear, and the justice system was riddled with incompetence. Already, it was clear to Villalpando that the investigation was stalling. "I wasn't surprised," he told me. "I know how it works." And so, instead of waiting, he began collecting evidence of his own, intent on building a case against Octavio. "I wanted him to go to jail and never leave," Villalpando said.

In search of leads, he rode by bus to Sonora to source toad secretion, which he planned to submit for toxicological testing. The journey took longer than twenty hours. He reasoned that if he could prove that the substance was poisonous, Octavio could be held liable—a flawed premise, because 5-MeO-DMT isn't toxic when smoked in standard doses. Villalpando managed to purchase a supply and stashed it in his wallet, but on the return journey he was mugged in a public bathroom, losing the sample. He later contacted a dealer who sent him more secretion by mail. Villalpando told me that he then spent around $8,000 on laboratory analyses. He insisted that the results showed that toad medicine had caused his wife's death, although this seemed to be a misinterpretation: Bufotoxins and other poisonous compounds are active only if ingested orally. (It was still plausible that Ramírez had died from other causes during the ceremony, such as a surge in heart rate or the inhalation of water and *rapé*.)

Villalpando also tracked down eyewitnesses and helped obtain depositions, accumulating a thick dossier. Eighteen months later, he delivered this to the prosecutor, only to be told that the material was inadmissible due to his personal involvement in the process. Villalpando petitioned to have the investigation reassigned; the case changed hands several times, with no discernible progress. According to Villalpando, one official divulged that Octavio's lawyer had pressured them to misplace the documents. These delays stretched late into 2020, when Villalpando eventually found a prosecutor willing to take the case seriously. That September, almost two years after Ramírez's death, a warrant was issued for Octavio. According to Villalpando, he was arrested in Guadalajara, where agents posed as clients and handcuffed him at a ceremony.

A few days later, wearing gray prison attire, Octavio was led into a windowless courtroom in León for a pretrial hearing. When Villalpando saw him, he was overcome by rage, leaping up and yelling insults. Octavio looked rattled at first, but when his turn came to defend himself, his oratorical charm resurfaced. According to Villalpando, Octavio portrayed himself as a visionary, boasting that people "adored and followed" him. The judge, a middle-aged woman, seemed taken in. "Octavio basically seduced her," Villalpando told me.

After consulting with criminal lawyers, Villalpando had been hoping to elevate the charge from manslaughter to culpable homicide, which would have made it harder for Octavio to settle out of court. The judge refused, and Octavio was allowed to walk free while the investigation continued. Weeks later, he called Villalpando to propose a deal—the first time he had reached out since Ramírez's death. The two men agreed to meet at a fast-food chain in the parking lot of a Walmart in León. Villalpando had become obsessed with "stopping Octavio from hurting more people." He wore a long coat to the meeting. Beneath the coat was a gun.

He sat near a window and watched Octavio enter. He thought to himself, "I'm going to shoot him." Octavio joined him at the table and launched into a monologue. He invited Villalpando to become his lawyer and offered healing ceremonies to his sons. He said that some of his clients were "like groupies," they were so devoted. Instead of apologizing, Octavio was touting his prowess as a healer. "I can give you a place in the family," Octavio promised.

As this went on, Villalpando felt his body growing hotter. Octavio's lips were moving, but he could no longer hear the words. His finger inched toward the trigger. But at that moment, a small boy came over from another table and tugged at his coat. The boy was around five years old, with a snotty nose and sticky hands. He lifted his arms, asking to be held. Night had fallen while Villalpando was recounting this story to me, and one of his neighbors was watching TV; as if on cue, a dramatic soundtrack filled the silence. Villalpando began weeping and told me, "Remember, I don't believe in supernatural things." He believed that Octavio had been saved by the boy's appearance, like some divine intervention. Villalpando accepted a settlement of $30,000 to drop the charges—about as much as he had spent on the investigation.

PART TWO

EVERYTHING IS CONNECTED

CHAPTER 5

The Sonoran Toad Rush

A wave of frantic, frustrated frogs, big ones, little ones, brown ones, green ones, men frogs and women frogs, a wave of them broke over the bank, crawled, leaped, scrambled. They clambered up the grass, they clutched at each other, little ones rode on big ones. And then—horror on horror—the flashlights found them.

—JOHN STEINBECK, *CANNERY ROW*

The swamps of Wisconsin—as well as Michigan, New York, Louisiana, and the Everglades—were once the domain of frog hunters. In the warmer months, vast blooms of frogs would appear, sometimes numbering hundreds of millions. Like their toad relatives, many frog species are opportunistic. When conditions are favorable, their populations can explode. In the summer of 1952, so many frogs inundated the western shores of Lake Michigan that *The New Yorker* dispatched a reporter. "A determined, green froggy army came pouring out," he wrote, "like creatures in a very strange and disorderly dream."

This riotous abundance of frogs became the basis for a fleeting seasonal trade. Frogs were prized for their meat, and people would go after them with ax handles and paddles, knocking them dead and tossing them in gunnysacks. Frog hunters took the animals home, dredging the legs in flour and frying them crisp, or sold them to buyers who paid by the dozen. In the 1930s, a man amusingly named Bernard Rog landed some five thousand frogs in a day, netting around $100—a hefty sum in the area, where the main industries were lumber and cucumber pickles. Diners clamored for frogs' legs in American cities, especially in the Midwest, which dealers dubbed "the Frog Belt." Frogs were easy money, and the slap of paddles rang out across the marshes.

Of all the frog species caught and sold, none were more prized than the bullfrog, whose legs looked most substantial on a plate. Bullfrogs grow up to eight inches from snout to rear and can weigh as much as a small rabbit, with hindlegs as long as their bodies when fully extended. Frog hunters posed with the animals like victorious fishermen, gripping them by the ankles. Yet the business faced all sorts of problems. The boom-and-bust life cycles of bullfrogs made them an unreliable quarry: In good years, they were so plentiful that prices collapsed, while in bad years they were scarce. Hunting also took a toll, leading to the disappearance of bullfrogs in many locations.

During the Great Depression, an entrepreneur named Albert Broel began touting a lucrative solution: frog farming. Broel was a disgraced medical doctor who had reinvented himself as a farmer and canner of frogs. He sold instructional handbooks and supplied prospective farmers with breeding pairs of bullfrogs, promising billions of dollars in profits—figures so inflated that federal officials eventually indicted him for mail fraud. In a four-month period, Broel cashed in orders worth $15,000, equivalent to $350,000 when adjusted for inflation. The steps to his cannery near New Orleans were flanked by frog statues with red eyes that lit up after dark. But the frog-farming business was such a risky proposition that after receiving thousands of queries from aspiring farmers, the U.S. Department of Agriculture issued warnings against it. The animals were vulnerable to diseases and required huge inputs of live feed, making large-scale operations commercially unfeasible. Broel himself relied on frog hunters in the Louisiana swamps for the bulk of his supply. When hunting was restricted to protect wild populations, his cannery shut down.

The world's appetite for frogs has only grown more voracious since then. The European Union imports as many as two billion frogs annually—the equivalent of more than five million frogs every day. The export trade has shifted to new countries as old sources have emptied out. Indonesia, with its richly biodiverse rainforests, is now the world's leading supplier of frogs, and scientists worry that new species may be harvested to extinction before they are even documented.

Toads, by contrast, have largely escaped this attention. With their bulging warts and noxious secretions, they have endured throughout evolutionary history by making themselves repulsive, not only to humans but to other predators. Only the most inventive creatures have found ways to circumvent their defenses, like the British stoats and weasels that "carefully snip away the irritant skin to feast on the edible flesh beneath," as one naturalist has written. In many cultures, frogs and toads were identified by the same name, prompting translators to tell them apart by connotation—frogs good, toads bad. Shakespeare described toads, in various contexts, as "ugly and venomous," "heavy-gaited," "foul," "loathed," and "swelling." Richard III is insulted by a vengeful queen as a "poisonous bunch-backed toad," while Othello laments that his wife has become "a cistern for foul toads to knot and gender in."

Some scholars have proposed that the toad skeletons unearthed from Mesoamerican sites—often interpreted as evidence of ritual psychedelic use—might instead suggest that the animals were eaten as a survival food, in times of desperation. In the 1970s, to test this hypothesis, a British archaeologist named Richard Cooke grilled and ate several cane toads after carefully removing their poison glands. He reported no ill effects. The toads tasted like smoked chicken. In another experiment that decade, an American biology professor fed the raw tadpoles of various toad species to his graduate students. They were instructed to hold the animals in their mouths for twenty seconds, delicately chew on them for just as long, and then bite "fully and firmly" into their bodies. The flavor of each tadpole was rated on a scale of one to five, from "tastes good" to "God-awful/emetic." The tadpoles of the cane toad—bitter, with a gritty texture—ranked last.

In modern times, some toads have been pursued for nonculinary reasons. The cane toad has been systematically hunted in Australia, where it spread with abandon after being introduced to control sugarcane beetles. In 2015, an environmental group on the front lines of the invasion reported removing some five million toads within a decade, averaging a toad every minute. The toads kept on coming, as one volunteer recalled, "hopping zealously west." Community organizations across Australia's east coast organize regular "toad-busting" events for catching and euthanizing the animals, with children encouraged to participate. The glut of toad carcasses has given rise to a distinctively Australian range of curios: taxidermized toads dressed in rugby jerseys, coin purses fashioned from the bodies of toads, leather bow ties with mummified toad faces.

The Sonoran Desert toad, too, has its human adversaries, mainly due to the threat it poses to pets and young children. These were documented as early as 1928, when a biologist at the U.S. Department of Agriculture encountered one of the toads in his garden. His dog, a small wire-haired fox terrier, promptly attacked and killed it. Moments later, she collapsed "with her feet crumpled under her and her face in the dirt," the biologist wrote. The dog was soon dead, foaming blood from the mouth. Pet hospitals in Arizona issue warnings each summer, although some dogs seem to enjoy the toad experience. I met a woman from Hermosillo whose aging crossbreed had a habit of mouthing the animals. She later texted me a picture of the dog holding its fourth *alvarius* toad of the month. "She seems to be better at ingesting that thing—she doesn't pass out anymore," the woman wrote, adding a string of laughing emojis. Other people are less tolerant, smashing the animals with baseball bats or throwing salt on them, which kills them slowly, like snails. A company in the United States advertises an irritant spray for deterring the toads, which are able to enter homes through pet doors. Their website makes the ominously casual observation that "destroying them is a viable way to get rid of them as well."

But around a decade ago, something unprecedented happened to Sonoran Desert toads: They became intensely desirable. Teams of collectors fanned out across the desert each summer, pouncing on toads and forcibly expressing their secretions. Dried flakes of the substance were weighed to the milligram and shipped in concealed packages—

incense boxes, pouches of dried herbs. More and more people wished to inhale the vapors; more and more toads were caught. The toads had run up against the ultimate opportunists: humans. Many toad smokers around the world believed that they were purchasing an ethically harvested Indigenous sacrament, but the reality was far bleaker, involving the exploitation not only of toads but of the workers collecting them. The numinous highs of a trip traced back to a ruthless scramble in Sonora, where the toads were vanishing from towns and villages. This irony was even starker for its lack of necessity, given that virtually identical states could be reached using synthetic 5-MeO-DMT. Yet many users preferred the idea of a psychedelic obtained from nature, which in turn colored how they experienced the drug. The toads, in effect, had become a marketing token. Their repulsiveness, once an adaptive asset, rendered them doubly vulnerable—investing people in their plight was far harder than selling the medicine. Even toad smokers who revered the species as something more like a deity seemed helpless to prevent its mistreatment. As one distressed user posted online, "People are trying to cash in on the toad rush."

. . .

In 2014, the conservationist Robert Villa—soon to become the world's foremost defender of psychedelic toads—paid a visit to the Yaqui, an Indigenous community in Sonora. The tribe, whose lands lie some 180 miles south of the Seri, was facing an array of environmental threats, including the construction of an aqueduct that would drain the Rio Yaquí, historically one of the few perennial rivers in the region. Representatives had filed legal challenges and, when these were disregarded, began protests that included blockading the state's main highway. The backlash was swift and violent: kidnappings, burned cars, homicides. Mexico was on its way to becoming the world's most dangerous nation for environmental activists; in 2021, an activist was murdered every week, on average. Amid this spreading tumult, Villa learned on his visit, a new and unsettling economy had taken root in Yaqui territory: the large-scale collection of Sonoran Desert toads.

Toads, known in Yaqui as *bobok,* feature prominently in the tribe's mythology. In one story, Toad borrows the wings of a bat to fly up into the clouds, where he tricks the Rain King into ending a devastating drought; in another, he brings fire to the tribe after stealing it from the gods and carrying the flames in his mouth. The Yaqui would decorate Sonoran Desert toads with ribbons and parade them ceremonially, praying for rain. In a far cry from this exalted status, toads were now being caught en masse for the psychedelic market. In one instance, or so the rumors went, a truck had been discovered carrying two tons of the animals.

Villa related this all to me the first time I called him, back in 2020, after several stories had quoted him raising the alarm about toad poaching. He introduced himself on the phone as a "freelance naturalist" and told me that he owned two Gila monsters—a giant lizard with black and orange scales—in addition to a Sonoran Desert tortoise named Virgil, whom a family member had given him at the age of five. He later acquired a pet gopher snake and took it along to catechism classes. He became especially fond of sea turtles. In middle school, on his first day of orchestra practice, both Villa and his teacher were wearing turtle T-shirts. She introduced him to some herpetologists, who became Villa's earliest mentors.

Like the tortoise, Villa is now in his mid-thirties. He serves as president of the Tucson Herpetological Society. He is small and puckish, with deeply tanned skin and a shock of black hair that he tidies into a topknot. He is a masterful violinist, even though he stopped taking lessons when his parents could no longer afford them. With his striking looks and eccentric interests, he is like a character dreamed up by Wes Anderson. In the summer of 2023, when I visited him during an Arizona heat wave, we went to an art-house cinema to watch Anderson's latest film, *Asteroid City.* At one point, a singing cowboy made a throwaway remark about a "toad swindle," and Villa turned to me with an expression of delight.

A few years after his visit to Yaqui territory, Villa appeared in a VICE documentary about the toads, speaking about their natural history. (This was the same episode that misidentified Albert Most, the modern pioneer of toad smoking.) Villa saw the flood of interest as deeply concerning—"a cognitive dissonance with the wellness motifs of the psychedelic renaissance," as he later wrote. It was difficult enough to control demand for wildlife products with more tenuous therapeutic effects, like rhino horn.* What hope could there be for an animal that delivered genuine states of transcendence?

Amphibians are the most imperiled group of vertebrates globally, with around 40 percent of the approximately eight thousand known species threatened by extinction. The outlook is especially bleak in Mexico, where habitat loss, climate change, and diseases like the chytrid fungus have already caused devastating losses. Villa heard of Sonoran Desert toads vanishing from certain areas and worried that overexploitation might drive further declines without anybody paying attention. Not long after the VICE episode aired, he met a Tucson artist who wished to print a satirical Nike T-shirt featuring a Sonoran Desert toad and the words "Just Smoke It." Villa urged him to publicize risks to the species instead. To raise awareness, he and the artist collaborated on a new design, based on the cover illustration of Albert Most's original manual. "Protect the Sonoran Desert Toad," the shirt read. "Please Trip Responsibly."

• • •

Villa wasn't the first to sound the alarm about Sonoran Desert toads. Albert Most himself had opened his 1984 booklet with a cautionary fable from Aesop: "A certain man had the good fortune to possess a goose that laid a golden egg every day. But dissatisfied with so slow an income, and thinking to seize the whole treasure at once, he killed the goose." Shortly thereafter, toad smoking was described as "an ethically dubious trip" in *The Entheogen Review,* an underground newsletter about psychoactive substances. Its editor had kept four of the animals

* Rhino horn is made of keratin, the same material in human hair or fingernails. There is no credible clinical or pharmacological evidence that it has any medicinal benefit.

in a terrarium for a while but given up milking them. "In extracting the venom one creates a lot of fear and stress in a fellow creature," he explained. But in 1994, the arrest of a California schoolteacher on toad-smoking charges set off a media frenzy, bringing new attention to the species. "Alas! Alas!" the *Entheogen*'s editor lamented. "The distorted publicity has now made it a hip thing." A reader from Arizona wrote in to express dismay about the "harm or decimation" that might result when "all the unhappy hordes pursue another way to 'get off' at the expense of the toad."

Through the deep passage of evolutionary time, Sonoran Desert toads have proved remarkably resilient to change. Fossils of their skeletons have been discovered alongside anteaters, camels, mammoths, ground sloths, capybaras, and other creatures that once roamed a lusher, greener region. Despite its ancient appearance, the Sonoran Desert is geologically young. As recently as eleven thousand years ago—an eyeblink in Earth's history—higher rainfall supported woodland trees and shrubs. Further back in time, tropical deciduous forests formed canopies during the wetter months. As conditions grew hotter and drier, many species died off or migrated, but the toads endured, burrowing underground.

Up to a point, the toads have also accommodated, and perhaps even prospered from, the rise of humans. Nearly fifteen hundred years ago, in what is now Arizona, Hohokam farmers created an expansive network of irrigation canals, excavating channels with perfectly sloping gradients. Hundreds of square miles of dry land flourished with corn and other crops, and the toads had abundant new waters to swim in. The Hohokam disappeared a few hundred years later; researchers believe their population grew too rapidly, outstripping the availability of resources. The channels remained behind, remnants of a lost civilization, and during monsoons the toads continued to breed in them.

In the nineteenth century, settlers in Sonora began using steam engines to pump groundwater. Rain that fell in the desert sank quickly through its permeable sands, filtering into deep and inaccessible aquifers; now some of that water was returned to the surface. In the 1940s, technological advances enabled the drilling of even deeper wells, driving a massive expansion of cotton and wheat farming west of Hermosillo. This was a welcome development for the toads, who congregated around reservoirs, ditches, and stock ponds. "With a few exceptions it is found only in the wet places around the cattle watering troughs of the ranches," some herpetologists wrote in an early survey. Electric lights acted as magnets for flying insects, serving as all-night buffets for the toads. During the rainy season, when the toads emerged, Sonoran residents would switch off their outdoor lights to avoid being inundated.

Yet as adaptable as they were, Sonoran Desert toads were not prepared for the onslaught of psychedelic interest. Humans are nimbler than other predators, with far greater appetites. Whether the toads hopped, scrambled, or froze, hoping to evade detection, their new pursuers could easily scoop them up and press on their glands. While toad smoking remained a fringe activity, this was a rare experience for the animals, and the rest went on with their lives—mating, feeding, hiding out from the sun. This fragile balance began to shift when Octavio was introduced to the medicine in 2006. With Gerry by his side, he set about milking thousands of toads each summer, amassing kilograms of dried secretion. "Octavio is simply unstoppable," a practitioner who went out collecting with him in 2014 recalled, "even enthusiastically doing jumping jacks between toad milkings."

The restricted habitat of the toad, an endemic species found nowhere else on earth, meant that the entire world's supply had to be sourced from the Sonoran Desert. As demand for the medicine exploded, a new economy took shape to provide it. People could catch toads in Arizona, but the epicenter was in Sonora, which itself was in the midst of a violent transformation. In 2006, the Mexican government had deployed military troops to fight narco-traffickers, who smuggled cocaine, marijuana, and methamphetamine worth billions of dollars each year to the United States. The cartels responded by professionalizing their security forces, acquiring AK-47s and mounted machine guns for shooting down helicopters. Mexico's drug wars intensified, and the national homicide rate tripled over the next five years. Vast areas of Sonora became no-go zones, and people who visited risked their lives.

This landscape of excessive violence also harbored the toad, an animal in demand globally for spiritual experiences and inner healing—including from addiction to the very drugs being trafficked. It was all but inevitable that these charged elements would come into contact. In 2016, Dean Jefferys, the Australian founder of the Facebook support group, spent several weeks in Mexico, shooting footage for a documentary about toad medicine. Jefferys is the personification of a New Age elder, with salt-streaked hair and a white beard; he usually wears colorful unbuttoned shirts. One night, while driving around, searching for toads, he was pulled over by armed men. "The cartels have a whole network," he recalled. "As soon as a strange car comes in, people are notified. I was staring down the barrel of a gun." Just a few weeks earlier, he reported, an unsuspecting woman from the United States had been kidnapped while looking for toads and was held for several days. In a Facebook post, Jefferys warned that the desert "is definitely not a place where you can just go and find some toads."

As Sonora became more dangerous, demand for the medicine only grew. Collecting toads had become perilous, creating an opportunity for local intermediaries who could move through toad habitats without arousing suspicion. One of the first to assume this role was a burly resident of Hermosillo named Carlos Barraza who, around 2014, began supplying buyers in Mexico and abroad. Barraza has a circular face and rounded shoulders, giving him a faintly toad-like appearance. According to his rivals, he has a ruthless streak. He soon rose to become one of the world's biggest toad medicine suppliers.

In the early days of this operation, Barraza began selling toad to Mario Garnier, a thickset former TV producer from Mexico City. Garnier had been introduced to toad smoking a few years earlier and "left everything behind"—his job, a voice-over studio, a production school where he taught—to begin what he later described as a spiritual journey with the medicine. He began serving toad and sourcing medicine for people in his network; one of his friends, a former corporate lawyer, was soon hosting as many as a thousand sessions a year. Garnier went from buying ten grams a month from Barraza (enough for several hundred strong doses) to ten times as much. But when Garnier tried to negotiate the price down, Barraza refused, and their relationship soured.

In Garnier's telling, Barraza was a "thug" who was seizing control of the toad market by force. "He was very violent," Garnier said, without elaborating further. Others have described Barraza to me in similar ways. (Barraza denied ever being violent, but said he had reported collectors to the police for "stealing toads" and personally chased after them on many occasions.) Garnier himself recalls experiencing a kind of mania at the time, "wanting to save the world with toad medicine." The God molecule had found another emissary. "I was in the Messiah state," Garnier said.

In 2015, seeking new suppliers, he set off deeper into Sonora, where the toads were even more plentiful. He met people who had formerly caught toads for Octavio. "He paid them with bottles of liquor," Garnier told me. "They were giving him the medicine without knowing what it was." (Octavio denies this.)* Garnier had formed relationships with practitioners in Europe and wanted to set them up with collectors in Sonora. Large orders started coming in—from Spain, the Netherlands, Germany. "I built the medicine bridge," Garnier said. "Then people became greedy." Later, in a text message, he seemed to acknowledge his own complicity. "The molecule is like the ring of Tolkien," he wrote, using a metaphor I'd heard from others. "Creates greediness. Thirst of power."

* Octavio has long maintained that he has never purchased or sold toad medicine, a point he raised repeatedly with me. He blamed commercial dealers like Barraza for "creating that black market and that underworld." He took no responsibility for his role in popularizing the substance. He confided to me that he had around a kilogram of toad secretion buried in underground caches around the world, like a squirrel hoarding acorns. "It's a treasure," he said.

. . .

It is possible to experience the visionary effects of 5-MeO-DMT without involving any toads at all. The molecule is inexpensive to synthesize in laboratories. Its high, many users report, is just as intense. But there is a reinforcing dynamic when it comes to psychedelics: One's expectations of a trip—set and setting—can profoundly shape the experience. And so for those who value natural substances or believe they're consuming an Indigenous sacrament, or both, smoking toad can feel radically different. "We imbue these molecules with such magic," the writer Michael Pollan told me in a conversation about natural versus synthetic demand. He speculated that toad medicine, in addition to its psychoactive properties, might be acting as "a super-placebo."

Once again, the psychedelic toad community found itself divided over a foundational issue. These tensions boiled over at the inaugural World Bufo Alvarius Congress in 2018, the same event where Octavio was confronted about his approach to serving toad. In one talk, Garnier, an organizer of the conference, interviewed the American man who had first introduced Dr. Gerry to toad smoking, inadvertently precipitating its global spread. "Poaching the toad must stop," the man, a dreadlocked figure known as Corvis, begged, looking stricken. "Toads must be kept free and wild."

Garnier told me, a little piously, that he had forbidden people from selling toad medicine at the congress, which he described as "a perfect setting for trafficking." At one point, he says, he ejected Barraza for trading out of a hotel room; he claims that Barraza then threatened to kill him. (Barraza denies this.) Yet despite this moral posturing, suppliers and buyers networked freely, negotiating deals. For all the rhetoric about protecting the species, the congress had become a marketplace. "I met people from Argentina, Africa, Australia, Spain," recalled one collector, who was soon shipping more than a kilogram of toad secretion annually, involving the capture of thousands of toads.

The mood turned more combative during a panel on toad conservation, where a man from northern Sonora disclosed that he caught up to a thousand toads every night in summer. He took them from urban areas "for protection," he said, and milked them on a private ranch. His name was Samuel Amistron. He had a hulking frame and a growling voice. He became defensive as people on the panel questioned him, and there was a feeling of the audience turning against him.

Amistron was a member of the Tohono O'odham tribe, whose lands span the U.S. border. Some associates of Octavio's had introduced him to toad smoking in 2015. He was living in poverty at the time, had twice been deported from the United States, and struggled with addiction to drugs and alcohol. Afterward, he began milking toads, smoking their secretions alone on a few occasions. The left side of his face had been partially paralyzed since a car crash in his youth; after one trip, he said, this miraculously healed. Another time, Amistron relived his ancestors being massacred by Spanish settlers. Like so many others before him, he felt called to share the medicine.

His prospects improved when Garnier fronted him money to go toading. That first summer, Amistron collected thirty grams of medicine; the next year, he collected ninety. He sold some of his possessions and purchased a car to cover more ground. Soon he was paying others to help him, bringing in hundreds of grams per week. When Garnier introduced him to more buyers overseas, establishing the "medicine bridge," Amistron invested the profits in an off-road vehicle. His wife and two young children often accompanied him, chasing after toads in the dark. The air was suffocatingly hot; mosquitoes attacked them in swarms. One night, tiring of the endless labor, Amistron had an idea: What if, instead of going out collecting himself, the toads were delivered to him?

With more borrowed money, Amistron acquired a piece of land near Caborca and paid locals to supply him with toads. He sank a well and built ponds. In dry years, he trucked in water from the municipality. "I don't know how many millions of toads we've brought to the ranch," he told me. Workers milked the toads on-site—thousands of toads, squirming in buckets and sacks—before releasing them at his property. It was Amistron's hope that the toads would settle and breed, but this was at odds with the impulses of the species. Sonoran Desert toads are bonded to the places where they are born; like pigeons or migrating salmon, their instinct is to return. They fled from Amistron's land, hopping away in their multitudes. Undoubtedly, many died. Amistron hauled in strings of toad spawn, hoping to hatch tadpoles, but these perished as well. "It doesn't matter what you do," Amistron lamented when we met in 2023. "The toad goes away."

Nevertheless, his business had prospered. Like Albert Broel, the frog-canning entrepreneur, Amistron brought in enough wild stock to offset his losses—an illusion of abundance that masked deeper depletion. He posted pictures on Facebook of sheets of toad medicine the size of serving platters. Before long, he was one of the biggest suppliers in the world, boasting about shipping to "the entire planet." He began hosting toad ceremonies in a teepee on his land or at nearby archaeological sites with petroglyphs carved by ancestors of the O'odham. Like some Seri practitioners, he began speaking of a lost tradition of O'odham toad smoking, something that had never previously been documented. He established a nonprofit, Bufo Alvarius: Guardián del Desierto, which styled itself as a conservation initiative even while he was exploiting the toads for commercial gain. The foundation's logo features a sacred O'odham symbol called the Man in the Maze; superimposed on this design is a toad, cradled by a giant pair of human hands. The image is supposed to evoke guardianship but instead comes off as ominously predatory, as if the toad were a target.

. . .

In 2019, at the second annual Bufo Congress, another panel convened in a darkened room to discuss the dilemma of toad harvesting. This time, they unveiled a solution: Fair Trade Toad, which they described as "Greenpeace for Bufo." "How does the medicine get ethically and sustainably from this sacred creature," a moderator asked, "to a person who wants to experience the medicine?" He added, with satisfaction, "Maybe you could call it God's assembly line."

Then Garnier, dressed in black, read from a long list of objectives, including preserving the species, setting fair prices, funding scientific research, fostering toad stewardship by Indigenous communities, and "developing a healthy and equitable working relationship with the collectors of *Bufo alvarius* secretion." Afterward, when the room burst into applause, Garnier wagged a finger. "That's just the dream, brothers and sisters," he said. "This is just a paper at this point."

At a later event, he announced the formation of a "union of collectors," who would supposedly unite with Fair Trade Toad to ensure a more responsible supply of the medicine. It was an ambitious exercise in governance, demanding cooperation among bitter rivals in a remote and lawless landscape. Who would keep them in line? Garnier was joined onstage by Amistron, Barraza, and a Seri man named Mario Lopez, introducing them as "the big players in the world of medicine collection." (Amistron and Barraza alone, he explained, were responsible for as much as three-quarters of the global supply.) Garnier began by reciting a formal pledge while the panelists fiddled with their translation headsets: "We, the collectors of the sacred medicine of the *Bufo alvarius,* do solemnly swear and agree to abide to be the caretakers . . ." This incantation went on solemnly for several minutes. Afterward, Garnier said, in a confessional tone, while peering around the room, "We are *all* learning. We have all abused the toads in the past, even buying medicine from unethical collectors. That makes us part of the problem."

Then Barraza grabbed the microphone. "We want to present you the reality of what's happening with the species in Sonora," he announced. Areas that had been rich in toads for many years were now barren; a team of collectors might search all night and find nothing. He blamed this on dishonorable suppliers abducting toads for their ranches. "Toads are just disappearing," Barraza said.

He cued up a screen recording on the projector, showing the audience Facebook posts by a rival collector. One featured a truck discharging water at a toad ranch; another advertised fresh toad secretion in January, when the animals were ordinarily underground. Realizing what was going on, Garnier stood up and waved for a microphone.

Another picture filled the screen: Amistron, holding a huge sheet of toad medicine.

"These are some strong, sensitive images," Garnier interrupted. "We have all made mistakes, but this is why we have created this union." Extending an arm toward Amistron, he added, "This is a new start."

"I don't see how we're ever gonna agree on this," Barraza shot back. He went on listing various complaints about Amistron, who looked on impassively, until Garnier cut him off again: "Carlos, this is not the place to blame somebody, okay?" It was clear that there would be no truce among the collectors. At the end, Barraza implored the audience to visit his Facebook profile for more evidence of toad abuse. "Just cut the supply to all the people who are doing this in the wrong way," he almost shouted. "Avoid buying their product." With these hostilities laid bare and no resolution in sight, the union was over before it even began.

. . .

One night in 2021, I arranged to meet up with Barraza in Hermosillo. He kept me waiting near a public park for several hours and forbade me from bringing an interpreter. "Be careful who you associate with," he warned in a cryptic message. "Everything will come to light soon."

I wanted to ask him about pictures he had shared on Facebook, purportedly exposing his rivals' misdeeds. The images appeared to be authentic, revealing not just carelessness but something closer to cruelty. One purportedly showed adulterated toad secretion, cut with sugar or the resin from mesquite trees; another depicted a toad with inflamed red glands, the skin raw and webbed by swollen blood vessels. Barraza said that some toads were recaptured and milked so many times in a season that their glands bled, staining the medicine pink. In a caption, he wrote, "Did you know that there are certain unscrupulous collectors who squeeze sick or dead animals?"

It was close to midnight and hotter than 100 degrees when he arrived, wearing a baggy tank top with a psychedelic print and a wide-brimmed hat that looked like the cap of a mushroom. We sat in a playground, opposite the swings. We had a halting conversation via Google Translate but could barely understand each other: The app kept mixing up our voices, blaring robotically from his iPhone speaker. Yet every now and then, Barraza indicated that he understood more English than he was letting on, and I began to suspect he was avoiding my questions. Several people had already suggested to me that Barraza was just as unethical as anyone else in the business. "Every accusation is a confession," Garnier advised, while accusing Barraza of violence, manipulation, and lying. (Garnier himself told me several lies, including that one of his closest friends was murdered in a dispute over toad collecting; the man actually died of a respiratory disease, and when I asked Garnier about this, he responded, "Just remember, there is a lot of misinformation.")

I had been hoping to accompany Barraza's team and see the first step in the toad medicine supply chain: a wild animal entering an economy for spiritual experience in the merciless borderlands of Sonora. But this was proving almost surreally elusive. My encounter with Barraza ended even more strangely, when one of my molars cracked and fell out, like an omen in a dream. I excused myself and found a dentist the next morning. "Oh!" she exclaimed, when I explained why I was in Hermosillo. "Many of our friends have smoked toad. My husband wants to try it."

I had more success joining a toad expedition a few days later, when I met up with a teenager whose older brothers had introduced him to the business. Both brothers were now missing, presumed dead—"forcibly disappeared," in the official parlance of Mexico, which had a register of more than 100,000 such victims, most of them recorded since the drug wars began in 2006. The boys' mother, Cecilia Flores, had founded a volunteer group called Madres Buscadoras de Sonora (Searching Mothers of Sonora) in 2019; in just over two years, they had exhumed the remains of more than 400 people, including mass graves with dozens of bodies. Her surviving son—aged seventeen, with the neat hair of a schoolboy—would sometimes help on these expeditions, digging with pickaxes and shovels in the desert heat. "By day, he searches for bodies," Flores told me. "At night, he searches for toads."

We left the city and followed dirt roads pooled with water from a recent deluge. The sunset was dark red, silhouetting the mesquite trees. We pulled over at a smallholding with a floodlit yard and clouds of swirling insects. Some farmworkers were in a dilapidated building, listening to accordion music on a tinny speaker. They had no interest in toads and waved us onto the property. A few toads had gathered around a water trough below a buzzing transmission line, reminding me of old men taking in the night air. They were fat and spherical, with leathery skins and resigned expressions. The boy swooped on them and pinned them with the flat of his hand, then dropped them into his sack.

We drove on, stopping for the boy to chase more of the animals. He sprinted after them, crawling catlike under wire fences and muddying his jeans. By the end of the night he had scooped up more than two dozen; in the past, he explained, there would have been many more. The toads were massed together in the bag, stronger toads on the backs of weaker ones, toads all the way down. Every few seconds, one of the toads would hop or squirm in an attempt to improve its position, provoking a flurry of jostling among the others. The boy fished them out one by one and expelled their glands onto a pair of glass dishes that his mother had purchased for him. Winged ants and termites tumbled into the light and became glued to the glass. They stuck to the boy's fingers and he crushed them as he worked. His headlamp cast enlarged toad figures on the ground, crisply outlined, like shadow puppets. After squeezing each toad, the boy let it fall to the ground and reached for another.

With his guidance, I milked a toad, feeling remorseful about how hard I had to press. The glands felt like gritty pebbles beneath the skin. "Harder," the boy said. A sebaceous substance burst out. Once it had dried, a contact would buy it for around $50 a gram and feed it into the psychedelic toad pipeline. Had the boy ever smoked toad?

Never, he said—no desire to. I tried to picture the tiny amount we obtained making its way to users in Mexico City or Sydney or Madrid, their epiphanies lighting up like dots on a map. The toads, after being freed, paused momentarily in the dirt, then fled for the darkness with muscular leaps.

• • •

Strictly speaking, toad medicine is a renewable resource. Sonoran Desert toads regenerate their toxins once their glands are emptied, and one could in theory milk the same toad over and over, allowing it time to replenish. But the commercialization and scale of the global trade are at odds with such restraint. In practice, the goal is to collect and sell as much secretion as possible during the brief seasonal window when the toads appear aboveground. This rush comes at a cost. Handling large numbers of toads can spread diseases; removing them from their home territories leads to disorientation and stress, as do repeat milkings. More than a century ago, some biologists remarked on the creature's violent reaction to being caught: "When held in the hand, this toad jerks spasmodically and vibrates the whole body, as if about to explode with wrath." Many toads, it seems, do not survive the ordeal.

Due to the clandestine nature of the business, nobody knows how much toad medicine is harvested and sold annually. Fair Trade Toad estimated in 2019 that worldwide demand was less than twenty kilograms, which would easily fit inside a single suitcase. Global production of cocaine exceeds thirty-five hundred metric tons—hundreds of thousands of suitcases. Compared with the volumes and profits of mainstream drug trafficking, the psychedelic toad economy is minuscule. But for the toads it is another story. The Fair Trade Toad estimates would require sixty thousand or more toad milkings every summer, or hundreds per day. This was the amount that Amistron claimed to be harvesting with his network of collectors alone, meaning the true scale of trade was likely far higher.

Yet assessing the impact of this activity is far from straightforward. Conducting biological surveys on cartel turf is prohibitively dangerous. Suppliers are guarded about their methods. God's assembly line, it turns out, is damningly opaque. (The words "secretion" and "secret" share a common root: to set apart, whether from the body or from public knowledge.) Researchers have documented toad medicine being traded on the dark web; one dealer, a man in Germany, shipped the substance onward to dozens of countries—including Egypt, Brazil, and a remote Pacific island—before being caught. (His brother, a policeman, had turned him in for trafficking illegal substances.) The dealer later appeared in a documentary with his identity obscured. When asked if he regretted his actions, he demurred: Toad medicine, he said, had helped him quit smoking.

Anecdotal reports of declines are not scientific evidence. It is still possible that the toads are holding out in remote parts of the desert—protected, perversely, by the deterrent presence of cartels. If their numbers are decreasing, this might be in response to other threats: pollution, development, the climate crisis. Distinguishing signals from the noise requires fieldwork, which in turn requires funding. How would you go about counting all the toads in the borderlands? Meanwhile, the market continues delivering toad-derived 5-MeO-DMT from Sonora to the neuroreceptors of users around the world, while money flows in the reverse direction, via practitioners and dealers and middlemen toward collectors who chase after toads in the darkness. Even if this was biologically sustainable—which seems unlikely—there are questions of ethics, from the welfare of collectors to toads being crammed into buckets.

As anxiety rose about the welfare of the world's only known psychoactive animal, support for conservation efforts arrived from an unlikely source. Hamilton Morris, the host of the VICE documentary on toad smoking, had come to regret his role in popularizing the practice. "I don't think there is a good, sustainable way to milk these toads," he said in a talk, urging people to switch to the synthetic molecule instead. (The reception was lukewarm, with one audience member arguing that the "spirit of a toad" improved the quality of the high.) In early 2021, Morris released an entirely new episode correcting the record about

Albert Most, whom he had previously misidentified. "I propagated a lie," he says in the opening scene. To coincide with the show, he arranged to reissue Ken Nelson's original pamphlet, pledging a portion of the proceeds toward toad conservation research. The most recent population assessment for the IUCN Red List of Threatened Species, a conservation database, had classified the toads as "Least Concern," but this was back in 2004—a different epoch for the animals, before they became a global spiritual commodity. Almost nothing was known about their present distribution or abundance, nor how these might have changed in response to collecting or other threats.

Robert Villa, the desert conservationist, received the funds at the Tucson Herpetological Society and circulated a call for proposals. One of the first projects he funded was by Ana Ortiz, the former youth counselor who had helped found Octavio's foundation. She had since parted ways with the group, judging Octavio to be a "sociopath," and felt a sense of culpability for her role in the trade. She had collected toad secretion for four years and hosted hundreds of underground sessions, including with public figures who had spread the word further. "I'm part of the problem," she told me. "This is my way of making amends."

To determine if the toad population was declining, she proposed a series of preliminary surveys, working toward updating the IUCN assessment. She had no training in biological fieldwork and enlisted the help of Georgina Santos-Barrera, a diminutive herpetologist with graying hair and the no-nonsense demeanor of a nurse. Santos-Barrera had conducted the original IUCN study, almost two decades earlier. When I asked her what she thought about toad smoking, she shot me a withering look and said, "It's ridiculous."

In the summer of 2021, I accompanied them on a trip to Álamos, an old silver-mining town with grand Spanish colonial architecture. Bougainvillea spilled over crumbling walls, and in the ornate downtown market area horse-drawn carts with tourists rattled over the cobblestones. On our first night, we marched up a dry riverbed traversed by arched brick bridges, waving flashlights in the dark. A man in reflective overalls was asleep beside a nest of beer cans, oblivious to the beams. We saw baby spadefoot toads the size of fingernails and some bigger toads with vivid mottled patterns, but no *alvarius*.

The next afternoon, black thunderclouds gathered and a driving wind whipped the tops of the palm trees. We began searching at dusk on the outskirts of town: orbs of light, thick torrents of rain. At first there were no toads; then there were dozens, calling to one another from the deepening puddles. There were fat brown toads and small green toads, but none of the psychedelic variety. We moved locations. We moved again. We encountered hundreds of toads—all the wrong species. Rocks and cowpats cast deceptive shadows. "Everything looks like a Sonoran Desert toad to me," Ortiz said. "Maybe it's just the desire of seeing one again."

Álamos is in southern Sonora, near the edge of the toad's range. After dropping me back in Hermosillo, the team drove north into more promising territory. Over the next two days, they encountered only two toads. They had to suspend further surveys when gun battles broke out between rival gangs in the nearby town of Magdalena. Vendors abandoned their market stalls, parishioners dived to the floor during Mass, and for several days afterward the streets remained empty, their storefronts riddled with machine-gun rounds. "We could only survey the private ranch we were at, because nothing else was safe," Ortiz texted me. "We didn't see any *alvarius*."

. . .

North of the border, different circumstances prevail for the toads and the people who catch them. Toad poachers have snuck into Arizona nature reserves, drawing scolds from the National Park Service: "Please refrain from licking." Border agents have intercepted toad secretion during customs inspections. I spoke with a circus performer from upstate New York who makes a pilgrimage to Arizona each summer to replenish his supply of the medicine, which he serves in ceremonies. "The authorities are alert to people going around with buckets," he said. To evade detection, he tucked a Pyrex dish into his pants and milked any toads he caught on the spot. He had learned to chase after them in a specific way—"kinda hustle but not beeline towards them"—to avoid causing them stress. "To have some giant come and trap you must be terrifying," he mused, likening this to his own experiences of ego death from smoking toad. While handling the animals, he spoke to them softly, thanking them for their medicine. I wondered, from the perspective of a toad, whether this made much difference.

In the monsoon season, the roads in southern Arizona are slicked with the carcasses of Sonoran Desert toads, their secretions smeared across the asphalt. The sun bakes their flattened bodies into brittle disks. A few years ago, a Canadian man with an interest in psychedelic toads drove around for a few nights, counting hundreds of fatalities. Baby toadlets sat in the headlights like shining little pebbles. Border Patrol vehicles roared by every few minutes, the man told me, "just running over toads."

The Sonoran Desert toad entered the annals of modern science through the establishment of the border. In the mid-nineteenth century, the United States seized more than half of Mexico's territory, including California and most of Arizona. Afterward, a scientific expedition set out to map the newly conquered terrain, led by a distinguished geographer who was once likened to a toad by a New England newspaper. The party covered some two thousand miles, from San Diego to the mouth of the Rio Grande. Along the way, specimens of an unfamiliar toad were collected near the confluence of the Gila and Colorado Rivers. These were shipped to the Smithsonian in Washington, D.C., where a taxonomist named Charles Frédéric Girard published a formal description in 1859. Noting the toad's prominent parotid glands and "pustular swelling upon the thighs"—later to be coveted by psychedelic enthusiasts—he placed it in the genus *Bufo* and gave it the species name *alvarius.* One of the toad specimens, preserved in ethanol, remains in the Smithsonian's Herpetology Collections, nearly six inches long and bleached a pale leathery color.

I visited Mexico for a second time in June 2023, entering via the remote border post of Sasabe, in an area frequented by migrant smugglers. Illegal border crossings were at a record high; U.S. authorities would report some 2.5 million migrant encounters that year, averaging nearly 7,000 people daily. Donald Trump had begun campaigning for his second presidency on an anti-immigration platform, vowing mass deportations and an end to birthright citizenship. The border wall he'd promised during his first term glimmered in the noonday sun. Its construction had involved blasting through a nearby mountain peak, leaving the slopes strewn with rock and construction debris; one conservation nonprofit likened the damage, replicated across much of the southern border, to "an unmitigated mining site." The wall impeded the movement of not only people but animals: Villa showed me photos of a Sonoran Desert toad that had become trapped and died in one section, as if symbolizing the species' entanglement with humans. Yet the wall remained unfinished, with dozens of gaps in the area. This had made Sasabe a coveted node in the border's flourishing illicit economy.

Mexican cartels, as the historian Rachel Nolan writes, have evolved into "fully integrated criminal organizations." Controlling migrant corridors—and charging fees to those who pass through them—can be even more lucrative than smuggling drugs. Not long after I passed through, fighting broke out over control of the town, a clutch of concrete and adobe buildings on the Mexican side of the border. Convoys of *sicarios* raced in from the desert; people were shot in the streets; houses were torched and strafed with bullets. Families fled in pickups and on foot, and within days virtually the entire population of twenty-five hundred had fled. The settlement stood empty for weeks, with dogs waiting outside the abandoned homes of their owners.

Villa dropped me on the U.S. side and I walked across, drawing bemused looks from both sets of officials. My driver was waiting for me on the other side, and we drove two hours south to his hometown of Altar, where violence between rival gangs had left hundreds dead since 2020: grenade explosions, executions, corpses laid out beside highways. We got tacos near a petrol station where sixty *sicarios* had opened fire on a military contingent the year before. Now troops wearing ski masks patrolled the main street on flatbed trucks. Signs everywhere advertised bare-bones hostels for migrants, costing as little as $2 per night, mattresses and blankets not included. The stores sold backpacks, water bottles, and soft booties for slipping over shoes, to avoid leaving tracks in the sand.

I had arranged to visit Samuel Amistron, the toad collector, in the neighboring town of Caborca, where cartel violence had been just as extreme. To my surprise, he texted me the address for an alternative medicine practice that offered acupuncture, osteopathy, ear candling, and other therapies. The office, a small building painted white, was in a poor neighborhood, with unfinished homes and several abandoned lots. Amistron came outside with a black shirt stretched over his belly. He had a ponytail, and the left side of his face, which he once claimed to have healed by smoking toad, hung limp.

He ran the practice with his wife, it turned out, who was on a video call in the reception area. There were framed diplomas on the walls and a display case with dozens of products, including massage gels prepared with marijuana and peyote. Amistron ushered us into an airless consulting room and shut the door. It was cluttered with pills and devices—massage guns, a chiropractic inversion table, indecipherable machines with dangling wires. We spoke there, sweating, for more than an hour; then Amistron's wife called out something indistinct, and we relocated to the yard. A little later, she beckoned Amistron back inside and I followed. She sat him in a reclining chair and pulled on surgical gloves. Without acknowledging my presence, she rammed two fingers up his nostrils and with the other hand began pressing hard on the roof of his mouth. Amistron groaned and spluttered. His wife spread cream over his cheeks and kneaded them vigorously. "For my face," Amistron grumbled afterward, his eyes streaming.

His house, a few doors down, was the grandest on the block, with sleek tiling, palm trees, and an enormous garage. An expensive Ford truck was parked outside—for doing the rounds and picking up toads from his collectors, Amistron explained. We headed out to his toad ranch early that evening. *Sicarios* were parked at various points beside the highway, watching the traffic. My driver wound down his window each time so that they would recognize him as local. I checked the rearview mirrors. The previous week, a Mexican American botanist had gone missing while doing fieldwork for his PhD. He was found dead, shot seven times, in his vehicle near the Sonoran town of Yécora. "Evidently he was in the wrong place," his father told a reporter.

As we drove, Amistron described his ranch as a response to this heightening danger. "You can't do what the toad community wants," he said. "They don't understand the context." From his perspective, the expectations of toad smokers around the world verged on sheer fantasy. They wanted their medicine gathered with reverence and care, preferably by Indigenous hands, but across much of Sonora this was impossible: Cartels, which operate by seizing and holding territory, wouldn't tolerate the presence of unfamiliar faces. In recent years, Amistron explained, the situation had grown even more volatile, and now the only way to collect large quantities of medicine was to outsource the work to locals in different areas. It had become so dangerous that he could visit his workers only by daylight, which caused other problems: Toads trapped at the bottom of buckets or sacks could be crushed to death in the wait. "All the toads are trying to climb," Amistron said, flapping his hands in imitation of their panicked movements.

His business model, while pragmatic, was also self-serving. The price for toad secretion was around $150 a gram. He could buy a bag of toads—sometimes yielding a dozen or more grams, once milked and dried—for around $5. He told me that he sold around a kilogram a year, although I suspected this was an underestimate. People familiar with his operation claim that he has collected five or more kilograms some seasons, potentially representing some $750,000 in product.

Amistron's collectors, for the most part, were migrant agricultural workers and their children on the commercial farms around Caborca, which produce table grapes, asparagus, and other export crops that require armies of seasonal pickers each summer. More than 100,000 laborers, many of them from Indigenous communities farther south, perform this work in Sonora annually. They are among the poorest and most vulnerable populations in Mexico, and child labor is pervasive.

"I feel very sad when I see the children in the fields," Amistron told me. Collecting toads, he claimed, enabled them to buy cell phones and laptops. (At $5 a bag, it would take a child many nights to afford either.) Yet the work remained deeply perilous. Amistron had heard of a collector being murdered by *sicarios* near Hermosillo, a story I'd heard from other sources as well. His own collectors, he reassured me with an incongruent laugh, had "just been slapped around."

We took a bumpy gravel road through marginal farmland, devoid of crops or livestock, and arrived at his property. A battered green truck with his foundation's logo was parked outside a squat dwelling. Cattle skulls hung from the unpainted walls. A farmhand was sweeping dust off rickety outdoor furniture, and a wind chime clinked forlornly in the breeze. Inside, the building resembled a migrant hostel: Cheap single beds, unmade, were crammed together in the rooms. The walls were streaked with dirt, and a handprint was smeared on one window. I noticed a human figurine with what appeared to be devil horns on display in the kitchen, its blank eyes gazing up at the ceiling.

Outside was the frame of the teepee where Amistron, wearing tasseled leather boots and a feathered headdress, sometimes hosted toad ceremonies. He offered "shamanic trainings" for aspiring facilitators, he said, serving them up to forty hits of toad in a day. The squalid rooms, it turned out, were for participants to spend the night.

These quarters were cast in more forbidding light by allegations I'd read, from a few years earlier, of sexual misconduct by Amistron. A woman from Canada had attended one of his trainings and, after smoking a large dose with him in the scorching heat, relived the trauma of being raped. While she was coming down, she said, he prepared another pipe. "We are going to release this trauma once and for all," she claims she heard him saying. "We have to stimulate your sexual organ." While still under the influence, she said, she consented and inhaled, but screamed when she felt him touching her.

She held back from speaking out afterward, in part because she was a toad practitioner herself and relied on him for access to the medicine. But she claimed that after witnessing him make similar advances on two women she knew, as well as hearing reports of other clients allegedly being violated, she posted detailed accounts on social media of what she said had happened to her. In contrast to the healing persona he cultivated, Amistron habitually drank "beer after beer during ceremony," she wrote. His approach to collecting toads was similarly unsettling, she said, describing it as "grab and bag, relocate, milk dry past sunrise." She declined to pursue legal charges, and Amistron later filed a criminal complaint for defamation against her. "Nothing like that happened," he told me in a text message, adding, "we are calm and working on the search for awakening consciousness, ha ha ha."

As the sun began to set, Amistron showed me the ponds he had built, now bone-dry, and dozens of tires sunk into the ground for catching water. In the coming weeks, when it rained, he would buy thousands more toads. The animals would be stored in large drums and milked before being released. "It's so difficult to run a toad farm," Amistron grumbled. Yet he always had medicine. I wanted to stay longer in this grim place where so many doses had originated, shipped around the world for psychedelic revelations, but it was getting dark and my driver was insistent: For our safety, we had to leave.

. . .

In around 2018, Karla Montaño Pérez, a researcher at the Sonoran Commission for Ecology and Sustainable Development, a government body, became interested in Sonoran Desert toads. Pérez grew up near a park where frogs and toads sang all night in summer. "But not anymore," she said, when we met in 2023. A biochemical engineer by training, she had once worked at an aquaculture laboratory south of Kino Bay, near Seri territory, experimenting with white shrimp genetics, until realizing that she was participating in an "ecocide," as she put it. Shrimp farms discharge some 200 million liters of effluent into the bay each year, including pathogens, antibiotics, and fecal matter. They have destroyed saguaro forests and wetlands. "So I went to work for the other side," Pérez said.

She pulled up at my hotel in Hermosillo one evening, where I had been sheltering all day. A heat wave had engulfed the city. The previous weekend, temperatures had risen above 120 degrees. "I felt as if my eyes wanted to burst," a resident told *The New York Times*. Pérez, who is in her early fifties, was wearing wire-rimmed spectacles and a cotton blouse embroidered with flowers. Her muddy jeep had a dream catcher dangling from the mirror, with crystals, feathers, and white sage in the console.

At the conservation agency, she was in charge of species monitoring and protection. But when it came to the toad population, "there are no studies," she said. And so, in 2020, she had begun some surveys, visiting sites around Hermosillo that were "anecdotally rich in toads" while avoiding the more dangerous areas. She and her colleagues noticed that there were very few large adult *alvarius* toads; the largest, whom they nicknamed Big Daddy, was four inches in length, just over half the maximum size for the species. In some places, there were barely any toads at all. "Many times," Pérez said, "the poachers get there first."

By speaking to locals, she had gained an understanding of how the system worked. A bag of toads was worth around $5, the same amount Amistron paid farther north. This was decent money on the *ejidos* and ranches fringing the city, where poverty is rife. Late at night, buyers would show up in expensive cars and make off with the animals. "Nobody knows where they go," Pérez told me. She and her team had sampled fifteen locations, hearing similar accounts wherever they went. Frighteningly, many of the people catching toads were unable to differentiate between species. "They grab whatever they find," she said. "Toads, frogs, whatever."

She took me to one of the collecting areas, on communal farmland bordering a sewage treatment facility. We bumped down a gravel road through fields of barley, arriving at a settlement of ramshackle dwellings. Horses were tethered in dusty corrals. A man with a drooping mustache strolled past, accompanied by a girl leading a kid goat on a rope. Outside one of the houses, an *ejidario* in blue jeans and a denim shirt was fixing his truck, blasting *corridos* from a flashing Bluetooth speaker. When he saw us, he moved slowly across the yard and lifted a cowboy hat from a nail on the wall. He narrowed his eyes and, with almost comic suspicion, said something to the effect of, "Toads? I don't know anything about toads." With the music still blaring, he turned back to the truck.

With night closing in, we wandered around, listening to frogs in the weed-choked ditches. The hoot of the Sonoran Desert toad was conspicuously absent. One of Pérez's colleagues had joined us and was telling an amusing story about his son smoking toad when he flicked on a flashlight. "Bufo!" Pérez cried. The beam caught the toad's olive-green spots and bulging parotid glands. Another materialized, then another, like stage magicians appearing in spotlights.

We drove on to another spot known for toads: the Hermosillo baseball stadium, home to one of Mexico's most celebrated teams. The car was air-conditioned, and when we climbed out the wind was Hadean. We were in a vast, empty parking lot beside a boulevard where joggers and cyclists were unfathomably exercising. A diamond-back rattlesnake lay coiled beneath a streetlight; Pérez warned one of the runners, who barely reacted. Enormous, swarming, aggressive ants were pouring from holes in the hard-packed earth beyond the road, a scrubby expanse that flooded most summers. It was dry and there were no toads whatsoever. A team was practicing at the stadium and the floodlights were blazing. I imagined toads gazing upward, watching insects in the beams. Pérez had submitted a funding proposal to the Tucson Herpetological Society for extending her surveys; a few weeks later it was granted. I happened to be with Villa when he read her application. "I feel like celebrating with champagne," he said. Then his face grew serious as he considered what she might find.

. . .

As of mid-2025, the population status of Sonoran Desert toads remained uncertain. "Clandestine markets confuse things," Villa wrote to me in an email. He had funded small surveys over four consecutive years, but these hadn't produced enough data to draw firm conclusions. Pérez had noted further anecdotal reports of declines, such as at an *ejido* known as El Sapo due to its former abundance of toads. Residents there spoke of armed poachers arriving at night in large trucks. Children were being asked to "trap as many toads as possible." As a countermeasure, Pérez's group had launched an outreach program, educating people about toads and offering them cupcakes with decorative toad frosting. Ortiz and Santos-Barrera, meanwhile, reported that Sonoran Desert toads "seemed to have disappeared" from at least three sites they had surveyed and "appeared to be in serious decline" at several others, although their findings had not yet been formally reviewed or published.

Others maintained, without presenting evidence, that the toads were still plentiful. "There are still plagues of toads in parts of the desert—millions and millions of them," Mario Garnier, whose reliability I had come to question, assured me. "The risk is not extinction but animal abuse, like factory-farmed chicken." This seemed equally misaligned with the all-is-one ethos of toad smoking, yet the commercial appeal of wild toad medicine remained undiminished. Garnier said that he had parted ways with Amistron, the collector he'd once championed, after visiting his ranch and observing that "50 percent of the toads were dying."

A ready solution to this demoralizing market existed: the pure molecule, synthesized in labs. But this supply came with its own peculiar conundrums. In the past few years, 5-MeO-DMT vape pens have become widely available online: innocuous-looking devices that, at the click of a button, deliver one of the world's most powerful psychedelics. In 2023, the practitioners' collective known as the Conclave issued warnings about the potential risks of this frictionless delivery system, ranging from accidental overdoses and psychological destabilization to the "desacralization" of the experience: the God molecule as direct-to-consumer product. (Given the rampant commodification of toad smoking, this seemed more a difference of degree than of kind.) On Instagram, advertisements began appearing for branded 5-MeO-DMT cartridges that promised to "unlock your ego." I contacted the page making the posts, hoping to find out more, only to receive a barrage of hostile messages in broken English, demanding to know when I'd be placing an order.

Not all producers of vape devices were so nakedly commercial in their ambitions. Rumors circulated about a legendary Silicon Valley engineer who, alarmed about the overexploitation of Sonoran Desert toads, had invented a bespoke 5-MeO-DMT pen he was distributing for free. By chance, at a psychedelics conference in 2023, I overheard a bald, gnomish man in his seventies animatedly discussing the topic with a small group of people. I realized it was him. He later agreed to talk with me via Signal, but only if I kept his identity secret. "There are Schedule I drugs in my home," he said. "I could go to jail for this." A veteran psychonaut, he had first smoked toad around 2017, describing the experience to me as "a psychedelic bungee jump." He later came to believe that 5-MeO-DMT offered "training wheels to teach you a divine state of being," regarding it as his life's work to share the molecule carefully and safely. He spent years developing and testing his pens, moving through more than a dozen designs; the final version included an analog flow sensor and a miniature onboard computer to regulate the temperature of the heating coil and avoid degrading the compound. ("I have a perfectionist streak," he explained.) Over the next few years, he gave away more than a thousand sets of the pens—calibrated across a range of strengths—to tech CEOs, therapists, and spiritual teachers. "The 5-MeO-DMT medicine quiets the conscious mind and opens up access to the subconscious," he wrote in a user guide. "One sometimes experiences becoming an eternal spiritual being having a temporary experience in a physical human body on planet Earth." In June 2025, he died of cancer, leaving instructions for his identity to be revealed: Bill Atkinson, a visionary Apple designer whose groundbreaking software helped usher in the personal computing era. His pens would not have looked out of place in an Apple Store.

Meanwhile, the rush for toad secretion continued. In Hermosillo alone, more than twenty suppliers were operating, each with their own network of collectors. "Thousands are involved" across the state, a major dealer told me in 2023. Barraza, the erstwhile toad kingpin, had organized a meeting to divide up turf and standardize prices, but this had gone about as well as the ill-fated union of collectors. As one dealer told me, "They just fought with their egos."

Once controlled by a few players, the toad supply chain had sprung open, with dozens of Facebook accounts openly advertising the medicine. "Collected with love and respect," one seller wrote. (This seemed highly improbable.) That summer, a dealer from Hermosillo promoted "sacred toad" at 750 pesos a gram, or around $45—less than a third of the usual rate. Others fumed about the low prices. After a practitioner had tried to bargain him down, boasting that he could source toad more cheaply elsewhere, a dealer I'd met fired off a heated post. A single gram, he pointed out, could yield fifteen ceremonies, easily worth $2,000 or more: a markup of around 5,000 percent. "How can you feel good about yourself?" he wrote. "Sonora is a state at war, and still we don't give up. We risk our lives for medicine." Someone replied with a GIF of the actor Ray Liotta laughing hysterically in *Goodfellas.*

Fearing instability in the market, some buyers had switched to placing bulk orders. Flor Bollini, the Argentinean "Corporate Shaman," had recently purchased a hundred grams of secretion from Barraza, paying him $10,000. She texted me a picture of the medicine stashed in her freezer. "It's like a brick," she said. Her clients were willing to pay exorbitant fees, and she earned back her investment in a single private session.

"Gringos want to pay us twenty dollars a gram," another collector texted me. "It's the same as Chinese kids assembling iPhones. The system is a shit." He had been collecting toads for several years but was thinking of quitting the business. One of his friends had been beaten by *sicarios* while toading; another had his car hijacked. "It's worse every year," the collector said. He was considering growing hallucinogenic mushrooms instead, which better appealed to his conscience. "Ninety-five percent of toad medicine is full of cruelty," he explained: toads layered helplessly in buckets, left for hours in the sun. Many toads died and were milked regardless. "It's sad how humans take advantage of other species, and of other humans. It's the same as the meat industry. But what can we do? Meanwhile, there is demand."

He introduced me to a friend of his who, as he put it, harvested "a damn lot" of secretion. He added, "This man is very cruel with the toads." The friend, who asked not to be identified, described his operation in businesslike terms. He had drivers making regular stops at around ten small towns, spread over a wide area, to buy toads. The price was 20 pesos, or around $1, per animal. They were taken to a ranch, where they were rinsed in clean water and milked. "This is not an aggressive way of manipulating the species," the friend assured me. "We treat them kindly." But his margins were shrinking. Orders used to start at 1,500 pesos a gram; now the rate had dropped to 350. Thankfully, he said, it was still possible to source toads so cheaply.

In earlier years, when profits were higher and the desert less violent, he had collected his own animals, but then he was threatened at gunpoint and "started hiring locals," he explained. He told me about a young couple who had gone looking for toads near Caborca a few years earlier. They were kidnapped and held for several days. The man was beaten. The woman was repeatedly raped.

Yet the ranch model had dangers of its own. At one property north of Hermosillo, where captive toads were nourished on mealworms, the local narcos began to take notice. They viewed the ranch as business in their territory and, as was typical, demanded protection fees. After a misunderstanding, the owner fled and locked himself inside his grandmother's house, fearing for his life. "The danger is real," said one of his friends, a U.S. military veteran who sometimes hung out at the ranch. Eventually a deal was brokered, and the toad venture resumed. Then, one day, the local cartel boss showed up. There was a problem. Some of his *sicarios* had become hooked on cocaine and were causing him problems. The boss had heard about a doctor named Octavio who used toads to cure addiction.

"Make them quit doing cocaine," the boss ordered. Then he left.

Two cartel members arrived soon afterward in a beat-up old truck. One was a young woman with cold eyes who "had seven bodies on her already," the veteran told me. The other was a thin, tattooed man with an even higher kill count. The ceremony took place outside at dusk. The assassins screamed and writhed, then began sobbing. "It was the most intense thing I've ever witnessed," the veteran told me.

A few weeks later, he ran into the man harvesting wild herbs near the ranch. He had quit being a *sicario* and become a spiritual healer for the cartel, he explained. In narco culture, spiritual beliefs often intermingle with violence, with cartel figures turning to *curanderos* or *brujos* for guidance or protection. The man's transformation attested to an inconvenient reality for the toads: despite all their mistreatment, their secretions remained spectacularly efficacious. At a local grocery store one day, the man's wife came over, looking mystified. "What did you do with him?" she asked the veteran. "He smiles all the time."

CHAPTER 6

Wild, Wild Country

Octavio lives in a neighborhood of Hermosillo with potholed streets and many drug users, some of whom occasionally call on him for free toad sessions. The front gate's handle is painted with a smiling blue toad. It opens onto an oasis of a yard with lush vegetation, a large shaded *palapa,* and a tiled patio inlaid with the same geometric toad symbol as the decals on Octavio's cars. The beams are strung with hammocks, Tibetan prayer flags, and a painted turtle shell from the Seri tribe. Octavio sleeps and plays video games upstairs, preferring first-person shooters. The room is cluttered with toad artworks, including a giant painting made by a friend under the influence of the medicine, working ambidextrously with a brush in each hand.

Downstairs lies a spartan dormitory with bunk beds and a small communal bathroom. This is where Octavio's longer-term patients—typically addicts—stay for the duration of their treatment, which can last for weeks. The walls are decorated with Octavio's framed medical certificates and photos of him posing with his hands clasped in prayer. In an unlocked chest on the floor, he keeps thousands of indemnity forms and testimonials from his toad sessions, creased and haphazardly stuffed together.

In an adjacent room, Octavio has a gym with weights and a collection of mountain bikes. When I visited him for the first time in the summer of 2021, he frequently stayed up all night and went riding the Hermosillo trails before dawn, posting videos to Facebook of himself launching off ramps. He had dislocated his shoulder in a recent fall but was eyeing an even bigger jump, which seemed in keeping with his approach to serving toad. "I can easily break my leg or something if I don't land properly," he told me one day. "I am fucking excited about it, because if I do it, this will only increase my level of confidence."

I had wondered, before traveling to Sonora, how Octavio would present himself and conduct his sessions. It had been two years since the public letter accusing him of malpractice. His stature in psychedelic circles had fallen. Had his approach to serving the medicine evolved? Over the next few weeks, I watched him hold sessions at home and in Seri territory, where the founding mythology of his practice originated. He still eyeballed large doses, performed little to no preparation or integration, administered *rapé* during trips, and left clients unattended. If anything, the volatility I'd heard about was on even fuller display, reinforced by a lurking defensiveness.

The first time I arrived at his house, a soothing New Age soundtrack was playing and around a dozen people were sitting in the shade with buckets positioned at their feet. Octavio was wearing a bright red shirt with Mayan patterns and the letters RETTIG on the back, like the captain of a psychedelic soccer team. He was in an animated mood, pacing the yard like a stage. It was a few days after Seri New Year, and many of the same clients were present, including his defense lawyer from the homicide case in León. The lawyer's name was Carlos Rojas. He was paunchy and had a trusting demeanor. Less than a year earlier, he had seen the widower Jorge Villalpando leap up in the courtroom, yelling at Octavio, "Son of a bitch! You killed my wife!" Rojas had left the trial so convinced of Octavio's healing powers that he brought his entire family to Sonora for treatment.

Two of Rojas's sons were in their early twenties; the third, Daniel, was a wiry boy of fourteen with hunched shoulders and a buzz cut with a horizontal line shaved above one ear. He had a veneer of toughness that failed to disguise his childlike features. He had been adopted at the age of four, "after his father died and his mother abandoned him," Rojas's wife, Gabriella, told me. Daniel had lately started using crystal meth, which consumed her with worry. Like any mother, she told me, she wanted her boys to be "at peace with themselves and follow their dreams."

Octavio frequently encouraged patients to bring their loved ones to ceremonies, either as witnesses or to participate. If this was conducive to healing, it was also good for business: Rojas's party numbered seven people, including two family friends in their twenties. "They have *issues* inside their family," Octavio told me, brushing past the specifics. "The whole family are coming to a healing process—the wife, the husband, and the kids. They have a whole *story.*"

The session began. Octavio picked up a butane torch and a small piece of wood with a pointed tip, which he heated until it glowed; he then moved around the circle, burning neat dots on the arms, legs, and shoulders of his patients. These were for administering kambo, a toxin obtained from the waxy monkey tree frog, a species native to the Amazon. The frogs are bright green, with bulging eyes and nimble digits. They protect themselves from desiccation by secreting a waxy substance and smearing it over their bodies—sun cream for frogs, as the naturalist David Attenborough once described it. This also defends them against predation. Ritual use of kambo was first documented in the 1920s, when a French missionary in Brazil observed frogs being tied above a fire to prompt them into releasing their poison, which was rubbed into fresh burn wounds to purge illness and misfortune. "The evil force exits the body by all the orifices," he wrote. "The sick man gains weight and regains his color."

Vittorio Erspamer, the Nobel Prize–winning chemist who detected 5-MeO-DMT in Sonoran Desert toads, performed the first laboratory analyses of kambo in the 1960s. In one paper, he and his colleagues noted the effects it was believed to offer: "increase in physical strength, heightening of senses, resistance to hunger and thirst." Despite scant clinical evidence, use of kambo as a detoxifying agent has exploded during the wellness era, touted as a cure for such diverse conditions as meningitis, Alzheimer's, chronic fatigue, and diabetes. In 2021, *The New York Times* quoted a media strategist in San Francisco whose face swelled up the first time she tried it. "It kind of looks like a celebrity plastic surgeon went to town on your face," she said, "like Kim Kardashian in a fun-house mirror."

As with psychedelic toads, the commercial market for kambo has reshaped the world in which this tree frog exists. There is an abiding belief in the kambo community that collection is performed in strict accordance with Indigenous beliefs about nature, but there are also reports of harvesters jamming metal implements up the noses of frogs or blowing smoke over them, agitating them into releasing more of the substance. Many frog collectors live in poverty, with financial incentives to extract as much kambo as possible. There is almost no data on its collection and use, although a recent study identified more than six thousand members of private Facebook groups dedicated to the substance, which is now available on every continent except Antarctica.

Running against his general aversion to client preparation, Octavio began incorporating kambo into his ceremonies in around 2014, believing that it purified the body to receive toad—an approach that involved little to no psychological engagement, and which sometimes bore resemblance to ritual hazing. "I am working with maybe the two best medicines on the planet," he told me, "and both of them come from amphibians. One from a frog that lives in the tops of trees in the jungle, and the other one is this toad that lives underground in the desert." He reeled off some of the benefits of kambo: "The color of your skin and nails changes. You feel more stamina. You feel it in the clarity of your mind." He has posted photos online of himself on the substance, his eyes puffy, his lips grotesquely engorged.

I asked how he determined when his clients were ready for toad. "You will see it from the buckets," he said. "There are many things we can see in vomit—the color, the amount, the characteristics."

After burning each of his patients—"to allow the medicine to get into the system"—he brought out a wooden Popsicle stick with daubs of kambo, which resembled dried glue. One by one, he instructed them to spit on it. Then he mixed the paste with a blunt scalpel and dabbed it onto the burns. (This was during the pandemic, and the mingling of saliva was jarring. Octavio said it potentiated the substance.) The kambo veterans were identifiable by the number of scars on their bodies; Oscar, the self-proclaimed Houston gangster and recovering addict, had more than two dozen fresh burns in a line across both shoulders. Octavio would not be serving toad today—this would come later—but what followed was no less dramatic to witness.

Within minutes of being dosed, everyone was dripping with sweat. Rojas, the lawyer, tugged off an enormous T-shirt he'd designed featuring an image of a Sonoran Desert toad; his belly rose and fell as he gasped for air. All around the circle, people began projectile vomiting. Rojas moaned, his lips swollen to cartoonish proportions. Daniel, his youngest son, seemed to shrink into himself, gulping water from a plastic cup. A woman nearing sixty with diabetes and high blood pressure threw up and urinated through her chair. Splashing noises came from every direction.

As he worked, Octavio became reflective, paying little heed to the chaos around him. "Sometimes I burn out with so much work," he said. "Because who else is going to help these people?" He was booked up for the next two weeks, he said—"every single day." Prior to the pandemic, he had been even busier, with international tours scheduled years in advance. (In fact, his travels had slowed earlier, following the backlash to his work.) I hadn't brought up these criticisms yet, but he alluded to them, gesturing toward his vomiting clients: "There is nothing, really, to dig up and see. If I was doing something wrong, *no one* would be here at my house."

He began telling me about some memorable toad sessions. He had introduced his son to the medicine at the age of 12; his daughter, Salvia, at 11. The oldest person he'd served was a Venezuelan tribal elder aged 102. Octavio's youngest patient was a 5-year-old boy who had been diagnosed with ADHD. "Serving little kids is more unusual," he said. "This is not something I'm putting on the web—*bring your kids to me.*" He explained that the medicine could be more effective for children because "they are not as polluted in their bodies yet." The idea of a

5-year-old smoking toad stunned me, though Octavio appeared not to notice. He clarified that he had given the boy a full breakthrough dose.

. . .

The next morning, I arrived at Octavio's house as planned, but the gate was locked and his phone rang unanswered. I called one of his volunteers, Gerardo, the engineer whom I had met before Seri New Year. "We're at the gas station in Kino," he said, with some panic in his voice. "Octavio just left. We don't know where he went."

At the kambo session, I had noticed Gerardo and his wife looking increasingly beleaguered, tending to anguished participants while their daughter toddled around. They had been with Octavio for a week, sometimes getting to bed after four in the morning. After one all-night session in Seriland, they had returned to Hermosillo as the sun was coming up, only for Octavio to head out mountain biking. Gerardo told me this during a break, laughing nervously. "This guy's batteries . . ." he said. "Maybe he slept for two hours." Saskia, who had rings under her eyes, looked less chipper, and I asked how she was doing. "Super tired," she said. She was pregnant, I was astonished to learn, with another baby.

Officially, Octavio was running what he called "a retreat" over three days, but the schedule was dictated entirely by his whims. A flyer advertised "Healing with Nature"—toad and kambo sessions, Tibetan singing bowl therapy, visits with the Seri tribe. There had been a proliferation of such retreats worldwide, with dozens of businesses listing toad ceremonies on sites like retreat.guru, which bills itself as the "world's largest collection of transformative experiences." These ranged from single sessions to catered multiday affairs costing several thousand dollars per person: "Seri Culture Immersion Excursion," "6 Day Men's Bufo Camp," "Kambo, Bufo Alvarius and Floatation with Magic Mushroom in Tulum."

On the phone, Gerardo guessed that Octavio had driven out to Punta Chueca. It was Saturday, and Gerardo was hoping to be back at work by Monday; I tried to picture him, sleep-deprived, in a corporate office. My driver and I made our way to the village, eventually locating the group on a remote beach belonging to some members of the Barnett clan, the custodians of Seri ritual whom Octavio had allied himself with a decade earlier. There were several cars parked beside the dunes and a huddle of people in the shade of a *palapa.* Gerardo, who had driven behind us, gave a helpless shrug. "Why are they here?" he asked, sighing.

Octavio stood on a wooden platform with a dozen people circled below him. He was bare-chested and had his sunglasses on, with a red peaked cap, cargo shorts, and a necklace of carved wooden toads. Most of the other men were shirtless as well, and it was noticeable that Octavio was the fittest among them, with ropy muscles on his arms and torso. One by one, his clients stepped up and he burned more dots on their skin for kambo, heckling them and cracking jokes. His tone veered between comedic and lightly bullying. Everyone laughed, as if on cue.

It was early afternoon and verging on 110 degrees. The air was humid and briny; the sea, scuffed by cross-shore winds, was a bright, milky blue. A row of tall sticks had been dug into the sand, each strung with blue, red, and silver streamers. They had been set up by Filomena Barnett, a Seri woman in her fifties who sometimes hosted ceremonies with Octavio. Filomena was a granddaughter of Miguel Barnett, the clan's long-haired patriarch, and like several others in the family had become a toad shaman. She did not look happy to be there. A few days earlier, at Seri New Year, Octavio had kept her waiting on the beach for several hours, dressed in traditional attire for a ceremony that never happened; she eventually gave up and caught a ride back to the village, where she found him partying. Now she sat on the edge of the platform, one arm draped over the railing, holding a shaker. (She ended up leaving early, after asking Octavio in front of the group when he was going to pay her.)

Octavio administered more kambo to Daniel, the lawyer's son, who smiled at him shyly. I asked Octavio if anyone would be smoking toad that day.

"I have no idea," he snapped at me. "I'm not Nostradamus, brother."

After being dosed, Octavio's clients wandered down the beach, gathering beneath another *palapa.* I walked over to find them sprawled on the sand, periodically throwing up. A few assistants went around dumping water on people's heads or wiping their mouths with toilet paper. Someone sounded a singing bowl. Gerardo, apparently relieved of his helper duties, came over with swollen lips and lowered himself to the ground, squeezing his eyes shut and rocking back and forth. His wife poured water on his neck, then calmly took out her phone and recorded a close-up video, as if this were a perfectly normal moment to capture. Their child was wandering around with a red lollipop. An older woman in a white blouse stained yellow with bile was groaning as her adult daughter stroked her arm and murmured, "Respira, respira." Brian, the Sri Lankan photographer, was crouched to one side with a zoom lens, snapping picture after picture.

A short while later, feeling the onset of heatstroke, I went back up the beach to get water and Brian rushed over. "Help me, brother," he stammered. "Octavio needs water. He's thirsty." He grabbed a bottle from a stash beneath the *palapa* and tried to unscrew it, but his hands were shaking and the lid slipped. Then he snatched the cup from my hands and dashed off. I followed and found Octavio cursing at him. "I need *mineral water,*" Octavio said, enunciating the words furiously, "and I need it now!"

By now, Octavio had finished serving kambo; more than a dozen people were throwing up. I came across Daniel, unattended in the sun, with black mucus issuing from his nostrils. Octavio had evidently given him another hit of *rapé.* Daniel was pawing at his face with a wad of disintegrating tissues. Others had staggered into the water and were rolling around in the shallows. I looked around and realized that Octavio was no longer on the beach. I found him in the parking lot, out of sight of his clients, smoking an oversized joint in his truck while blasting psychedelic trance music. While he sat there, several of his helpers—the word "toadies" came to mind—were bent over in the dust, changing a punctured tire. The kambo patients, I guessed, were looking after themselves. As the track reached a crescendo, Octavio cranked up the volume, leaped out, and began stomping around to the beat. A few other people came up from the beach, including Brian with his cameras. When Octavio saw this, he announced that it was time for a photo shoot.

He strode off down the dirt road, tugging on a red Seri jacket. Brian hurried after him, fussing with his lenses. The music was still thumping. Octavio set his joint down and began striking various poses—hands in prayer, arms and legs outstretched like the Vitruvian man—as Brian frantically clicked. Then, without warning, Octavio sprinted toward us and launched himself into the air, crashing with full force into Brian, who cried out and fell backward, cradling a camera against his chest. He struck the ground with a thud and got up, winded and smiling sheepishly. "Watch out, Brian!" Octavio shouted, slapping him on the back. Octavio had dislocated a thumb in the collision and tugged it back into place with a grunt. Then he marched away to pose for more photos.

As the afternoon went on, I was reminded of something Octavio had mentioned a few days earlier. Without prompting, he had brought up the documentary *Wild Wild Country,* about an increasingly sinister cult that formed around the spiritual leader Osho, whom Brian had once devoted himself to. "It might be considered a cult," Octavio told me, "but if you see the whole picture, I don't think that guy was dangerous himself." Osho's devotees had stockpiled weapons, poisoned hundreds of people, and plotted the murders of perceived enemies. Octavio described him as "one of the main spiritual leaders of the twentieth century." Octavio also recommended that I watch *Murder Mountain,* a documentary about a utopian cannabis-growing community in Northern California that descended into violence, paranoia, and black-market chaos. "This is not a cult," he stated, of his own work with toad medicine. "I don't have followers, or a team."

"It's interesting how something that starts with good intentions—and maybe even helps people—can still turn harmful," I said, perhaps a little transparently.

"Absolutely," Octavio said. "And I'm aware that what *I* am doing might look like this kind of thing. Some people admire what I do. Some people think I am special. Some people hate me."

The next day, Brian pulled me aside and surreptitiously showed me a tattoo of Octavio on one shoulder. He knew of six or seven people with similar designs, he said. The tattoo was of Octavio in a cowboy hat beside a Sonoran Desert toad. Brian was talking quickly, twisting around to see if anybody was watching. He seemed eager that I understand something about Octavio, though it wasn't clear to me what. "He's in another realm—easily misunderstood," Brian said. "Everyone has a different opinion. He's unpredictable." Nobody served the medicine better than Octavio, he went on: "He takes you on a deeper dive. He makes sure you hit rock bottom, and he makes sure you don't die. He brings you back." Yet this praise was undercut by small, pointed details, as if Brian were sending me a coded message. "I treat him like a friend," he said, "but the thing about him is that he has no space for anybody. He's focused only on this work. All the time, he tells me, *Fuck off! Fuck off!*"

Brian was documenting Octavio's sessions for free, which he referred to as his job. "I have to be on the ball all the time," he emphasized. "Batteries charged, everything ready." When I asked what Brian got out of this, he didn't hesitate: more opportunities to smoke toad with Octavio. It was natural, he said, to feel devotion toward those who showed you the path.

"Whoever gives you the milk," he whispered, "the mother becomes."

. . .

Early in his relationship with the Seri tribe, Octavio would bring clients to Punta Chueca and serve them toad in the middle of the village, watched by large groups of residents. Now he was skirting the edges of the community. The alliances he touted in public seemed more fragile on the ground. At one point during the retreat, Octavio pulled over at the home of one of Chapo Barnett's sons, who had himself become a prominent toad shaman. The property, known among Seri people as the hippie house, had a large toad mural painted on one wall. I had stopped by during the New Year celebrations to find a firelit jam session under way, with dreadlocked white people coming and going while a small pig nosed through beer bottles in the yard. Now, as I moved to follow Octavio inside, one of his assistants stopped me. There were tensions, it was becoming clear, between Octavio and the Seri.

The same night of my visit, Octavio had served *rapé* to a local known as Puma. Puma was a son of Antonio Robles, the leader who originally welcomed Octavio into the community. Puma had a history of crystal meth abuse and was drunk; after inhaling the snuff, he stopped breathing. Members of the Seri traditional guard arrested Octavio, in part for his own protection. Had Puma died, multiple sources in the community told me, people in Punta Chueca were prepared to kill Octavio in revenge. Octavio related parts of this story to my driver but later played it down, texting me a pair of photographs he'd posted to Facebook a few months after the incident. One showed Puma as a young man with plump cheeks; the other showed him aged and haggard. "Maldito cristal," read the caption. ("Fucking meth.") According to Octavio, Puma had requested *rapé* at the party. "Obviously he was puking," he told me, "and very weak and sweaty because he was so intoxicated. But nothing happened, brother."

Puma recovered, but this was only the latest in a series of charged encounters between Octavio and the tribe. These went back to 2012, when Octavio first went to live in Punta Chueca. At the time, an anthropology student named Jesús Ogarrio was conducting an ethnographic study of Seri rituals. He and Octavio were the only outsiders living in the community, and for several months they shared a small room. Initially, Jesús said, he found Octavio to be "credible and trustworthy," adding, "He was there to help with a very grave issue." The village had no basic medical services; here was a doctor, offering treatment. Of the roughly four hundred residents, Jesús estimated that dozens were addicts. "It was a pandemic of addiction," he told me.

But as time passed, he became increasingly disturbed by Octavio's behavior. Octavio smoked toad throughout the day and often came across as irritable and anxious—"like an addict," Jesús said. Many people in the village were afraid of the substance, and Octavio sometimes declined to inform his patients what they were being dosed with, saying only that it would help with their recovery. "So people would come there in need," Jesús told me, "and because they had no preparation, they would scream and run around." This caused upheaval in a community where most people identified as Christian, he went on. "Some people said this was a thing of the devil."

On at least eight occasions, Jesús witnessed Octavio tricking people into smoking toad by pretending that it was crystal meth. Octavio's attitude seemed to be that any route to the toad experience, no matter how coercive or misleading, was justified by the outcome. (He later denied ever deceiving people into smoking toad with him.) One day, according to Jesús, Octavio slipped a toad pipe to one of Robles's sons, who had been lounging on a relative's couch. The man "started to go crazy," Jesús recalled, hurling furniture around, attacking Octavio, and running off into the desert, only to return after dark. His addiction worsened afterward, and he died in 2019. Another of the Robles brothers—Miguel, the young heroin addict who became one of Octavio's first success stories in the community—later relapsed and was imprisoned for attempted murder. A third continued using meth and became a commercial dealer of toad secretion until dying in a car crash in 2018.

To the world, Octavio portrayed himself as having the support of the entire tribe, but in reality he was aligned with a small and influential faction. On the winter solstice of 2013, when Octavio hosted a large group ceremony with members of the tribe on Tiburón Island, even these relationships came under strain. A year had passed, almost to the day, since his girlfriend had gone missing and drowned in the

Yucatán cenote. The group gathered in a circle and some Seri elders chanted; then, while serving toad, Octavio took a hit and became violent. According to an eyewitness, he started yelling, "She's not dead! She's still in the water!" He raged and cursed at the group, punching people and breaking the nose of a Seri woman. (Octavio acknowledged becoming angry during the ceremony but said that he had only raised his voice and cursed. He dismissed the allegation of violence, which I had also heard from Seri sources, as a "funny story.") The following day, the tribe's leaders issued a letter denouncing Octavio for his "lack of respect, ethics, and professionalism" at the event. "Dr. Octavio Rettig Hinojosa is not authorized to represent, promote, or disseminate our tangible and intangible cultural heritage anywhere within or outside our territory," the letter stated, "and is prohibited from using, promoting, disseminating, and handling the sacred medicine from the species *Bufo alvarius.*"

This letter, I subsequently established, was authored by Odily Fuentes, the friend who had originally introduced Octavio to the Seri. I first spoke to her via Zoom, where she appeared on-screen wearing purple lipstick. A giant print of the toad artwork in Octavio's lounge—a lurid Technicolor design in thick brushstrokes—hung behind her. It had been painted by her husband, Xixi, she said, blowing smoke from a joint. We later met up in Hermosillo, where Fuentes cast Octavio's work with the Seri in an unflattering light. Besides providing treatment, she said, he was searching for something: a narrative of Indigenous toad use. "We needed a tribe to protect and promote the toad," Fuentes recalled, with no evident embarrassment. "Any Sonoran tribe embracing the toad would have been fine."

In 2012, the OTAC Foundation had also visited representatives of the Yaqui, another community where meth abuse was rampant; children as young as eight were becoming addicted to the drug. According to Anahi Ochoa, a Yaqui activist who was present for the meeting, Octavio arrived barefoot and smoked pot during his first meeting with the tribe's elders. "It was shameful," she said: a white visitor acting as if he owned the place. Octavio later brought a film crew to the village without asking permission and began boasting publicly about his relationship with the tribe, using the Yaqui term for toads, *bobok,* to promote his work. He held some toad sessions in the community, but these were also contentious; in one instance, he passed smoke to a Yaqui woman by placing his lips against her own. Octavio had requested a formal letter from the tribe to authorize his ceremonies, but Ochoa demanded that he stop using their name. After that, Octavio stopped visiting. "He was looking for validation as a shaman," Ochoa said. "But he's nothing more than an actor—a fake."

The following year, when the Seri disavowed him, Octavio found himself without Indigenous partners at a pivotal moment of his career. He had recently spoken at Burning Man and was receiving invitations to travel the world. "Imagine Octavio without this tribe," Fuentes said. "He needed that document to keep moving." Octavio has used formal letters from the Seri to legitimize the collection and the transport of toad medicine across borders, as well as to validate his role to external organizations such as TED, which provided him with a platform to broadcast his claims about the ancestral roots of toad smoking. After the Tiburón Island episode, according to multiple sources I spoke with, Octavio began paying for letters from the tribe, which he has periodically renewed. ("I just give what they ask," he told me. "I don't bargain. I'm fair. I gave a car one time; I gave them TVs." He called this system "a code of honor.") Some men in the Robles family, including the brothers who have since died, charged a few hundred pesos for such documents whenever they wished to buy meth, Jesús Ogarrio told me: "They saw that what Octavio really wanted to do was business." One month after the solstice, a new girlfriend of Octavio's posted pictures to Instagram of him posing with Chapo Barnett, another of his allies. "Chapo signs the paperwork!" she wrote. "Octavio Rettig has the Seri blessing."

. . .

After his photo shoot with Brian, apparently energized by the attention, Octavio was ready, at last, to begin serving toad. It was mid-afternoon and the heat felt unendurable. We trooped down to the beach, where Octavio's kambo patients lay limp in the shade, no longer purging. Two helpers held up a picnic blanket to shield him from the wind as he unscrewed his medicine jar and prepared a pipe, sprinkling flakes into the bowl. There was precious little ceremony. One by one, his clients perched beside him on a wooden bench and inhaled, followed by Octavio briefly chanting and shaking his rattle; assistants or family members then led them down to the water on wobbling legs while Octavio summoned the next person.

Earlier in the day, he had been animated and engaging, but he now had an impulsive, almost tyrannical manner. He berated a broad-shouldered schoolteacher for refusing a second hit of toad—"You need to do it again! You did it wrong. That's how you're going to educate your students?"—before sending him away with a disgusted expression. Minutes later, he ordered the lawyer's fourteen-year-old son to come over for more *rapé* and became furious when the boy hung back. "Come on, you bastard," Octavio said, pointing a finger in his face. "And make your back straight! You're too young for this hunchback." The boy hid behind his hands and glanced at his parents. "You will do it," Octavio commanded. "Don't make me stand up and go for you. If you resist, we will force you." He began counting: "Una. Dos . . ."

The boy sat down next to him. His whole body jolted when the snuff hit his nostrils. Tears welled up in his eyes, and he was soon curled up on his side, cradled by his mother. Octavio announced with contempt that he was "not ready for toad."

A few others in the Rojas family smoked the medicine that day. One of the older sons sat upright and smiled peacefully during his trip; the other collapsed face down in the sand, monitored by Saskia, who was simultaneously breastfeeding her daughter and holding a jar of *rapé* for Octavio. A friend of the Rojas family's began trembling all over his body—lips, diaphragm, thighs—before Octavio blew *rapé* up his nose mid-trip and he began vomiting. Octavio's assistants left him lying with his feet in the surf, like a shipwreck casualty. (I later found the man comforting another client who had keeled over nearby.) Rojas himself, after taking a large hit from the pipe, nearly toppled backward off the bench: Octavio had been supporting him with one arm but then shut his eyes and let go, lost in song. One of Rojas's sons leaped forward to catch him and stayed there, braced like a goalkeeper, until Octavio opened his eyes again, oblivious to the averted danger.

The next day of the retreat was on Tiburón Island. Some members of the group had left; a few new faces had arrived. The mood was expectant and charged with possibility. We drove back to Punta Chueca and piled onto a wooden boat belonging to Filomena Barnett's husband, who steered the outboard motor with a purple scarf draped around his head, looking piratical. Octavio, who once again seemed amiable and relaxed, took selfies as we crossed the channel. We waded ashore on a beach flanked by mangroves; in the distance rose peaks where the Seri had once sheltered from their enemies. A film crew from Hermosillo, hired to shoot promotional content for Octavio, was waiting in the only scrap of shade, a tarpaulin held up by four poles of driftwood. It was 2:00 p.m.; an oppressive wind was sweeping over the water, and thunderclouds massed on the horizon. Filomena's husband departed with the boat, the drone of its engine fading in the distance.

There was no first aid kit on the island, and we were more than an hour from the nearest medical facility. The previous evening, I had been dizzy with heat exhaustion, and I was one of the few who hadn't been purging violently. From what I had observed that week, Octavio hadn't altered his approach to serving toad at all. A few days earlier, at the villa in Kino Bay, I had seen one man throw up, start choking, and slam his forehead on the tiles before one of Octavio's assistants rushed over; Octavio then slapped him on the rear and said, "C'mon! Stand up!" During another session, while being filmed by strangers, a woman had menstruated through her white shorts and vomited repeatedly. Octavio blew *rapé* up her nose a few times; when she waved her hands in front of her face, trying to block him, a helper restrained her. Afterward, he handed her a Seri pouch stitched with a toad pattern and said, "Welcome to the tribe." The woman later posted a picture of herself and Octavio on Instagram overlaid by a frog sticker with the words "Love you."

By now, Octavio had repeatedly brought up the allegations against him, yet he seemed unperturbed by such things happening in front of me, as if he couldn't conceive of his work being interpreted critically. For more than a decade he had been surrounded almost constantly by a revolving cast of disciples, as if trapped in the bubble of his own ego. At no point had he introduced me to the group as a journalist, despite the extreme nature of the toad experience and the intensely personal reasons people had for putting themselves through it. I made a point of doing this myself, and to telegraph my presence further I wore a collared shirt every day and conspicuously held a notebook. I also made voice recordings, and sometimes during interviews I handed my phone to Octavio and asked him to hold it, not wanting him to forget why I was there. It hadn't inhibited him in the slightest.

On the inland side of the beach was a saltwater lagoon. The videographers erected a tripod at the edge as Octavio lit another joint and began serving the medicine. The first man to receive toad lay on his back in the shallows, thrashing his arms and roaring, as water poured into his mouth; then he floated off into the distance, gazing slack-jawed at a circling bird. I was the only person watching him in this seemingly vulnerable state; Octavio had moved on to the next client and was being filmed by six people.

As the afternoon wore on, my head began spinning and I went to try to find some shade, wedging myself into the mangroves. When I returned, Octavio was holding court in the lagoon, pausing only to relight his joint. Or was it a new one? He spoke uninterrupted for nearly an hour with everyone facing him in a semicircle, a winding monologue that became more defensive and conspiratorial the longer it went on. He was speaking in Spanish, so it didn't seem as if I were the intended audience, but he furiously dismissed many of the criticisms against him. Araceli Ramírez had died because she ate breakfast on the day of her ceremony—participants had apparently been urged not to—and also due to medical negligence from the authorities, he insisted. "Ambulances don't come for dead people," he added darkly, intimating that the paramedics had been responsible for her death. Another patient had died because he was fat and unhealthy—"like him," Octavio said, pointing to one of his helpers, an overweight young man with a lost air about him. Octavio's tone was becoming harsher and more aggrieved. Almost everyone listening had smoked toad with him, many of them that very afternoon. I had the sensation of watching a narrative being seeded as they murmured assent.

"I've never walked around with a pistol killing people," Octavio declared. "I've never walked around with a toad drowning people."

Missing from the group was his defense lawyer's family, who had hastily departed that morning to catch their flight home to León. We had been hanging around at the beach in Punta Chueca, waiting for the boat to the island, when the lawyer announced that they had to leave. Octavio sprang into action, whipping out his glass pipes and jar of toad secretion, which he served right there in the parking lot. After the buildup of the past few days, it felt abrupt, almost perfunctory. Rojas's wife screamed during her trip, sinking to her knees and rocking forward on the dirt, as if expelling something buried deep inside her. Daniel, the boy, drew on the pipe and looked stunned, gazing around blankly at the people filming him. His mother was weeping. Afterward, he was led down to the sea, where he played like a carefree boy in the shallows. He had an innocent smile and his eyes were shining. "A child is reborn," Oscar, the Houston gangster, said raptly. The family pressed together for a group hug with Octavio, who howled like a wolf and posed for more photos. A short while later, after a rushed farewell, they were gone, and we were motoring across the channel.

. . .

The uptake of toads among the Seri, singular though it may have seemed, had a kind of historical precedent. In 1961, a Seri man named Jose Astorga began carving ornaments out of ironwood, a desert tree with extraordinarily hard timber. Ironwood is so dense that it does not float in water; the Seri traditionally used it for clubs and harpoons. One day, Astorga presented a polished rectangular block to an American tourist who sometimes visited Desemboque. "Something to hold your papers down," he explained.

Even by the nonconformist standards of the Seri, Astorga was whimsically eccentric. He had striking features, with a large nose and prominent cheekbones. He habitually wore a policeman's cap and carried a venomous Arizona coral snake in his pocket. He told yarns about flying around at night and traveling to the moon. Astorga was a master of Seri chants, and at fiestas he could sing all night and all of the next day without repeating a song. He was friends with Miguel Barnett, the patriarch of the Wolf Clan, and as young men they had devised a scheme to avoid paying customary bride fees: They swapped sisters. Astorga's wife had peculiarities of her own, among them rearing a pet javelina (a porcine desert creature also known as a skunk pig) that snored at Astorga's feet while he carved.

After the paperweight, Astorga progressed to making sea creatures: a turtle, some porpoises. These were eagerly purchased by visitors, and Astorga, who had an entrepreneurial bent, enlisted his family to help him. The carvings were strikingly modernist, with an economy of detail that showed intimate knowledge of the animals being depicted. Other Seri began carving ironwood, and within five years half the population of Desemboque was involved in this new activity. "Their transition was from hunting and gathering to commercialism," one historian noted. Seemingly out of nowhere, a distinctive art form had emerged, finding a ready market among admirers of Indian crafts.

A flood of interest in the tribe ensued. "They are tested, studied, painted, questioned, photographed and written about, and they have almost no privacy," a scholar named Bernice Johnston wrote in 1970, attributing this in large part to the new enterprise of wood carving. The Seri had become renowned for a practice oriented explicitly toward outsiders, and as commercial fishing declined, their economy became increasingly reliant on ironwood. Soon there were shortages around the villages, and the Seri had to buy wood at ever-inflating prices. The species grows extremely slowly; an established tree can live for hundreds of years. Dense stands along the floodplains inland from Desemboque were felled, followed by trees on Tiburón Island.

As the trade evolved, so did its origin story. In one version, Astorga said that he had been fasting in a cave when a bat-like spirit appeared and commanded him to carve ironwood "to save his people." In another, he had accidentally shot himself while hunting and was rescued by extraterrestrial beings who, after treating his injuries aboard a spaceship, told him to save the Seri by carving ironwood for tourists. There are also more prosaic accounts of American tourists requesting designs and demonstrating woodworking techniques. Regardless, ironwood carving became a vital source of revenue for the tribe, even as it was becoming more precarious. Not long after it began, Johnston warned that this new industry "could collapse as suddenly as it was born."

Fifty years after Astorga produced his first carvings, Octavio arrived in Punta Chueca, setting in motion a new economy involving the Seri. Like ironwood carving, psychedelic toads became a part of Seri culture, but there was an important distinction. One was a new innovation, despite conflicting stories about its inspiration; the other was said to have ancestral roots. And yet there were reasons to doubt that the Seri had ever used toads at all. Researchers have documented a rich set of medicinal and cultural traditions among the Seri, and there is no evidence that toads were considered important, let alone sacred. Several toad species live in the tribe's historic territory, yet these were never differentiated by name. *Otac,* the word Octavio used for his nonprofit, is a generic term for amphibians, translating as "thing that sits in water." As Gary Nabhan, an ethnobiologist who has spent forty years documenting Seri Indigenous knowledge, told me, "It's like saying 'some frog.'"

Nabhan, now in his seventies, is a wide-ranging scholar who received a MacArthur "Genius" Fellowship in 1990 for his work on desert ethnobiology. Among other things, he is a writer, an activist, and a connoisseur of mescal. He has spent so much time among the Seri that he earned an honorific title: *Hant Coáaxoj,* or "Horned Lizard." Nabhan has a special affinity for reptiles and amphibians, having begun his career as a desert herpetologist. During a raging summer thunderstorm, he once floated on an inner tube for miles down a flooded arroyo alongside thousands of Sonoran Desert toads. The toads were in a frenzy of mating, and their spawn "looked like suds from a good draft ale on top of the water," Nabhan told me. "These little eyes are poking out, like the toad is drowning in a big flask of beer. And they're just darling."

Among the many books Nabhan has authored is *Singing the Turtles to Sea,* a treatise on Seri ethnoherpetology that makes no mention of psychedelic toads. When I first emailed him, he responded with a thoughtful message. "A lot of rituals emerge in a pan-Indian or cross-cultural context that we can't trace back as a traditional practice, but are accepted now as valid by contemporary Indigenous peoples, either for their own therapeutic use or for profit while administering to others," he wrote. "That is fine. But that should not be confused with an ancient tradition well integrated into a community's cosmovision and characteristic ritual practice. If it depletes wildlife populations and distorts or eclipses truly traditional ceremonies it may be disruptive or harmful."

Nabhan happened to be in Sonora around the time of Octavio's retreat and invited me to accompany him to Desemboque, where he was holding a food security workshop. We arranged to meet at a hotel in Kino Bay, but he wasn't there when I arrived and sent me a series of confusing emails, some of them in all caps. I tracked him down the next morning. He had recently suffered a stroke and was still recovering; one side of his face sagged, although he remained cognitively sharp. He was accompanied by some affable Mexican permaculturists and an older American with a druidic beard. Their vehicles were decorated with left-wing activist stickers—"No Hablo Republican-o," "Coca-Colonization," "Resist"—and piled messily with buckets, seedlings, flip charts, tools, and an assortment of bicycles. We set off.

In contrast to Punta Chueca, Desemboque lies in formidable isolation, situated on a vast desert plain beyond a rim of rust-colored mountains. A coastal dirt road from Punta Chueca had been washed out, so we took an inland route, passing through swaths of abandoned farmland. Groundwater pumping for agriculture had depleted the coastal aquifers, causing an intrusion of salt water that contaminated the earth, leaving behind a ghostly patchwork of fallow ground. The fields had been taken over by jumping cholla, a tall cactus with a mangled, hunched-over appearance. The air, as usual, was scorching.

As we drove, Nabhan spoke about the tribe's economic situation. The average family income was less than $10,000 annually; many families survived on far less. Power failures were common, and both villages routinely ran out of water. "They're desperate for any new source of income," he told me, "and so they make room for it." A handful of Seri had established themselves as toad shamans, modeling themselves on Octavio. Many more had become collectors, gathering the medicine during summer monsoons. The toad economy was concentrated in Punta Chueca due to its proximity to psychedelic tourists, and Nabhan wanted me to hear a wider range of Seri perspectives. "Desemboque folks aren't directly gaining income from it, so they may be more balanced on pros and cons," he said.

He invoked the historical example of Carlos Castaneda, whose book *The Teachings of Don Juan* became a worldwide bestseller in the 1960s. Purportedly an anthropological account of peyote rituals among the Yaqui, it had inspired a wave of hippie tourism that "turned the Yaqui villages into comedy hour," Nabhan told me. The book was later unmasked as a work of fiction. The Yaqui didn't even use peyote, it turned out, but the Huichol tribe, in central Mexico, did, so "everyone put on their favorite psychedelic soundtrack and drove their Volkswagen buses further south," Nabhan said. Similar scenes were playing out in the remote Oaxacan villages where psilocybin mushrooms had been popularized, with rock stars like Mick Jagger and John Lennon arriving for ceremonies, backpacker bungalows springing up, and psychedelic merchandise—magic mushroom postcards, faux-traditional clothing with mushroom designs—being hawked on the roadsides. Gordon Wasson, a banker and amateur mycologist who had instigated the entire spectacle with a feature story for *Life* magazine, later decried the "mob of thrill-seekers" who were "altering and corrupting the lifestyle of what used to be an idyllic indigenous town."

Nabhan was the second person that week to mention Castaneda, who had gone on to preside over a cultish group of followers, mostly young women who identified as his "witches." An editor of Castaneda's once described him as having "a kind of charm that was partly subtle intelligence, partly a real affection for people, and partly a kind of innocence, not of the naive kind but of the kind one likes to suppose saints, holy men, prophets and gurus have"—a passage that could have been written about Octavio, during his better moments. Coincidentally, it had been Octavio who brought up Castaneda a few days earlier. "That guy was a fucking fraud," he told me.

. . .

We arrived in Desemboque, a clutch of government houses with fishing gear, car parts, water drums, AC units, bricks, rusting bicycle frames, and other jetsam in the sandy yards. Fishing boats bobbed in the bay, and the beach was thickly spread with fish heads from the cleaning tables, picked over by packs of skittish dogs. Along the shore and among the houses lay mounds of trash. Thick clouds of flies buzzed aggressively. As soon as we stepped out of the cars, some older women came over with carvings and shell necklaces. The smell of rotting fish blew in from the bay.

The dogs were some of the most abject I'd ever seen, calling to mind a description from Seriland decades earlier: "They are mostly a slinking crew, submissive and cowering, scavenging around the huts and along the beach for a bit of fish or other scraps to fill their chronically empty bellies." Nevertheless, the Seri held the animals in high regard, believing them to have supernatural powers. A Seri dog once learned to walk on its front legs after being run over by a truck, balancing its paralyzed hindquarters in the air. Nabhan told me about a veterinary service that had once arranged to conduct vaccinations in Desemboque, only for the dogs to disappear. There had been a miscommunication, it turned out, when one of the visitors announced, in broken Spanish, "We are coming tomorrow to shoot your dogs." The dogs had been evacuated by the tribe and hidden in faraway caves.

That afternoon, Nabhan took me to see a former governor of the tribe, a brusque and guarded man who seemed impatient with my questions. He told me that he had known about the psychedelic properties of *sapo* since he was a child; that their ancestors had used toad skins to treat pain and sickness, placing them on affected parts of the body; that the Seri had been smoking toad in a medicinal way since the 1950s. None of this had been mentioned in ethnographic studies of the tribe, and I got the impression he was improvising, or perhaps telling me what he thought outsiders wanted to hear. When I asked him about Octavio's story—that all knowledge of *sapo* had been forgotten—he disputed it, but later reversed course and said that Octavio had taught the Seri about toad smoking. We were sitting outside in his yard, and as we spoke, more women arrived with crafts to sell. The whole encounter was uncomfortable. I was trying to clarify what the old governor was saying, thinking I'd perhaps misunderstood, but he continued giving irreconcilable answers.

He told me that many tourists came to Desemboque to smoke toad, and that only two people in the community served the medicine. Later that evening, I met one of them, an affable and smooth-talking younger man named Gabriel who showed me a little zippered purse of toad secretion. Gabriel had formerly been involved in Seri politics; during another phase of his life, I heard from others, he had dressed tough and hung around with narcos. Now he wore beads and spoke in the grounded manner of a therapist, demonstrating an impressive capacity for reinvention. He began by telling me that the Seri were no longer culturally isolated, and that by incorporating new skills into the community, they were "rebalancing what it means to be Seri in the modern world." Seri culture had never revolved around hallucinogenic plants and animals, he continued. Then he recounted a mythological story that Nabhan, who was translating, had never heard. Toad had "asked permission to come to earth and help heal people," Gabriel said. "And God replied, 'You can only be outside three months of the year. Nobody will like you. You'll be the worst animal.'" At some point during the genocidal wars with the Spanish, a Seri shaman had started using toad secretion for healing trauma in the community. "Nothing had been forgotten that Octavio reintroduced," Gabriel insisted, contradicting what he had just told me. "A lot of secrets went underground."

This raised a few problematic questions. If toad smoking had been deliberately kept secret, why had the Seri decided to share their knowledge when Octavio arrived in Punta Chueca? And why were there so many differing tales about the tradition? Pancho Barnett, one of Chapo's brothers, had already told me that the Seri historically consumed toad medicine inside *temazcales,* or sweat lodges, vaporizing the secretion on heated stones. But the Seri have no long-standing tradition of sweat lodges. A Seri woman I spoke with said that bygone shamans had sprinkled toad secretion on bundles of wild sage, then lit them and wafted the smoke over warriors to instill a sense of fearlessness before they went into battle. The stories I heard didn't accord with each other at all.

Questioning purported Indigenous customs is a delicate undertaking. But it was becoming clear that the story of toad smoking and the Seri was more nuanced than the version being presented to the world. A young Seri man from Punta Chueca told me that toad smoking was a divisive issue in the community, with only a small number of families benefiting directly from the business. "It's offensive selling this so-called magic recipe," he said, arguing that psychedelic tourism was obscuring actual Seri traditions. "It's all marketing," he added. By most accounts, only a minority of the Seri had smoked toad since Octavio's arrival in 2011; most of the community were members of an evangelical church that forbade such behavior. (Near the entrance to Punta Chueca, dwarfing any signs advertising toad ceremonies, white shells on a hillside spelled out the word CRISTOS.) But Seri culture was so individualist—the young man's word for it was "anarchic"—that dissenters generally tolerated the toad boom. "The Seris hated authority," Richard Felger, the ethnobotanist who documented the tribe's traditional knowledge, wrote decades earlier. "You were supposed to mind your own business. You didn't tell someone else what to do—that was the cultural ideal." At one point, exasperated by the spread of toad murals in Punta Chueca, Nabhan had commissioned a Seri woman to paint a rebuttal featuring the words "Comcaac culture is more than *sapo.*" But the woman had since become a toad shaman herself, losing interest in the project. Nabhan guffawed at the memory.

When I asked Gabriel, the Desemboque shaman, about some of these ambiguities, he evaded the question, telling me instead about his own work with the substance. People had come to him from all over the world, with clients including an eighty-nine-year-old woman with Alzheimer's and a three-year-old autistic child. Like Octavio, he betrayed no unease sharing these extreme stories with me. The child had been healed, he offhandedly claimed: "Normally it would take many years of regular therapy, but *sapo* can do it in one session."

Gabriel then pivoted to denouncing the commercial toad medicine market, which he said was harming the toads and making life more dangerous for Seri collectors. Just days earlier, two Seri men had been abducted by narcos while harvesting the medicine and had to pay for their own release, as well as forfeit their stash of toads. "People have poor methods of extraction," Gabriel went on. "They don't know how to do it right." A few years earlier, Gabriel had appeared in a YouTube video, filmed by a Spanish toad practitioner, demonstrating what he described as the "traditional way" of milking toads. The footage has the tone of a promotional reel. Gabriel, wearing Seri attire and face paint, chants over a pair of wriggling toads before milking them onto a glass tray. At one point, he empties the front-leg gland of a toad, only to warn against doing exactly that because it compromises the animal's defenses. "We must have a lot of love for this being, because it is a very important element in the life of the Comcaac," he explains. "Some people who do it commercially try to extract as much as they can. They end up drawing blood."

"This is the reason I always get the medicine from people in the Comcaac community," the Spanish practitioner responds. "The medicine is ritualized from the beginning, and the animal is treated with total respect. The intention is very important."

I heard a more complicated reality from Fernando Suárez Bleck, a Mexico City man who moved to Punta Chueca in 2020 as part of Fair Trade Toad, the ill-fated conservation initiative. In an almost perfect inversion of the narrative Octavio presented—that toad medicine had helped the Seri overcome addiction—toad medicine had become a new source of cash for addicts in the community, Suárez said. If anything, addiction to meth and other drugs had worsened since Octavio's arrival, according to numerous people I spoke with in Seriland. "They don't have a consciousness about the sacredness of the species," Suárez added. "It's just a hustle business. If they see a toad, they will milk it till the last drop."

The two Seri villages lie at the periphery of the Sonoran Desert toad's habitat, and so pickings for local collectors are thin, even before factoring in any losses due to overexploitation. There are more toads inland, in the irrigated agricultural zones west of Hermosillo—along with a persistent criminal threat. Suárez, who often goes out toading himself, told me more stories of Seri collectors being held up at gunpoint after trespassing on cartel turf. Their medicine had been confiscated each time, causing Suárez to speculate that "drug lords" were becoming interested in the substance. "In the past," he said, "they didn't care about the toad; they just didn't want you in their area. They started closing the desert, and only locals could come and go." Now this seemed to be changing. I later read an account by a journalist who was accosted by gunmen while collecting toads. The gunmen—riding a quad bike, holding assault rifles—turned out to be friendly, sharing their beers and a stash of toad medicine they'd collected. "Sometimes we milk as many as nine hundred toads for big orders," one of them boasted.

For Seri collectors, access to the toad economy was becoming increasingly precarious. Obtaining a supply had become more challenging even as prices had fallen—a consequence of rising competition and an influx of new dealers across Sonora. I met a Seri community leader who had purchased around fifteen grams of secretion from impoverished collectors in Punta Chueca, simply to provide them with an income. He had no interest in serving the medicine himself. "I don't know what to do with this," he said, shrugging. The local market had effectively collapsed.

In many ways, toad medicine had followed the arc of the Seri ironwood trade, which imploded in the 1970s amid rising outside competition. As the carvings grew popular with tourists, Mexican artisans began copying them, mass-producing crude imitations. "The buzz of power tools seemed to emanate from every yard around the Mexican workshops in Old Kino," a journalist wrote some years later. The oversupply of artworks drove down prices at the same time that ironwood stocks were being depleted, and the Seri were steadily squeezed out of the market. Today, outside the seafood restaurants in Kino Bay, roadside vendors sell Seri-style carvings; almost none of the sellers are Seri.

I kept thinking about how, before Octavio's arrival, the tribe had no known tradition of toad use; a decade later, they were viewed as stewards of a psychedelic ritual that few Seri had ever practiced. "This is thanks to Octavio," Suárez told me. "He went and gave toad to the tribe, and by doing this he gained a lot of respect from people outside the community. He built this idea that he was helping the Seri, but my guess is that this was really about his own image; it helped him travel the world."

I'd already grown skeptical of Octavio's framing, which contradicted the ethnobiological record and aligned so neatly with his interests. But even in Desemboque, where there was supposedly less influence from toad tourists, I kept being steered toward Seri with a stake in the trade. This posed a reporting dilemma: I wanted to remain open-minded while trying to reach beyond the version of events I'd been presented. One afternoon, I spoke to a young woman named Gabriela Molina whose father had once been the tribe's governor. Molina had studied Indigenous law and become an activist, protesting against proposed mining projects in Seri territory. She had smoked toad herself, guided by a Seri practitioner, traveling down "a tunnel of light" to a place where she met her ancestors. "It was as pure a Seri experience as I could have had," she told me. She was open to the idea that her tribe had used toad in the past, but was wary of the economy that had grown around it. "*Sapo* isn't the problem," she said. "Selling it is." Psychedelic tourism was drawing outsiders who brought other drugs into the community. They dressed in Seri clothes and sang sacred chants out of context. Molina blamed Octavio for "manipulating the story" and redefining the tribe in the eyes of the world. "It's hurt our culture," she told me. "It's out of our control."

. . .

On the outskirts of Hermosillo, Octavio owns a smallholding where he is developing a retreat center. He acquired a portion of the land in 2011 in exchange for a yellow Mustang convertible that "did five girls per kilometer," as he fondly put it. I met him there a few days after the retreat, arriving at a scrubby plot beneath some high-voltage electricity towers. He was busy with some new clients: a young man streaked with dirt from a recent toad ceremony, and two middle-aged women who had driven nine hours to be there that day, having departed at three in the morning. One of the women had come because she'd lost a son to drug addiction; she had been in rehab eighteen times. She was wearing a floral shirt and had a steely expression. When I arrived, she was sweating profusely beneath a *palapa,* a pool of vomit at her feet.

Octavio's vision for the property was to host people from around the world for toad treatments. Its name, he said, would be the Otac Healing Center. Several of his supporters had donated funds, including a Mexican businessman who practiced Buddhist meditation and, a few years earlier, had introduced Octavio to some visiting Tibetan monks. "I received their blessings to keep doing my work trying to heal society," Octavio told me, while showing me around the site. I asked if the monks had smoked toad. "Uh, not yet," he said.

A short distance away, some contractors were toiling in the heat, building dormitories, bathrooms, a communal dining area. Octavio led me to some excavated pits of muddy water holding thousands of Sonoran Desert tadpoles; they ranged in size from lentil to raisin, with fat spherical bodies and thin, whiplike tails. Within a few weeks, they would metamorphose and burrow into the earth. "I love this magical toad," Octavio mused. He spied an empty beer can in the water—from one of the builders, I guessed—and reached for my hand so he could lean over the edge and retrieve it. He held on tightly, surprising me with the vulnerability of the gesture.

I hadn't yet broached the allegations that had been leveled against him, from psychedelic malpractice to the embellishment of his relationship with the Seri. I began doing this the next morning at his house. Octavio was wearing his hand-painted toad cap and a shirt decorated with luminous mushrooms; incense swirled around us, and more New Age flute music was playing. He brought his palms together in a gesture of peace. "What I am doing is bringing light, life, hope, healing," he said. But the longer we spoke, the angrier he became, reminding me of his outburst on Tiburón Island. He was perched on a barstool and I was on a chair, and he leaned forward, looming over me. Brian grabbed his phone and began filming the encounter, like a fight primed to go viral.

"My work has been misunderstood, misinterpreted, and misused," Octavio said. "Everything is overexaggerated. Everything is out of context." He acknowledged that certain videos might look "barbaric or violent," but argued that, as a practitioner, playing that role was sometimes necessary. "I cannot play by the same rules of conventional therapy," he told me. "Most of my patients already went to many rehab centers. They already tried many drugs. I don't have time to fool around. I just need to be very straight, very direct"—he clapped his hands—"to stop the bullshit."

When I pressed him, Octavio expressed no remorse about his record with toad medicine. "I have nothing to feel bad or guilty about, brother. I was doing my job," he said. "I didn't shoot anyone, I didn't stab anyone. I didn't wake up any day saying, 'I'm gonna kick this guy's ass because I am evil.' I am just doing what people are asking, requiring, seeking." He saw opposition to his work as confirmation of its righteousness and described the public letter as a blessing: Now only "people without fear" would seek him out. When I asked if he regretted the deaths in his care, he replied, "They made me a better human being."

As we spoke, I remembered a conversation with Alan Davis, the psychologist who had conducted early research with 5-MeO-DMT. Davis warned me about a risk involving the compound: "When the ego is dissolved, and you are completely at one with what you're perceiving as God or the universe, there is no difference between you and that thing. You *are* that thing." Davis continued, "When your ego reasserts itself, there's a potential to hold on to that belief—that there's no difference between you and God."

Davis saw Octavio as an especially dangerous manifestation of this impulse, and the psychedelic toad community as especially vulnerable to its consequences. "When it comes to 5-MeO-DMT, people can be preyed on more easily," Davis said. "One of the hallmark effects of the substance is openness—feeling more connected, sharing deeply meaningful experiences. This naturally creates a sense of trust. For people steeped in these communities, it almost becomes a value system: This is how they approach relationships, by trusting others." Introducing someone like Octavio into that kind of environment, Davis added, was "like letting a wolf loose in a henhouse."

As early as 1960, a psychiatrist named Sidney Cohen had observed a similar pattern among psychedelic therapists using LSD (which was still legal at the time) during their sessions. "An unusual number of those dispensing these drugs have themselves come down with psychiatric disturbances," Cohen later wrote. "A few have gone on to a psychotic breakdown or to megalomaniacal ideas of grandeur." Cohen had taken LSD himself and initially believed in its therapeutic promise, but as use of the drug spread, he grew increasingly concerned. "The ability to induce the transcendental state is a heady and powerful endowment," he wrote. "Only well-adjusted therapists without personal needs to play God will be unaffected by the potency inherent in the situation."

Other would-be toad gurus, many of them less famous than Octavio, have succumbed to these same forces. In around 2021, Bruno Cluzel, a French real estate agent who had defrauded investors in Miami, reinvented himself as a bufo practitioner, adopting the name Gabriel. He moved to Mexico and opened a retreat center, offering ceremonies and facilitator trainings. As the journalist Jules Evans has reported, Gabriel would smoke toad throughout the day and yell at his clients, insisting that they called him Jesus. One participant recalled, "He would smoke it, drop the pipe, glass would go everywhere, and he would get up and go to each person, look them in the face, and yell 'What's my name?'" Another said, "I was so high on bufo and in such a vulnerable state, I thought 'maybe this motherfucker really *is* Jesus.'" Evans interviewed Victoria Wueschner, a 5-MeO-DMT practitioner who focuses on harm reduction. "We've seen multiple times where facilitators think they're the Messiah and start cults," she said. "This is the medicine of the ego."

After I left Sonora, fact-checkers at *The New Yorker* contacted Octavio—along with everyone else I had spoken with—and went over my reporting with him in exacting detail. He disputed numerous points, which the story noted. When the piece came out, he sent me a furious voice note on WhatsApp. "I think it is just very sad that you spent all this time and energy, and also my time and energy, to write something so mediocre and filled with so much mistakes," he said. "I don't think you will be known as a good journalist because of this lack of honesty and integrity." Then, with defiant bombast, he added, "I will be remembered as someone whose work was important for the world in general, not only psychedelics but in the future, even for medical science."

When I asked him for specific inaccuracies, he said that his mother had never bought him a pharmacy, and that his brother hadn't described their father as "good at marketing." (Neither his mother nor his brother had objected to these points with the fact-checkers.) He promised to send me a fuller list, but never did. In a feature that detailed allegations of malpractice, the deaths of multiple clients, and his fraught relationship with the Seri, the only corrections Octavio offered concerned his family; this seemed oddly revealing, both of what mattered to him and of what he chose not to refute. A few months later, I texted him that I was working on a book. "My trust in you as a journalist doesn't exist at all," he replied. "There is nothing else I can discuss with you." I understood this to be the last contact I would have with the toad doctor.

From the depths of a crack addiction, he had shot to fame by promoting a lost tradition of toad smoking, building a global following around a substance from the far margins of psychedelia. Thousands of his clients credited him with life-changing experiences. One of the most powerful psychedelics in the world became widely known through his efforts. Forces beyond Octavio's control had worked in his favor, from the timing of the wider psychedelic renaissance to his introduction to the Seri, a tribe whose ruptured history and cultural adaptiveness enabled his narrative to take hold. He had the look and manner of a charismatic savior. Yet Octavio's work was ultimately overshadowed by flaws he denied even existed. For more than a decade, he demonstrated a recurring pattern of recklessness, refusing accountability for traumatic trips and deaths alike. He serially began sexual relationships with women after serving them toad. He bullied clients during ceremonies. He presented himself as having the support of the Seri tribe when in reality he leveraged—and often paid for—a handful of strategic relationships, profiting disproportionately from the arrangement. He did all this without apparent reflection or remorse, even when confronted with the consequences. This was a level of delusion I found frightening.

In the 1980s, an American psychotherapist and Buddhist teacher named John Welwood coined a term, "spiritual bypassing," for a tendency he observed in which people avoided unresolved emotional issues or psychological wounds using spiritual practices. He warned about the dangers of "premature transcendence"—attempts to rise above the messy realities of being human without adequately reckoning with them. The God molecule can work as a potent accelerant for this dynamic, delivering even spiritual neophytes to breakthrough mystical realms. Octavio, who has likely smoked more toad than anyone else in history, seemed to embody the contradictions that could result: divine self-belief matched with lingering, unexamined darkness.

And yet without his manic self-regard and ambition, how might this story have unfolded? As Mario Garnier, the organizer of the World Bufo Alvarius Congress, told me, "Only an ego as big as Octavio's could take toad medicine as far as he did." At some level, the conflicts erupting around 5-MeO-DMT felt archetypal—spiritual experience being codified into something like organized religion, with schisms widening over how to access and interpret it. But in this case, the experience was pharmacologically mediated and almost instantaneous, triggered by molecules flooding into the brain. If Octavio was a divisive early prophet, the movement was now moving into an even more contentious phase, with 5-MeO-DMT entering clinical trials as a mental health treatment. Billions of dollars, potentially, were riding on the outcome. The pharmaceutical era of toad medicine had begun.

CHAPTER 7

Rocket Ship into the Void

Beckley Park, a country estate in Oxfordshire, lies at the end of a narrow drive that winds through pastures and farmland, flanked for several hundred feet by concrete statues of mushrooms. The house, an austere brick building with three gabled towers, is partially encircled by three concentric moats. It was built in the sixteenth century as a hunting lodge for British aristocrats and has peculiar dimensions, standing three stories tall but only one room deep. From the front it has "the look of a fairy-tale castle," *House & Garden* once noted, but from the side is curiously narrow, as though it might topple over. Enormous topiaries crowd the grounds outside, looming overhead in dreamlike forms: hallucinogenic spirals, a bear, a tilted top hat. In 2005, the house appeared in a Harry Potter film as the site where a young Lord Voldemort murdered his father and grandparents.

I visited on a gloomy spring morning in 2024. The owner of the estate was Lady Amanda Feilding, a spry countess in her eighties with a long-standing devotion to LSD. She had spent decades orchestrating the return of legitimate psychedelic science and was often described in the international press as "the hidden hand behind the psychedelic renaissance." She was also notorious for her advocacy of trepanation, the ancient surgical procedure of having holes drilled into one's skull, once thought to release evil spirits and alleviate pressure from brain swelling. In 1970, she was filmed performing the operation on herself while under the influence of LSD, boring into her forehead with a dentist's drill and smiling exultantly as blood streamed from the hole. She had been inspired by a Dutch lover who believed, dubiously, that trepanation increased the flow of blood to the brain, producing a permanent high. When the footage was screened in New York, a reviewer wrote, several people in the audience fainted, "dropping off their seats one by one like ripe plums." Feilding later ran for Parliament twice on the platform that trepanation be made freely available on the National Health Service.

The British media delighted in such antics from a member of the peerage, dubbing Feilding, who claimed descent from the Habsburg monarchy, "the crackpot countess" and "Lady Mindbender." Yet she seemed impervious to derision. "My family were in the ruling class, if you know what I mean," she told me. "It gives one a certain bearing."

After reporting for four years on toad ceremonies and the illicit global networks that supported them, I was seeking a glimpse of a more formalized, but no less radical, future market: 5-MeO-DMT as a psychiatric medication. We were sitting in a room cluttered with antique furniture and stacks of books on consciousness. Logs were smoking in an enormous stone fireplace, tended by a solicitous member of the household staff. Feilding called to mind a Quentin Blake drawing, with beady eyes and wizened features. She produced a wooden pipe and smoked some charas, a potent form of hashish "from the mountains of India." As we spoke, I became distracted by a human skull on a dresser behind her, displayed on a velvety plinth with its hollow sockets pointed toward me. It had belonged, she said, to a Celtic chieftain who had been trepanned half a dozen times, possibly as a treatment for migraines. "He's a beautiful skull," Feilding remarked in an airy tone, showing me the coin-sized holes. "And funny enough, some wretched scientist in Los Angeles took his jaw because he wanted to do a test on it, and hasn't returned it."

Feilding's highborn eccentricity was cultivated at Beckley Park, where her grandparents had entertained writers like Aldous Huxley, whose book *The Doors of Perception* aroused popular interest in psychedelics in the 1950s. Her grandmother was a trailblazing architect who "went after what she wanted without letting social niceties get in her way," as one historian noted, "using her connections when it was to her advantage." Feilding's father, a lover of the arts and lifelong diabetic, "would have daily swoons," she told me, falling into ditches or swerving the family car over roundabouts. At sixteen, Feilding dropped out of school and attempted to hitchhike to Sri Lanka, where her godfather—a British spy-catcher during World War II—had become a Buddhist monk. Feilding made it as far as Syria, where she briefly lived with a tribe of Bedouins before returning to England and enrolling in art school. Not long afterward, she was introduced to psychedelics. In 1965, she moved into an apartment in Chelsea, on the banks of the Thames, where she hosted riotous multiday parties attended by Allen Ginsberg and the Rolling Stones. "The flat was a centre for all the lunatics in London, popstars, artists, speedfreaks, junkies, smokers and acid-heads," one of her boyfriends wrote in a memoir. "Amanda herself was usually too stoned to get up off the bed, where she reclined like an Egyptian sphinx-queen, surveying the havoc around her with eyes like black searchlights." At one point, the key to Feilding's front door went missing, and for months she and her guests scaled the Victorian facade, coming and going through windows on the fourth floor.

"I would say I was one of the original microdosers," Feilding once said, "because I was microdosing in the '60s by taking big trips every day." (This is not the conventional understanding of microdosing.) She has spoken of being high on LSD for months, playing the Chinese strategy game Go and reading the works of Freud and Nietzsche. "I was living, really, on LSD," she told me in her sitting room.

Through these experiences, Feilding came to believe that psychedelics not only heightened consciousness but enhanced cognition, and she made it her life's quest "to break the taboo surrounding psychedelics." In 1998, she established a nonprofit, the Beckley Foundation, to promote drug policy reform and fund psychedelic research—a field that was almost nonexistent at the time, after decades of prohibition. She had recently married a wealthy earl (soon to be trepanned himself) who was close to the royal family; over the next decade, she convened a series of drug seminars at the House of Lords, where topics ranged from the neurobiology of psychedelics to the social role of altered states. Feilding usually described herself as an artist, and the Beckley Foundation, she said, was a conceptual artwork—"a Trojan horse" for infiltrating the establishment. In 2011, she coordinated an open letter advising governments around the world to reconsider their drug policies. Its signatories included Jimmy Carter, Archbishop Desmond Tutu, and Noam Chomsky.

Then, in around 2018, popular attitudes toward psychedelics underwent a radical shift. New research—some of it supported by the Beckley Foundation—had demonstrated the promise of psychedelic therapy for treating addiction, depression, and other disorders. *How to Change Your Mind,* by Michael Pollan, became a worldwide bestseller. A host of biotech start-ups began raising capital to turn psychedelic compounds into licensed medicines, enticing investors with the prospect of lavish returns; in just four years, investments rose more than tenfold, exceeding $1.2 billion in 2021. Media coverage of the psychedelic renaissance hailed Feilding as a visionary: "The Queen of Consciousness," "The First Lady of LSD."

Yet the sudden emergence of a psychedelics industry posed a threat, paradoxically, to Feilding's foundation. Donors now had the option of investing in for-profit companies instead of giving their money away. "People asked, *Why should I put it in a bottomless well?*" Feilding said. She'd grown increasingly wary of the direction the field was taking, mistrusting many of the wealthy investors involved. "The for-profit model can be abused," she said. "You have to go for maximum money. Whereas I've always been guided by what's best for society." She fished a small Rescue Remedy dropper out from her bag, filled with a substance she asked me not to identify, and licked a few drops off the back of her hand. Amid the transformation of psychedelic culture, she had clung to her vision of nonprofit research and lobbying, working fifteen-hour days while taking small doses of acid. She complained of being "endlessly and absolutely always without any money." And so, in 2019, she had helped one of her sons found a drug development company called Beckley Psytech, aiming to bring new neuropsychiatric treatments to market and funnel a portion of the profits back toward her foundation. The molecule they decided to work with was 5-MeO-DMT.

. . .

Attempting to convert the God molecule into a pharmaceutical product is manifestly a strange, even fraught, endeavor, but there are several compelling arguments for doing so. The first is that clinical development would make 5-MeO-DMT safer. Obtaining regulatory approval for a new drug requires a battery of trials for detecting the kinds of risks that can be overlooked or suppressed in underground settings. What is the optimum dosage range for different patients? Are there contraindications? How does 5-MeO-DMT interact with other medications? Such questions can be explored through rigorous scientific analysis.

The production of medical-grade 5-MeO-DMT would also ensure its purity and strength more reliably than existing supply chains, especially compared with the lawless market for wild-harvested toad medicine. "Would you trust the Sinaloa cartel to provide you with pure cocaine?" one biotech entrepreneur working with 5-MeO-DMT asked me. "As a medical doctor, I wouldn't trust a source just because it's natural." A facility in the United States that legally produces 5-MeO-DMT for biomedical research manufactures the drug in five-kilogram batches, enough for around a quarter million doses. Obtaining a comparable supply of toad secretion would require capturing and squeezing more than fifty thousand Sonoran Desert toads, during the vanishingly brief summer rains, on turf warred over by cartels. There is an incalculable difference in efficiency, to say nothing of danger.

From the perspective of patients, a far larger population would be able to access the potential healing benefits of 5-MeO-DMT through formal medical channels than via the prevailing ecosystem of retreats, guides, and self-experimentation. As rapidly as psychedelics have moved toward the mainstream, the reach of the field remains limited.

Many people would never willingly attend an underground ceremony; many more will never be able to afford one. Recent surveys have indicated that more than ten million people in the United States use psychedelics each year—around a fifth as many as suffer from substance abuse disorders (nearly fifty million) or mental illnesses (nearly sixty million). For companies, this gap represents an alluring opportunity: An effective psychedelic medicine would be enormously lucrative. "They're betting on commercial success," a former executive in the psychedelics industry told me. "That's where the megabucks are."

Yet bringing such drugs to market is charged with uncertainty, involving squeezing psychedelia through layers of regulatory and financial control, often with contradictory incentives and values to the counterculture. Critics have coined a term for this emerging phenomenon: "corporadelia," defined by one researcher as "manifesting corporations to commodify psychedelic experiences."

Major early investors in psychedelics included the Silicon Valley libertarian Peter Thiel and Christian Angermayer, a German billionaire who was once likened to "the Darth Vader of the psychedelics galaxy" for his unashamedly capitalist bent, including vigorous attempts to secure intellectual property. Many psychedelic molecules occur in nature and have been used for centuries, placing them outside the scope of traditional drug patents; instead, companies have focused on patenting synthetic analogues, along with proprietary methods of use and delivery systems. In 2021, one industry publication warned of an unfolding "land grab" over psychedelics, warning, "The future of the psychedelic renaissance may be at stake." Retail investors flocked to buy shares in psychedelic start-ups, posting on Reddit pages with names like "Shroom Stocks." (Tagline: "Let's ride the mush rush!") Seemingly without irony, the investment bank Jefferies released a briefing in 2022 titled "Capitalizing on Consciousness?"

Lady Amanda Feilding was proudly of an older, less commercialized psychedelic era. She was not, however, an early convert to 5-MeO-DMT. Octavio once met her at a conference and tried to talk her into smoking toad with him. "I didn't like his insistency," Feilding recalled. Her first and only experience with the substance was in 2017, at her same apartment in Chelsea, guided by Flor Bollini, the Argentinean practitioner who served toad to CEOs and billionaires. The two women had met a few years earlier and become friends. "I saw her as a mother figure," Bollini told me. She would visit Beckley Park for sleepovers, smoking hashish while strategizing how to fund psychedelic ventures. Feilding had been wary of smoking toad but ultimately agreed to try a small dose. When I asked her about the experience, she waved away the question, saying only, in an offhanded way, "Well, I prefer LSD . . ."

. . .

Numerous clinical trials have shown that LSD can be an effective treatment for alcoholism and other psychiatric conditions, but its prolonged effects, which can last ten hours or longer, constrain its use in therapeutic settings. A typical 5-MeO-DMT trip, in comparison, is over within thirty minutes. In theory, this would make it considerably less expensive to administer, requiring briefer periods of supervision. The economic logic was appealing to Beckley Psytech: If the drug were available to more patients, this would make it more profitable. A compound that had only recently risen from obscurity was poised to become a front-runner in the psychedelic drug development race, spurring hype in new circles. "Have you ever done 5-MeO-DMT? You need to do 5-MeO-DMT," an investor would later write to the founder of a psychedelics venture capital firm. "Once you do 5-MeO-DMT you'll realize that no drug, clinic, program, therapy or research matters. Nothing can compete with 5-MeO-DMT. We don't need any innovation in psychedelics. People just need to do 5-MeO-DMT."

Beckley Psytech was founded by one of Feilding's sons, a trim and affably laddish man in his thirties named Cosmo Birdie Feilding-Mellen. (He shares his second name with a pet pigeon Feilding had kept for many years, proclaiming the bird to be her lover.) Cosmo has joked that he and his elder brother were "fairly brainwashed from an early age," adding, "Psychedelics were the topic of conversation ad nauseam, one might say." He had gone to Oxford and become a filmmaker; his first documentary was a critique of international drug policy, made with a son of Sir Richard Branson. Several people described him to me as an easygoing trustafarian sort. "Cozzie didn't know how to either pay money in or out of a bank," his mother disclosed. But in 2018, he demonstrated a streak of business acumen, establishing a medicinal cannabis start-up that raised $10 million—and was promptly acquired by the world's largest cannabis company for eight times as much. His next move was into the psychedelics sector. "There was this burst of activity," he explained, "and there were lots of people getting involved, and we wanted to continue to try and help shape it." He has described Beckley Psytech, somewhat vaguely, as an "ethical beacon" for the industry.

The company positioned itself as a foil to the opportunists: a family business with deep roots in psychedelic culture, equipped to balance commercial ambition with principle. Cosmo became CEO; his mother was less involved, but her name carried weight. They appointed some of the most experienced and credible figures in psychedelic research to their advisory board and recruited executives from the pharmaceutical giant Janssen, which had a market value several hundred times larger than the entire psychedelics sector at the time. For psychedelics to win medical approval, it would be necessary to work with corporate suits who were able to navigate the system. Other early hires were veterans of the underground; one told me in detail about her most memorable trip, on the drug salvia, in which she had experienced the full life cycle of an Antarctic penguin, from hatching to rearing chicks and dying in the snow. She thought of psychedelics as medicines, while other colleagues referred to them as "assets." The company had considered working with psilocybin, but a rival firm backed by Angermayer had already secured patents involving the compound, effectively blocking competition. Instead, the team was tasked with identifying short-acting compounds to focus on.

At least one other psychedelic start-up had already passed on developing 5-MeO-DMT, which they considered too extreme for clinical patients. "It could be a mini-trauma of its own," the company's founder told me. But a view formed within Beckley, a former executive at the company told me, that "a trip is a trip is a trip." Numerous studies with psychedelics had identified a correlation between therapeutic outcomes and so-called peak experiences, which often include feelings of mysticism or transcendence. 5-MeO-DMT was a reliable vector for inducing such states. The molecule is able to slip through the blood-brain barrier, a protective net that encircles the brain, where it binds with a different serotonin receptor from most other psychedelics, shutting down neural networks associated with one's sense of self. A 2025 brain-imaging study, in which participants consumed 5-MeO-DMT while hooked up to electrodes, described this state as "deconstructed consciousness."

Just as the drug could seemingly spring open the mind, like a pick in a lock, it could conceivably slot into the existing mental health-care framework. For all the promise psychedelics had shown in academic studies, there were concerns about their "commercial tractability," as one investor put it to me. Prolonged dosing sessions would be prohibitively expensive, requiring medical staff and therapists to be present for hours. "Fast-acting compounds are the only viable way," the investor said, with a note of apprehension. Josh Hardman, the founder of *Psychedelic Alpha,* a publication that covers the industry, described 5-MeO-DMT as "the most extreme incarnation of this impulse to shoehorn psychedelics into the system we already have."

To bring a new drug to market, companies require a recognized diagnosis to target. Beckley chose treatment-resistant depression, a hole in the market thought to be worth billions of dollars annually. Typically defined as a major depressive episode that has not responded to at least two different rounds of antidepressant treatment, TRD had only two approved medications at the time: a combination antipsychotic-SSRI and Spravato, a ketamine nasal spray developed by Janssen, which was on track to become a blockbuster success. Beckley, too, opted to use a nasal spray, which slows the onset and duration of 5-MeO-DMT trips. Preclinical testing began with rodents and beagles, a dog breed favored in lab studies for its docility. At higher doses, the dogs stiffened their muscles and became aggressive; they gnawed at the wire of their cages, and the males got erections. These effects were transient, with no signs of toxicity. Satisfied by these findings, the company progressed with plans for human studies.

In a pitch deck to investors, Beckley Psytech declared itself "an early mover in 5-MeO-DMT." In May 2020, the company raised $4 million; later that year, it raised another $18 million. Clinical trials are divided into different stages, called phases, which must be completed one after the other, like checkpoints in a race; starting before potential rivals is competitively advantageous. "We thought we were the only ones working with 5-MeO-DMT," the former executive said. But on a subsequent call with investors, Cosmo was blindsided by a question: How did the company differentiate itself from a competitor named GH Research? The team looked them up, finding a website that had only recently gone live. The landing page featured stock footage of clouds drifting over a lush mountain landscape. Beckley soon learned that GH had filed expansive patent applications involving 5-MeO-DMT and was already running clinical trials for TRD. A press release announced that the firm had just raised $125 million in funding.

. . .

Two months later, in June 2021, GH listed on the Nasdaq. Its market valuation swiftly rose above a billion dollars, making it one of the biggest psychedelics companies in the world. "They emerged as this leviathan," a Beckley investor recalled. Other companies hired PR agencies and networked at conferences, but GH was in stealth mode, declining even to respond to basic media queries. "They're literally the only company I've never managed to get anything out of," Hardman, the industry analyst, told me in 2024. Even within the close-knit 5-MeO-DMT community, where people typically knew one another, GH remained an enigma. I spoke with around two dozen researchers, practitioners, and investors who were intensely curious, and often wary, about the company's operations, but nobody had any leads. Amid this dearth of information, one speculative take came from a YouTube channel that analyzes psychedelic stocks via tarot readings. After drawing a disturbing sequence of cards and issuing a disclaimer—"we're just scoping out what the universe is saying"—the hosts surmised that the company's founder was living "a karmic nightmare," warning, "There's some serious stuff going on behind the scenes."

With some effort, I managed to trace the company's origins in more detail. The driving force behind GH was a Danish biotech entrepreneur named Florian Schönharting, the son of a German baroness; he had co-founded the company in 2018 along with two business partners. The competition between GH and Beckley, at some level, was one of aristocrats, though of quite different sorts. Schönharting's family owned a historic estate in Bavaria, complete with a brewery, mill, and forestry operations. In the 1970s, when Schönharting was a child, his father, a geophysicist, took an academic job in Copenhagen. There, Schönharting later recalled, he faced harassment lingering from World War II, with people shouting anti-German slurs at him on the streets. "I wasn't one of them," he said. "I was second-class. That was probably the worst part." This experience left him with a deep-rooted sense of defiance, as he explained to a Danish interviewer: "Either you get broken by it, or you say to yourself that you will *show* them. I chose the latter path."

In the early 1990s, Schönharting graduated at the top of his class from the Copenhagen Business School and began his career at an investment fund. He was tall and blond, with cool gray eyes. He competed in triathlons and played Bach suites on the cello. A colleague once described him as "one of the best stock pickers in the world." In 2000, in his early thirties, Schönharting launched a venture capital firm that became notable for its secrecy. "Who are they and how do they operate?" a reporter wrote. Schönharting described this approach as the firm's "black box."

With a knack for converting innovative medical research into businesses, he founded a string of successful biotech start-ups that worked on more conventional diseases: cancer, diabetes, autoimmune disorders. As an early pioneer of Nordic biotech, he helped shape the industry that would later give rise to drugs like Ozempic, now among the most valuable pharmaceutical products in the world. In interviews with the Danish press, Schönharting was tersely efficient; one profile described him as working fifteen-hour days and struggling to make time for his girlfriend and new baby. "When he smells blood," another journalist observed, "he seems unstoppable."

In 2017, a company Schönharting chaired netted $1.25 billion in a patent dispute with a rival. He grew increasingly wealthy. He reportedly stocked his Copenhagen apartment with Eames furniture and was knowledgeable about the arts. He would later like Twitter posts by right-wing culture warriors, climate change denialists, and anti-vaxxers such as Naomi Wolf and Robert F. Kennedy Jr., which could hint at certain political leanings. Contradicting screenshots I'd saved, GH disputed this, noting that Schönharting had a track record of "investing in companies pursuing rigorous science, including in multiple vaccine companies."

By mid-2018, Schönharting and a circle of trusted collaborators had identified a promising new market. Commercial interest in psychedelics was awakening. "To raise money in this industry, you have to chase trends," a fellow biotech entrepreneur, who knows some of GH's founders, told me. After reviewing potential compounds, the team zeroed in on 5-MeO-DMT. Like Beckley, they saw commercial potential in using the molecule for TRD, which affects roughly nine million people across the United States and Europe. (In corporate filings, the company would later frame the condition in starkly economic terms: "Patients are often unable to perform daily tasks, are less productive at work and have higher rates of unemployment. They are also more likely to receive disability or welfare benefits.") The first scientific survey of 5-MeO-DMT users, published earlier that year by Alan Davis and colleagues, had found that more than three-quarters of those with depression reported improvements in their symptoms. Although formal research into the drug was only beginning, anecdotal accounts also hinted at its efficacy. In one online report, a man who had been enduring "conditions of the psyche for which one normally suffers incarceration in a mental ward" described 5-MeO-DMT as a "miracle drug that restored the sanity which grief and time had destroyed."

An insider at GH told me that the company had been "open-minded" with their sources of information, consulting YouTube videos and web forums. Inevitably, they became aware of Octavio, who was facing a growing backlash at the time. "He was present everywhere," the GH insider recalled. That June, members of the team attended a psychedelics conference in Prague, where Octavio presented a characteristically volatile talk. He played a fifteen-minute clip of himself smoking toad in an outdoor setting and entering a violent rage, throwing himself to the ground while screaming gutturally. "We are not making any change," he narrated to the audience, casting his pain as collective suffering. "We are still trying to illuminate ourselves—to escape." Later in the talk, he furiously defended himself against malpractice allegations and lashed out at his critics. He also appeared on two charged panels about "shadows" in the psychedelic renaissance, refusing to change his approach to facilitation or to accept responsibility for any deaths.

It was another presenter who caught the eye of GH's founders: Malin Uthaug, a doctoral candidate in psychopharmacology at Maastricht University, in the Netherlands. Uthaug, then in her mid-twenties, had smoked toad with Octavio and conducted a study of the practice, observing him and other practitioners in underground ceremonies: eyeballed doses, chanting, flutes. Her research showed, remarkably, that a single inhalation of toad secretion caused improvements in stress, depression, and anxiety lasting at least a month. Uthaug ended her talk with a quotation from Buckminster Fuller, the visionary designer and systems theorist: "To change something, build a new model that makes the existing model obsolete."

Though quick to grasp the clinical potential of these findings, the GH team was dismissive of the context in which they arose. "All these hippie connotations," the company insider told me, "are not a strength for medical development." The team generally avoided using the term "psychedelic," instead referring to 5-MeO-DMT as a "central nervous system neuromodulator." There would later be signs that they had an antipathy for psychedelia more broadly: One scientist who consulted on trials for the company described its leadership as "disdainful of the psychedelic community," while a major investor in the industry told me that Schönharting was "contemptuous" and "completely disregarding of the psychological and spiritual experience." A spokesperson for GH denied these claims, pointing to its use of a "Mystical Experience Questionnaire" as evidence to the contrary.

As disclosed in subsequent patent filings, the company believed that 5-MeO-DMT worked on the brain by modulating so-called resting state networks, or RSNs, a set of neural systems associated with emotional regulation and cognition. Prior research had shown that patients with a range of mental disorders, from depression to eating disorders, frequently demonstrated unusual activity in these networks, as if their internal circuits had become stuck or miswired, with the same pathways being reinforced over and over. Psychedelics appeared to offer a reset, temporarily unplugging certain brain regions and giving them a chance to reconnect in new ways. Scientists referred to this phenomenon as neural plasticity. GH speculated that mystical experiences correlated with the shutting down of RSNs, and that the strength of this effect could help drive therapeutic outcomes. From this perspective, it was possible that the revelatory power of 5-MeO-DMT was little more than a by-product—"a surrogate behavioral marker for the underlying mechanism," the company wrote. This technical language masked what it might feel like for patients to be hurled within seconds into an experience indistinguishable from death.

Seeking to explore the molecule's effects in more controlled settings, GH approached Uthaug's professor, a psychopharmacologist at Maastricht University named Jan Ramaekers. A rangy, bespectacled man with a cerebral manner, Ramaekers had treated the original study with caution—"there were many potential confounding variables," he recalled, limiting what conclusions could be drawn from the data—but was excited by the prospect of a new antidepressant medication. For the past fifteen years, the field of neuropsychiatry had been a drug development graveyard. "The industry basically shut down," Ramaekers told me. He signed on as a scientific adviser with GH and, when Uthaug declined to work with them, recruited another PhD student to run trials funded by the company. Quietly, and with a sense of urgency, they set about designing their studies.

There are strong commercial incentives for being first to market with a new drug, such as laws that slow the development of generics. A space race was developing over 5-MeO-DMT. Yet many people acquainted with the molecule balked at the idea of it as a clinical treatment in the first place. One practitioner I spoke with compared the intensity of the trip to proximity flying, where daredevils in wingsuits soar perilously close to mountain cliffs. "So are we giving wingsuits to the masses?" he asked, with a mirthless laugh.

GH, like Beckley, was positioning itself to capitalize on a contradiction: that the most cost-effective and medically scalable psychedelic compound was also among the most formidable. The company heightened these stakes even further with a decision that would horrify many 5-MeO-DMT experts when it came to light. Since the modern study of psychedelics began, researchers have followed the lead of traditional and underground practitioners by designating therapists or guides to care for patients. GH, however, would not mandate any therapy at all in its trials, asserting that there was no need for "lengthy and complex patient preparation prior to treatment" or "psychological integration work" after the experience. As the company stated in public documents, trial participants would receive "only limited required support" from a health-care provider, without "any planned psychotherapeutic intervention before, during, or after dosing." (In what seemed like a change in position, a spokesperson later told me that the company was "fully committed to providing therapeutic support" on its trials, including "before, during, and after dosing.")

At one level, the decision to omit therapy was strategic. The FDA and international bodies that approve new drugs don't regulate counseling, and its inclusion in trials can make results difficult to interpret. If some of the benefits of psychedelics stem from the therapeutic encounter, how can regulators assess their efficacy as medicines? But the choice may also have resulted from a notable blind spot among the company's leadership. A spokesperson wrote to me, "We are not commenting on most personal and biographical details." But according to my sources, neither Schönharting nor the company's CEO had any personal experience with psychedelics.

• • •

In March 2019, two years before GH revealed itself publicly, its first clinical trial began at Maastricht University. This was a study involving paid subjects with no known mental health problems, many of them students. Dosing took place in the psychopharmacology department, on the second floor of a drab institutional building, upstairs from a busy dining hall. The room was bare and white, with linoleum flooring and whirring air vents; for a measure of privacy, cubicle dividers were placed in front of the windowed doors. On the floor was a mattress with pillows and blankets. A bright mandala tapestry hung from one wall. Johannes Reckweg, the PhD student who conducted the research, told me he'd been struck by the severity of the room and brought the decoration from home.

A courteous and reserved German in his late twenties, Reckweg had been advised, before joining the trial, to watch YouTube videos of toad ceremonies where people screamed and writhed around. And yet GH, he later recalled, was aiming to treat 5-MeO-DMT "as much as possible like a conventional medicine, not a psychoactive drug." The difference was that, while regular drugs worked behind the scenes of consciousness, this fundamentally disrupted one's experience of reality.

The company had elected to deliver a proprietary formulation of the molecule via a medical vaporizer called the Volcano—an unwieldy contraption, resembling the base of a kitchen blender, that inflated a crinkly three-liter plastic balloon. Reckweg set up the device across the hall, in an office he shared with other graduate students, and would hurry over to the dosing room, where participants received the drug individually. Some were given a single dose—strengths varied—while others received multiple hits of escalating strength until they achieved a peak experience, defined as scoring 75 or higher on a proprietary scale devised by GH. (This approach was possible due to the rapid action of 5-MeO-DMT and its apparent lack of tachyphylaxis, or the tendency for a drug to lose effectiveness with repeated dosing; if required, people could be dosed multiple times in a day.) The scale consisted of three questions, which participants rated out of 100 after their trips: *How intense was the experience? To what extent did you lose control? How profound was the experience?* Reckweg conceded to me, with some humor, that the measure seemed rather arbitrary. "Like what's an ego dissolution of 80?" he asked. "What kind of question is that?"

The study protocol called for minimal intervention, and Reckweg recalled standing at the ready with pillows, darting around to prevent people from slamming their heads on the walls and floor. Several of them, Reckweg told me, manifested behavior like a cross between an exorcism and an epileptic fit. On trial days, Reckweg said that he took to knocking on the doors of nearby offices and reassuring his colleagues, "If you hear screaming, it's fine."

Participants seldom had any memory of these reactions, although some declared their experiences euphoric. Reckweg told me that one young woman thanked him by baking him muffins; another gifted him poppers and a bottle of wine. He later denied ever making these statements, saying only that he had received "small tokens of appreciation."

GH denied these claims, saying that there were always two or three observers, including a medical doctor, present, recording the sessions minute by minute. They said no observations of behavior akin to exorcism or an epileptic fit were recorded or reported as per their protocols by the study team, adding that the evidence is stored in confidential patient files. The company said both Reckweg and Ramaekers state these claims are not true.

Reckweg's work became more freighted when, later in 2019, GH progressed to a phase 2 trial, recruiting patients diagnosed with treatment-resistant depression. There were strict exclusion criteria, including prior diagnoses with psychiatric disorders or medical conditions like uncontrolled diabetes, and more than two hundred people who signed up were disqualified from participating. Some had been severely depressed for decades and saw the study as their final hope. After being screened out, a number told Reckweg that they would apply for euthanasia, which is legal in the Netherlands.

Those who made it onto the study were evaluated using various mental health metrics. On average, around a decade had passed since their first major depressive episode, and their current symptoms had persisted for nearly a year. Prior to dosing, many lacked facial expression or spoke with a flat affect. But less than thirty minutes later, "they totally looked different," Ramaekers, the supervising professor, told me, his own cheeks reddening with excitement. "Some radiated," he added.

GH released a data readout from the trial in December 2021. The sample size was tiny at that point, but the results caused a minor sensation, sending the company's stock price soaring. Among the eight participants who'd received escalating doses, seven were in remission from their severe depression a week later—an astonishing finding, given that this was among people who hadn't responded to two or more rounds of prior treatment. There had been no serious adverse events, GH said, although the company stopped monitoring these after a week. Two of the participants had experienced flashbacks.

Yet beyond a basic press release, little was known about the study until June 2023, when it appeared in the peer-reviewed journal *Frontiers in Psychiatry.* Its publication coincided with the world's largest-ever psychedelics conference, Psychedelic Science, which drew some fourteen thousand people daily to a convention center in Denver. The event billed itself as "a bridge connecting the medical, the mystical, the marginalized, and the mainstream." It had the flavor of a political rally crossed with Burning Man and a trade show. There were investment bankers, yogis, influencers, neuroscientists, military veterans, alternative healers, Indigenous activists, and a head-spinning variety of psychoactive swag on offer, not all of it legal: psilocybin gummies and LSD sprays and disposable vape pens filled with obscure stimulants. One day, a jam band set up in one of the hallways and interpretive dancers writhed around on the floor while businessmen in suits walked briskly by. Never before had I appreciated the extent to which the term "psychedelic community" no longer seemed to make sense. This was less a community than a collision of worlds.

On the final morning of the conference, before an attentive audience, Reckweg presented findings from the GH trials. His hair was neatly parted and he had chosen a buttoned shirt with a floral design—"a bit more playful," he told me—to take the edge off his scientific demeanor. One of his slides showed that participants varied widely in their sensitivity to 5-MeO-DMT, and I reflected on how risky Octavio's eyeballed breakthrough doses could be. But when Reckweg mentioned that the study participants had received no mandatory psychotherapy, the crowd grew restive, with a man behind me exclaiming, disbelievingly, "Why?!"

Afterward, standing politely beside the stage, Reckweg was mobbed with questions and comments for more than an hour. A barefoot man in beads and a wide-brimmed hat, identified by his name tag as "Donkey Love," wanted to know if Reckweg had personally experienced the drug. Reckweg declined to answer, and Donkey Love acknowledged him with prayer hands. "If you say yes, the scientific community doesn't take you seriously," Reckweg told me afterward. "If you say no, the psychedelic community says, 'You have no idea what you're talking about.'"

We escaped to a quieter room, where Reckweg reflected on his mission as a researcher. "Everyone here is already hugely convinced of the effects of psychedelics," he said. "I would rather educate people who are *not* in this field. I want to try to remove the stigma around many of these substances." He saw medicalization as the most effective way of doing this. "But as an academic institution you cannot fund this research on your own," he went on. "You need the companies.

And there's no lying to ourselves—these companies are there to make money." Above all, he believed that the research had to be conducted with scientific neutrality, even if this was at odds with the more emotive outlook of many psychedelic advocates. "The only way we can get these substances legalized or approved is by being rational and scientific about it," Reckweg told me. "Regulatory agencies don't care about an emotional plea."

His hadn't been the only presentation on 5-MeO-DMT that day. Before him, on the same stage, Ana Ortiz—the former member of Octavio's foundation who had gone on to perform toad population surveys—spoke about the "false narrative" of ancestral toad use by the Seri tribe and how this had driven global demand for the medicine. "Far from protecting the toad," she said, "we were the ones who put it in the ecologically precarious situation it now finds itself in." When she urged the audience to use synthetic 5-MeO-DMT instead, a hippieish older woman beside me rolled her eyes and whispered, conspiratorially, "But who builds the lab where those chemicals are made, and where is the material mined? We're not looking at the full picture."

• • •

In contrast to GH, Beckley made structured therapeutic support central to its work with 5-MeO-DMT. During its phase 1 trials, which began in February 2022 at a medical facility in northwest London, each participant met twice with a trained psychedelic therapist to discuss their hopes, fears, and intentions. The trips took place in softly furnished rooms—salt lamps, nature photographs—with ambient music playing in the background. Participants were invited to bring along meaningful personal objects to anchor them during the experience. After a guided breathing exercise, the nasal-spray dose of 5-MeO-DMT was administered by a nurse.

One of the therapists told me their role was to "maintain a steady presence," reassuring participants that they were safe. Two days after dosing, they met again for focused integration sessions, helping distill lessons from the experience and, as a company insider put it, talk through any "destabilizing events or dissociative reactions," although these were said to be rare.

Yet for all these safeguards, one aspect of the study design struck many observers as distinctly incautious: None of the thirty-one dosed participants had previously taken psychedelics. (In GH's phase 1 trial, by contrast, at least twenty-one of twenty-two participants had prior psychedelic experience.) "There's a perception that 5-MeO-DMT is the most extreme final frontier," Cosmo, who has spoken openly about his own use of psychedelics, explained to me later, "or that you need to be a seasoned psychonaut to try it." The company had decided to test that assumption, predicting that many patients would be similarly inexperienced if the drug ever made it to market. The trial therapist likened this to "throwing people off the top diving board," adding, "You need to learn to swim first."

I was introduced to Cosmo one evening of the Denver conference at a private event celebrating his mother's foundation. Amanda Feilding seemed tired; Cosmo was posh and a little tipsy. A few days later, when we sat down for a brief interview, I was struck by his candor. "There's a tension between the ideals that a psychedelic experience can engender in people versus the business of making drugs available in the real world," he told me. "Unless there's a return on investment, it's nearly impossible." He paused, carefully considering his words. "The challenge," he went on, "is that the industry is all about growth. As soon as you scale one mountain, there's another. And you're just trying not to lose the core mission."

The trade-off between pragmatism and principle was especially pronounced when it came to therapy, yet developing a therapeutic infrastructure for clinical trials came with complications of its own. This was dramatically underscored in August 2024, when the FDA issued its first-ever ruling on an application for psychedelic-assisted therapy, rejecting MDMA as a treatment for PTSD, in part due to concerns about the role of therapy in the trials. Psychedelics stocks tumbled following the news, and a sense of disillusionment spread across the field. The application had been submitted by a for-profit arm of the Multidisciplinary Association for Psychedelic Studies, a driving force behind the psychedelic renaissance and a staunch proponent of therapy. "The treatment is the human interaction. It's the therapy. It's not really the drug," the founder of MAPS, Rick Doblin, argued prior to the ruling. "And the pharma companies don't make money on that, anyway. They only make money selling the drug."

Beckley took a similar view, theorizing that psychotherapy would work synergistically with its 5-MeO-DMT treatment, improving both safety and clinical outcomes. Yet the company's approach soon drew its own criticism. In 2021, Beckley announced that it would be training eighty therapists with a company specializing in psychedelic integration, but it later came out that the program took place entirely online and was designed by people who had never personally experienced 5-MeO-DMT. In light of this information, a leading authority on the substance, who spoke with several trainees, pronounced the program to be "absolute dogshit." In a statement, Beckley said that its clinical trials and training programs had been "developed with expert partners to adhere to best practice, prioritize patient safety and generate robust scientific evidence." There were also internal tensions about developing a standardized therapeutic approach for Beckley's trials, which was necessary for logistical reasons but also struck many practitioners as absurd: a standard operating procedure for delivering the God molecule. The company went on to produce confidential manuals for its trials, each longer than a hundred pages and updated with feedback from dosing sessions, although therapists were also encouraged to "use their intuition," a Beckley scientist told me.

Even as the company forged ahead, a number of the practitioners it had consulted remained uneasy about developing 5-MeO-DMT into a pharmaceutical product. The clinical psychologist Joseph Barsuglia, who is widely considered an expert on the molecule, warned that proper integration could take anywhere from three months to a year. "This is like the graduate school of psychedelics," he said. "It's so fast, so potent. It can be too much for people." Over time, he believed that patients were at risk of "severe depersonalization, dissociation, and even psychosis."

In 2022, Barsuglia replied to a Beckley post on LinkedIn—in which the company had promoted the brevity of 5-MeO-DMT trips—by writing, "You don't want to advance the world's most powerful psychedelic experience on the time scale of a dental cleaning."

Many experts who had advised Beckley during its planning phase also came away feeling that the company had taken advantage of them. I spoke with four who accused the Feildings of appropriating their insights without any compensation or credit, and of overall, as one put it, "building a company on the coattails of the community." One researcher recalled multiple lengthy meetings in which Amanda Feilding pressed for detailed information—dosing ranges, contraindications, integration strategies—while making vague offers of a job that never materialized. Another said they'd been "ghosted" by Beckley after answering "all kinds of questions." Yet another described themselves as being "mind-raped by Beckley." A spokesperson said that "anyone involved in making meaningful contributions" to the company's work "has been contracted with the company and appropriately remunerated."

"They pissed off a lot of people in the underground," Bollini, the Argentinean practitioner, told me in 2023. She had since fallen out with Amanda Feilding, her old friend, and come to regard Beckley's approach as disingenuous and extractive. "Always around the light," Bollini added, "there are so many flies."*

According to Beckley's published findings, its phase 1 trial went smoothly, with nearly 90 percent of participants saying they would take the drug again at the same dose or higher. Beckley also reported, however, that participants generally struggled to "let go and surrender to the experience," and the therapist I spoke with said that many found 5-MeO-DMT to be overwhelming. "I was prepared for a skipping rope," one participant declared afterward. "You handed me a bungee jump." I established separately that, following a subsequent phase 2 trial in the United States, some Beckley participants had reached out

* Bollini died in 2024 at a party in Ibiza. She was forty-three.

for support from an independent psychedelic integration specialist. "They felt the people serving them did not understand the medicine," the specialist told me.

Still, the trial therapist in London believed that Beckley's approach was vastly preferable to that of its rival. Beckley's maximum dose, twelve milligrams, had been chosen through conversations with long-time experts. GH had given some of its own participants 50 percent more, via the more aggressive route of inhalation. It was "highly unethical to give such large doses," the therapist told me, with support as minimal as what GH offered. In a comment, GH said that its dosing was "safe and well tolerated." But the therapist believed that the company was in for a "nasty shock" as it moved forward with its larger trials. To date, GH has reported no treatment-related serious adverse events from these studies.

Compared with toad medicine sessions with cavalier facilitators, no medics, wildly varying doses and methodologies, loose screening and preparation, possible combinations with other drugs, patchy integration, and a general reluctance to call emergency services in case of trouble—which Barsuglia summed up as "the nightmare of the underground"—both sets of clinical investigations were notable for their precision and care. But the idea remained disconcerting, as one psychedelics investor had described it to me, of "blasting the masses into the deep end with 5-MeO-DMT." I later spoke with a researcher who said that they had been cold-contacted by more than ten "highly distressed" trial participants, most of them from studies run by GH. Some, according to the researcher, said they had reached out to the company. GH denied this, emphasizing that it takes safety seriously, provides participants with "means to directly contact study investigators," and "received no phone call or any emails by any patient." Ramaekers, the professor, said that he and Reckweg had never been contacted by any participants, noting that 5-MeO-DMT trials were "running at multiple sites across the world" by the time my source was contacted. When I asked him if he ever worried about the psychological aftermath of the drug, he said, "It's a fifteen-minute intervention, of which most people don't even remember what happened. In that sense, there's not too much to integrate." He, too, had never tried the substance.

By the time I visited Maastricht University, in 2024, GH was enrolling participants for a larger phase 2 study, to be conducted at multiple sites, as well as trials for bipolar disorder and postpartum depression. The idea of serving 5-MeO-DMT to the depressed mothers of young infants had drawn complaints to a British health-care agency, but these concerns had been dismissed and the trials were proceeding. Some of the sessions were planned to take place at the university. The testing room was to be in a basement, adjacent to a garage where staff parked their bicycles. "Down there," Reckweg said, half jokingly, "nobody can hear you scream."

. . .

GH and Beckley Psytech, while furthest ahead in the race, were not the only companies developing 5-MeO-DMT. Reconnect Labs, based in Zurich, was working on a slow-absorbing sublingual formulation, believing this would be gentler for patients. Its co-founder Daniel Claussen told me in 2025 that his priority was minimizing long-term risks, including "severe psychological destabilization, which we know from real-world evidence can last for months." His rivals were following "the standard rules of hypercompetition," he went on. "The capitalist machine will absorb anything and create abstract value out of it."

This embrace of market logic marked a sharp turn from earlier fears about psychedelics. In the 1960s, as Josh Hardman of *Psychedelic Alpha* pointed out to me, drugs were seen as a threat to social order, driving people to "drop out" and become less productive members of society. "It's basically the opposite now," Hardman said, describing an implicit goal of the psychedelic renaissance as "creating better, shinier, happier workers." (Sometimes, as in GH's investor materials, this was stated directly.) If religion, as Marx wrote, was "the opiate of the masses," then a pharmaceutical product that induced mystical experiences might serve much the same purpose. "Without addressing the systemic issues that cause people distress, we risk using psychedelics as a Band-Aid," Rafaelle Lancelotta, a longtime 5-MeO-DMT researcher, told me. "And ending up with another form of psychiatry to pacify people caught in the gears of the industrial machine."

Not everyone subscribed to the vision of psychedelics as commercial medicine. The Usona Institute, funded by private philanthropy, was testing 5-MeO-DMT and psilocybin in clinical settings but had no plans to profit from their distribution. In 2020, it published an open-access method for synthesizing 5-MeO-DMT, in part to reduce harvesting pressure on Sonoran Desert toads. (Lancelotta was a co-author.) Yet for all their idealism, nonprofit ventures struggled to match the speed and scale of corporate players, who were rapidly patenting more and more psychedelic terrain.

The earliest effort to turn 5-MeO-DMT into a pharmaceutical came from Alvarius Pharmaceuticals, formerly known as Tryptamines Overcoming Addiction and Depression, or TOAD. The company was founded by a curmudgeonly Irish biochemist named James Linden after he met Octavio on tour near Dublin in 2014. "Here was this handsome Jesus-looking fuck, serving toad medicine and riding all the girls," Linden recalled to me. "It was a bit lawless. He just brought chaos." Octavio claimed to be busy with "clinical trials," Linden told me, bursting into laughter at the memory, "but what he *meant* was serving toad to people with clinical conditions." Octavio somehow got hold of a dozen patients from an addiction treatment center and gave them the medicine. "Cocaine, heroin, benzos, pills," Linden said. "But the outcomes were phenomenal." Galvanized by what he'd witnessed, Linden approached a professor at University College Dublin and received funding from the Irish government in 2015 to pursue research into 5-MeO-DMT. "We kept it stealth, though," Linden explained, "because the world is full of jealous, judging cunts."

GH was their first competitor with 5-MeO-DMT, and at one point Linden had a conversation with the company's founding CEO, a fiercely competitive medical doctor named Theis Terwey. "I asked how they'd landed on the substance, and he said they'd analyzed the market, the IP, the stats, the data," Linden told me. "I asked if he'd ever tried it and he said no. So I responded, 'You've picked the world's most powerful psychedelic without really knowing anything about it?' Then I offered him a toad pipe. He still hasn't taken me up on it."

Linden was similarly unimpressed with Beckley, whom he dismissed as "old-money cunts who like psychedelics." Of Amanda Feilding, he said, "People seem to kiss up to her. There's a darkness there." The entire premise of using 5-MeO-DMT as a depression treatment affronted him, in fact, even though this had been part of the original name for his company. "Depressives don't need to be blown wide open," he argued. "They need ayahuasca or a psilocybin cuddle." He went off on a tangent about various spy agencies—Mossad, "the Russians"—trying to entrap him with honeypots over the years, coveting his research for nefarious purposes, but then the call cut off and I imagined we had been intercepted by Pegasus, the Israeli surveillance software. (In reality Linden had driven out of range and was running late for a meeting with Northern Ireland's health minister about legalizing cannabis.)

Incidentally, there was another company named Alvarius working with 5-MeO-DMT, although its operations had stalled by the time I made contact. When I met the founder, a genial and absent-minded Canadian named Tim Harvey, on a video call, he had a corpulent Sonoran Desert toad perched on one shoulder. He quickly stooped to pick up another. "This one weighs eighteen ounces," he boasted. The toads lived with him in British Columbia, where he fed them on earthworms, beetle grubs, and baby rats reared by his nine-year-old daughter. A single toad could devour six baby rats in succession, he said. "There'll be a head and a tail sticking out each side of the mouth. The toads will stuff as much into them as you can give them and just fatten right up."

The goal of all this, Harvey explained, was to develop tissue cultures from toad cells that could produce full-spectrum defense toxins, eliminating the need to harvest toads from the wild. "There's a false binary," he told me, "between synthetic 5-MeO-DMT from a lab and natural toad medicine." He added, borrowing a phrase from Buddhist teachings, "This is the third path."

In theory, this Frankentoad assembly line would resemble the production of lab-grown meat, but Harvey had run into various obstacles and was now keeping the toads mainly as pets in a heated shed; one had escaped in winter and frozen to death in the snow, more than a thousand miles north of its natural habitat. Harvey's interest in the species dated to the early '00s, when he became obsessed with the writings of the anthropologist Wade Davis, who had revealed its identity a decade earlier. Harvey set off to look for the toads in Mexico but didn't find any. He ended up living in South America for much of the next decade. In an odd coincidence, he then settled on Salt Spring Island, where Octavio would later lead his first international tour. He didn't attend any of Octavio's sessions but heard about "people being broken open without any support." It was only in 2017 that he smoked toad for the first time, on a surf trip with some friends. "It changed our lives," Harvey said, with an astonished expression.

Intent on getting some toads for himself, he located a seller in the United States and drove down to collect them. On his return, a border agent asked if he had any animals in the car. "They're kind of jumpy," Harvey warned, gesturing to a cloth bag on the front seat. He opened it and a giant toad leaped out, knocking the agent in the face. The genus *Bufo* was illegal to bring into Canada, dating back to the toad-licking furor of the 1980s, but Sonoran Desert toads had since been reclassified as *Incilius.* In a taxonomic loophole, the one true psychedelic toad species in the world was free to enter the country. After checking the rules, the agent waved Harvey and his new pets through.

• • •

Linden was not the first to suggest to me that Amanda Feilding's exalted reputation was more complicated than it appeared. A former employee of hers advised me to consult LinkedIn for a sense of how rapidly staff turned over at the Beckley Foundation. I tracked down several former employees who described a freewheeling and often fractious working environment, frequently while expressing fears of being identified. "Not many people last longer than six months," one told me.

"You're her serf while you're there." Another, with British restraint, said, "Working with her sent me mad."

The offices of her nonprofit were in a converted cowshed at Beckley Park, behind the family residence. According to one ex-staffer, Feilding would burst in and announce, "A fox chased away the swans," and the rest of the day would be spent searching the property. She was said to have dictated quarrelsome emails, including to Yoko Ono, whom she'd known for years; the employee who typed the message told me that Ono had refused Feilding the use of her New York apartment for a fundraiser after guests at a previous event damaged a priceless Egyptian sarcophagus, which Ono believed to be a former incarnation of herself. Representatives for the foundation and for Ono deny this.

One day at the Denver conference, Feilding took the stage in front of a packed audience of several hundred people, who crowded into the available chairs and spilled onto the floor. Here, it was clear, she was still a countercultural hero. Feilding was small and stooped, wearing a green cardigan and white blouse. The title of her talk was "A Life of Science and Dreams: The Dawn of the Psychedelic Age," with the *L, S,* and *D* offset in bright yellow. Quietly and hesitantly, stammering in places, she read a speech about her decades-long fascination with altered states of consciousness, receiving a standing ovation at the end. "I hate public speaking," she told me afterward. (She had fortified herself, I later established, with a small dose of LSD.)

Afterward, Feilding was joined onstage by Cosmo and her eldest son, Rock, for a discussion titled "A Family Legacy: From a Mother to Her Sons." A tall man with gray curls and a starchy manner, Rock had spent much of his life disavowing psychedelics. "He was a bit more of a rebel, in a kind of weird way," Cosmo said, to uncertain laughter from the crowd. Rock blushingly described how awkward his childhood had been, "having a mum trying as much as possible to be in the press, talking about the benefits of taking LSD and drilling holes in her head." He once joked on a podcast, "If you asked any of my therapists, they would say that's where all my problems started."

After graduating from Oxford and the London School of Economics, Rock had worked as a property developer, going into business with Feilding's husband, an earl twice over who donated tens of thousands of pounds to the right-wing UK Independence Party. (The earl, Feilding told me, had courted her by playing the lute.) Rock soon entered conservative politics himself, rising to become deputy borough leader of Kensington and Chelsea. His mother described him to me as "bright and bossy," adding, "We called him the future prime minister." And so it had been a striking reversal when, in 2021, Rock founded Beckley Waves, a venture studio for incubating psychedelic start-ups. "I don't really think of psychedelics as a medicine in the traditional Western sense," he once said. "They're not some panacea that is going to fix all our mental health problems. Instead, I think of them as gateway drugs to the deep inner work that our planet and society needs all of us to engage in."

His conversion to psychedelics had come about, he explained onstage at Psychedelic Science, through a tragedy. "I ended up in a slightly dark and nihilistic hole," he said. "And eventually I found my way to psychedelic-assisted therapy. Needless to say, it was life-changing. And I had to come back to my beloved mum and say, 'You were right all along.'" It was a polished line, and the audience applauded. "I feel blessed to have found a new calling," Rock said.

He was referring, obliquely, to a disaster that had occurred while he was a politician. One of his duties was overseeing the refurbishment of public housing in a gentrifying neighborhood near where he lived. This was the Grenfell Tower, where a fire broke out in June 2017, killing seventy-two people. Emails revealed afterward that Rock had urged contractors to save costs on cladding, which had contributed to the spread of the blaze. When activists put up posters accusing him of "social murder" and protested outside his home, Rock fled the city with his wife and children.

Although he didn't relate any of this detail in Denver, Rock later published an astonishingly tone-deaf piece in *Newsweek* promoting his new company. "The life I had been building was blown apart," he wrote. "The trauma of Grenfell was an earthquake that upended my life. Yet it led me to a form of healing that I would not have considered otherwise. Psychedelics, it turns out, are not merely an avenue for escape or a remnant of rebellious youth. For me, they became a path toward recovery, acceptance, and a new beginning."

. . .

When I visited Beckley Park, Lady Amanda Feilding had seemed uninterested in discussing 5-MeO-DMT. She kept steering the conversation back toward acid. She was enthralled by the idea that LSD increases blood flow in the brain, an unfounded conviction she had held for decades. "Blood is unfashionable," she said, with haughty indignation. "It's all about neurons. No one wants to talk about blood."

We sat down for lunch, prepared by a private chef, at a table where Aldous Huxley and other intellectuals had once dined. Feilding picked at her salmon and took small sips of red wine. The more we spoke, the more aware I became of a detachment to her gaze and a kind of watchful, fidgety remove that felt at odds with her reputation as a psychedelic matriarch. For someone who had probably taken more LSD than anyone else alive, she projected curiously little warmth. Feilding had often spoken in interviews about a formative trauma in her early twenties, when a man named Michael Hollingshead laced her coffee with a massive dose of LSD; she described the resulting trip as "like a stab in the back—but it was in the brain. And it did lasting damage, I'd say." Hollingshead, a notorious early figure in the counterculture, had introduced Timothy Leary to LSD and was known for using the drug to sleep with women. When Feilding brought this up with me, she did so unemotionally, as if it had happened to someone else. "I kind of died, in inverted commas," she said.

The motto of the Beckley Foundation is "Know thyself." Its logo is derived from the Feilding family crest, a double-headed eagle long associated with the Habsburgs, one of Europe's most powerful dynasties. The Feildings have long traced their descent to a German count who had purportedly settled in England in 1228, yet this heraldic claim was discredited more than a century ago. In 1901, a British genealogist and "debunker of bogus pedigrees" named John Horace Round dismantled the story, attributing it to a seventeenth-century act of forgery. "The Hapsburg descent is an absurd fiction," Round wrote of the Feildings. The family crest was not a birthright but a social gambit. That it later became the emblem for a project devoted to inner truth and higher consciousness was an irony that mostly went unremarked.

"I love philanthropic work," Feilding once said in an interview, "because it leaves you completely free to do the research you think is best for society, regardless of the profit at the end." But in the new era of psychedelics, that attitude was a luxury. A few months before my visit, a firm called atai Life Sciences, founded by Christian Angermayer, the "Darth Vader" capitalist, had acquired a third of Beckley Psytech for $50 million. The head of a smaller psychedelic start-up described the sale to me as a "deal with the devil." Feilding, sitting on an old sofa after lunch, considered Angermayer a moment: "He's rather sweet, isn't he?" It was true that he was charming. "I disapprove of his morality, sadly," she added.

Just two weeks after atai's acquisition, GH was granted a sweeping European patent for its 5-MeO-DMT program, which, among other things, gave the company ownership of intranasal delivery of the drug—the same method being pursued by Beckley. This was, in the words of an expert on psychedelic IP, "an existential crisis" for the Feildings' operation. According to corporate filings, atai subsequently challenged the patent, along with a nonprofit research group called Porta Sophia. A protracted legal dispute was brewing over the God molecule. When I commented on how incongruent this seemed, the IP expert replied, wearily, that psychedelics had "just become another pharmaceutical commodity."

. . .

In February 2025, GH released data from a larger phase 2 trial for depression. Around 60 percent of the participants were in remission a week after dosing; this rose to nearly 80 percent among those who'd taken part in a voluntary extension of the trial, receiving up to five additional doses. The average improvement in depression scores two days after dosing was more than five times greater than in studies using ketamine. Within a few days, shares in GH almost doubled, and the company raised another $150 million in a second public offering.

Yet many analysts believed Beckley was still in the running. In the United States, where both companies will need large successful trials before they can obtain FDA approval, GH's work had been stalled for more than a year, with regulators demanding further toxicology studies for a new inhalation device developed by the company, in part to further strengthen its IP position. In an additional blow, GH had a wide-reaching patent application provisionally rejected in the United States, for, among other reasons, trying to claim existing underground knowledge as its own proprietary information. Beckley, meanwhile, had reported promising results from its own phase 2 trials, with 55 percent of patients in remission a month after dosing. Josh Hardman, the industry analyst, told me that the race "was too close to call."

In May 2025, Amanda Feilding died of cancer. I spoke with many, including those who'd criticized her, who expressed admiration for her years of work, advancing the serious study of psychedelics. She had seemed indefatigable. A week later, as if to underscore the ending of an era, atai announced that it would be taking over Beckley, conditional on the company's next round of trial data, in a deal valued at $370 million. Beckley had tried, unsuccessfully, to thwart the bid by raising more money. "Sadly seems they couldn't get the cash," an investor in the company texted me.

That same month, I finally spoke to a member of GH's leadership on the record: the new CEO, Velichka Valcheva, its former chief medical officer. She denied that GH had been intentionally secretive in the past—"There was no black box," she insisted—but declined to answer several questions, such as when its founders had first considered working with 5-MeO-DMT. ("For patent reasons," she said, "I don't want to get into that.") When I asked what had led a group of traditional biotech investors to such a powerful substance, she said only that they had been guided by unmet medical need, describing depression as "a good space for innovation." Given their coldly clinical reputation, she spoke of the founders in surprisingly messianic terms: "A group of believers who endured."

Valcheva had a lifelong fascination with astronomy, she told me, but since joining GH had come to believe that "the mind is much bigger and more complex than any universe out there." I remarked that this sounded like something a 5-MeO-DMT user might say, but she, like many of her colleagues, had never tried the drug. She pointedly avoided naming the compound during our conversation, instead using the term "GH001," which refers to the company's proprietary formulation and dosing protocol; it had been GH001, she explained, that produced such incredible trial data. I pushed back: Surely regular 5-MeO-DMT would have yielded similar outcomes? She equivocated. Not for the first time, I felt a wearying cynicism. An attribute of the peak 5-MeO-DMT experience, like other modes of heightened consciousness, is the sense of being at one with the universe, that everything is connected. But this was also true in more disillusioning ways. The molecule was thoroughly bound up with human reality—money, power, ego, the rest of it. Whether in underground or clinical settings, no experience was too enlightening to be commodified. In a telling comment, Valcheva spoke about "vaporizing the IP."

CHAPTER 8

All the Darkness Is Vanished

In 2023, after the conference in Denver, I returned to Punta Chueca for Seri New Year. Two years had passed to the day since my first visit to the village, and I wanted to see where the story of toad medicine had led. My driver parked where the lawyer's sons had thrown up at Octavio's feet. The sea was the same electric blue. Tourists were milling around the dusty square on the beachfront, where an elder was chanting into a microphone. A Seri man was performing a dance to the chants, stomping intricate rhythms on a small wooden platform. He stepped aside and sipped from a bottle of liquor in an ornate gift box, showing it off to his friends, while some tourists in Seri face paint took turns inexpertly stomping on the platform.

I was wondering what would happen if I ran into Octavio, but I couldn't see him in the crowd. There were Mexican men in cowboy hats and tight jeans, Seri girls in bright skirts, a posse of soulful youths with musical instruments. A woman with a mushroom tattoo on one thigh drank beer with some buff men in tank tops. Dream catchers had been strung up around the square, swinging in the breeze. Commemorative T-shirts for the event were on sale with a design prominently featuring the toad.

Shortly before sunset, a Seri man took the microphone to announce the inauguration of the tribe's new governor. The crowd pressed closer, cameras and cell phones aloft. I found myself behind a Mexican woman of about thirty, dressed in all black with skinny jeans worn low. She seemed inebriated or unwell, talking loudly and slurring. As the incoming governor was being presented with a ceremonial wooden staff, one of the elders resumed chanting, and the woman began dancing erratically, kicking her legs and shuffling her sneakers. Locals edged away from her, but she carried on for several minutes. Whenever the crowd applauded, she balled her fists and howled at top volume. In another context, she might have been asked to leave, but here, where the lines between ritual and tourism had become blurred, her behavior passed without comment. She was there as a client of a young toad shaman from the village: a paying seeker. Scenes like this were becoming more common in Punta Chueca, where a fragile local economy and the cultural phenomenon of toad medicine were colliding in unpredictable and sometimes dangerous ways.

After the inauguration, I ran into Saskia, the woman who, during my first visit, had been helping Octavio with his ceremonies while pregnant. (That baby was now eighteen months old.) It was an awkward reunion. I asked if Octavio was around; Saskia said she wasn't sure, "but probably."

"He might not want to chat," I said, mindful of his last messages to me, "but if you see him, please let him know I'm here."

"I also didn't like your article," Saskia answered, before walking off. My piece on him, published the previous year, had evidently made me unpopular.

A little later, I looked up and saw Octavio gazing in my direction from across the crowd. He was wearing a colorful wide-brimmed hat tilted over his face and had grown a full beard, so it took me a moment to recognize him. He looked away and I reflexively did the same, but after a beat I walked over. As I greeted him, he turned his back, so I found myself speaking to his shoulder. Quickly and almost under his breath he replied, "How are you, bro?"

A Seri woman approached us then and sold him an orange jacket in the traditional style. "This is great," he told me, tossing it over his shoulder. "I didn't have this color." Saskia snapped some photos of him, which Octavio soon posted to Facebook. He looked at me and asked, in an edgy tone, "So how's it going with the book?"

I told him I'd just been at a conference where people were discussing the commercial development of 5-MeO-DMT. "Like all synthetic drugs, this is not something I promote," he said, before I'd finished my sentence. "I still think there is enough toad medicine to create a world movement. If you just squeeze the glands and leave the toad alone, the next year they will be there. So it's completely sustainable." He became more animated while speaking, as if unable to hold himself back. "I'm not worried about the toad being extincted. I'm worried about the toad being mistreated." People were spreading the narrative of toad overharvesting to promote the use of synthetic 5-MeO-DMT "because it's a big business for them." Their motivations were no different, he said, from the Mexican cartels flooding the market with fentanyl, which had recently eclipsed meth as their primary product. "There's a link between the persecution of plant medicines and the promotion of synthetic drugs," Octavio concluded.

It seemed we were transitioning into an interview, and when I checked with him, he made a why-not expression, so I took my phone out to record our conversation. We walked a few paces down the beach and sat on an overturned fishing boat, facing a golden sunset over Tiburón Island. I thought back to Octavio's arrival at Seri New Year in 2021, flanked by an adoring entourage—the cameras, the fist bumps, the radiant aura of celebrity. Now his presence felt diminished. His body language was more muted, his voice less commanding. There were fewer people surrounding him: I saw his daughter, Salvia, his mother (wearing a toad T-shirt captioned "OTAC Bufo Alvarius"), and a handful of followers.

As we spoke, a brawny middle-aged man randomly approached us and, in a thick Bronx accent, struck up a conversation about toad smoking. The tattoos on his bare arms included a toad, a kambo frog, and a psilocybin mushroom; around his neck he wore an ornate beaded sash patterned with a frog. His name was Tony, and in a former life he'd owned a restaurant in Atlantic City, New Jersey, where rival mob bosses met to hash out deals. "There was sex, drugs, rock 'n' roll, and threesomes," Tony said, of his own revelries. A decade ago, he'd been introduced to peyote and now described himself as "a certified medicine man through working with various tribes, such as the Seri." He explained that he was half Italian and half Puerto Rican, with an ancestral connection to the Taino people of the Caribbean, who had made ceremonial use of plants containing 5-MeO-DMT.

After speaking for some time, Tony expressed curiosity about whether we had ever smoked bufo. Octavio looked at him with a prickly expression. The moment was so absurd that, without thinking, I joked that Octavio had only recently smoked toad for the first time.

"He's making fun because I was the guy who introduced the toad here to the natives," Octavio explained.

"What's your name?" Tony asked.

"Octavio."

"Oh, I heard about you, bro," Tony said, in a disinterested way, then told us about a YouTube documentary, *Journey to the Ego Death: The Life of an American Medicine Man*, about his own work as a healer. "It's not really going viral, but it just hit three thousand views," he declared. "For three thousand people to watch my documentary was pretty humbling for me." Tony's mission in Punta Chueca was "putting together a training program for people who want to serve bufo to learn the Indigenous way," he said. "It's becoming so mainstream now with these 'facilitators' and 'shamans'"—he used air quotes—"but they have no training in Indigenous teachings."

Watching this unfold, I was struck by the warp of time and sheer strangeness of history: a new toad evangelist telling Octavio the Seri origin myth at a tribal celebration increasingly associated with toad smoking. The story had begun with Octavio but moved far beyond him; where it would end was unknowable. Amplified chants rang across the beach as the sky grew darker. A fire was being lit for a sweat lodge ceremony. "But I *heard* of you, brother," Tony went on. "You been around a long time, huh?" He interrupted Octavio's answer and spoke more about his documentary. "I don't serve medicine," Tony insisted. "I do *ceremonies.* Completely different."

"This concept of a healer is completely distorted in society," Octavio muttered. "Nobody can heal anyone. It's self-healing."

"Aho! *Axatipe,* brother. I tell them, 'My job is to provide a safe, sacred space to guide you through your journey.' That's it."

"We don't have any power, any authority, nothing. Sometimes the facilitator is an obstacle, because they're trying to possess the process."

"I even said in my documentary," Tony cut in, "that in the first two years I made a lot of mistakes with these medicines. Because your ego gets out of control. It takes time to rein yourself in and realize it's not about you." The Seri chants were getting louder, and Tony raised his voice. "I want to find a way to regulate these out-of-control New Age hippies that are taking this medicine to a level that has no respect for it," he half yelled. "They wanna do all these crazy things with people putting their lives at risk. It's not necessary. I have people prepare for three to five days."

Tony said this with such guilelessness that I realized he knew little about Octavio's reputation, and I felt a sense of vertigo witnessing their bizarre exchange. Octavio was murmuring assent, an irate resignation about him. "People used to talk a lot about integration," he said, "but it's more important the preparation."

It was around this point, as I became aware of a faint buzzing around my eyes, that I realized I'd made an error of judgment. Before Tony appeared, I'd noticed Octavio holding a small glass vial and asked what it contained. "It's essential oil that my daughter and I are gonna share, because she's having her seventeenth birthday next month and I won't be here," he explained. He was heading to Spain, he said, at the invitation of a former student of Carlos Castaneda's, where he would be serving toad to a group of people aged sixty to eighty ("healthy, most of them retired"). Salvia had perched herself beside him on the hull of the boat, and as we spoke, Octavio unscrewed the lid and shook a few drops onto her tongue, followed by his own. "¿Quieres?" he said, proffering the bottle. "You want?"

"What is it?" I asked.

"It's essential oil."

"Not drugs?"

"No."

During my first reporting trip, Octavio had repeatedly pressed me to smoke toad with him. I declined for various reasons (not while I'm working) and kept others private (not my first choice of facilitator). I eventually consented to a dose of *rapé,* which he blew up my nose one afternoon at his house. My eyes began streaming and claggy black mucus gathered in my throat. Brian, Octavio's Sri Lankan acolyte, noticed this happening and spent the next few minutes circling me, whispering, "Burns, huh? He-he. You pussy, you pussy." The experience was miserable, although watching Brian morph into a bully was interesting.

"What essential oil?" I asked Octavio again, on the beach in Punta Chueca.

"It's from trees, just for relaxing."

I had no reason to trust him, yet in that moment I chose to, perhaps because the offer felt sincere, even conciliatory. It had been a long day; I was caught up in the rush of the scene. Without thinking further, I opened my mouth and swallowed.

• • •

Octavio whispered something to his daughter and they soon left, leaving me with Tony. Whatever I was experiencing came on in waves, like the onset of an edible, and in the lulls I wondered if I was playing tricks on myself. Tony was listing Mafia dons who had dined in his restaurant and rhapsodizing about toad medicine. I was suddenly gripped by the urge to leave. I found my driver and we returned to our accommodations in Kino Bay, racing down the dark road with bats swirling in the headlights. When we arrived, I looked around the truck for my backpack, which contained my passport, wallet, and reporting notebooks from the past two weeks. It was missing.

Mortified and self-conscious, with a rising sense of paranoia, I told my driver what had happened. "Wow," he said, with a laugh. We headed back to Punta Chueca and from the opposite direction came speeding vehicles with their high beams on, drifting into our lane. A man flashed into view around one bend, changing a tire in the darkness. My driver swerved around him and opened a beer.

The sensation of being affected by an unknown drug was not a pleasant one. Whatever it was kept getting stronger, and I had no idea how long the trip would last or what direction it would take. I was hyperalert; my eyeballs felt twice their usual size. "The worst thing to do is resist," I kept telling myself, but I couldn't relax into the experience. I believed that I had lost irreplaceable material—interviews, ideas, jotted scenes—and wondered, somehow, if this was Octavio's revenge. I thought of toads in buckets and the God molecule and cartels and venture capitalists and the Seri chants, all blurring together into narrative overwhelm. Yet in a corner of my mind was an awestruck realization: that Octavio, knowing I was working on a book about him had chosen to reveal himself so damningly.

We drove into Punta Chueca. The village square had emptied out and a few Seri people were stacking away chairs. The fire from the sweat lodge burned low on the beach, where I found the backpack, untouched, on the hull of the boat where I'd left it. This felt like a miracle. Then a burst of loud music came from up the beach. Another party had started. My driver and I wandered through streams of people to a stage with Mexican *cumbia* music blaring and a dazzling light show. Several Seri men were chanting into microphones and the crowd was hopping up and down. Tony materialized in front of me, his face contorted in horror. "People have *died* with that guy!" he shouted. "I didn't know it was him!"

Still feeling the effects of whatever Octavio had given me, I couldn't sleep that night and stayed up for hours on the beach in Kino. Some drunken men were strumming guitars and chorusing mournfully on a veranda with lights that changed from purple to orange to green. I floated in the water and watched the starlit sky trying to make sense of the night. The next morning, I got a text from Octavio.

"Man. Was good to see you again. Let me know if I can help you with anything." He seemed to have forgiven me for what I'd written about him: "Nothing to regret. Always gratitude."

Disarmed, despite myself, by his friendliness, I asked again what the essential oils in his little bottle were.

"Why?" he replied, as if this were an unusual question.

Eventually he told me: an extract of morning glory seeds, revered by the Aztecs as *ololiuhqui,* described to science in 1941 by the ethnobotanist Richard Evans Schultes, containing a natural counterpart to LSD. "Natural, organic and gentle," Octavio texted. "No alcohol or synthetic drugs, bro." He, Salvia, and his mother had all taken a dose, standing at the water's edge and watching flashes of phosphorescence.

He was packing for Spain and in an expansive mood. He commented on Tony and his enthusiasm for serving toad, decrying the proliferation of inexperienced bufo facilitators. "It's the wild wild west," Octavio wrote.

"And here I thought you were the wild west," I replied, still processing what had happened. "It gets even wilder?"

"Out of control."

• • •

Later that afternoon, a humid breeze dragged across the shore at Punta Chueca. A camper van belonging to some Spanish content creators, emblazoned with social media logos, was parked beside a drum kit coated in dust from the previous night's party. Throngs of tourists sheltered under shade cloths and *palapas* along the beach, a short distance from the encampment of a Seri meth addict: a few ragged tarps strung up between pieces of driftwood. It was 105 degrees and getting hotter. The summer rains had not yet begun.

Around a dozen Seri women had set up stalls at a sandy promontory where fishermen stored their boats. Their tables displayed baskets, wood carvings, sage bundles, and shell jewelry, each assortment of souvenirs indistinguishable from the others. There were no customers. One of the vendors was chanting while shaking a wooden rattle. A young woman with a camera came up to the tables and photographed the singer, who stopped and offered to sell her the rattle.

I had heard that there was going to be a public meeting about toad smoking and the Seri, that the tribe would be asserting its sovereignty over the tradition and demanding that outsiders stop harvesting toad medicine or performing Indigenous rituals without their permission. "It will be big, easy to find," one of the organizers promised. But by 2:00 p.m. there were still no signs of the meeting. A sweltering torpor lay over the village. I ran into one of the newer Seri toad shamans, a handsome youth with long hair tied up asymmetrically on one side, giving him a modish appearance; I had seen him with a group of clients the previous evening, including the woman who had been yelling while the new governor was sworn in. He was slender, draped in beads, with ornate tattoos spreading up both arms. When I asked if he knew anything about the meeting, he was coolly dismissive. "We already did all that years ago," he said, informing me that "government inspectors only allow Comcaac collectors to gather toad medicine." This was starkly at odds with what I had learned about Sonora's lawless toad market, but he made it clear that our conversation was over. He resumed slicing up some marine snails, a traditional Seri dish, to serve his clients for lunch.

Later that afternoon, at a large *palapa* near the water, I found Fernando Suárez Bleck, of Fair Trade Toad, setting out chairs. I'd met him on my previous visit: an elfin man with straight dark hair whose speech slowed when he smoked pot, which was often. "There cannot be fair trade if people here are struggling with poverty," he had told me in our first conversation. "We should take care first of the people living in the territory of the toad, then think about how to do sustainable collection of the medicine." He had realized this after the debacle of the World Bufo Alvarius Congress in 2019, where rival toad suppliers had bickered onstage and Indigenous representatives accused Suárez and his partners of "trying to make money or take control of everything," he recounted. After raising some funds he had come to the village with plans to install a water purification plant, which broke down after six months. He never left. "I arrived with a very romantic idea about how tribes are," he reflected, "but to my surprise it wasn't like that. It's a very difficult society."

A few people trickled in for the meeting. Suárez spread a Seri flag over a table and fussed with his cell phone, setting up a Facebook live stream. While we were waiting, I spoke with a woman in her thirties from Mexico City who was visiting Punta Chueca for the first time. Her name was Naytxe, after a Mayan love goddess, she explained, adding, "My grandfather loved Mayan culture." (I was unable to find any references to this deity afterward.) She had formerly worked for the Mexican government and as a corporate social responsibility consultant for Coca-Cola, but quit her job and moved back home with her mother after smoking toad for the first time earlier that year. "I'm rethinking my whole life," she told me. Hearing about her professional background, I made a remark about the poverty of the village—the water shortages, the uncollected trash—and asked what she made of its development needs. She shot me an admonishing look and said, "They don't want or need it."

"Help" from the "developed" world, she went on, would be damaging for the tribe. "They begin to *believe* they're in poverty. But they were abundant; Mother Earth gave them everything. We're imposing something they don't know." She had been in Punta Chueca for two days and smoked toad with Raymundo Barnett, Octavio's first patient in the community. "The Comcaac have so much wisdom to share, but as humanity we're not ready to understand," she continued. "You have to know them—but *really* know them from the inside. Then you can understand them, and then you can respect their traditions."

When it became clear that nobody else was arriving, the meeting got under way with ten people, at least three of whom were not Seri. Five stray dogs napped in the shade. Suárez, a former corporate lawyer, launched into a technical explanation about legal papers he'd filed with the Mexican government to secure exclusive protections for the Seri tribe to harvest toad medicine, using legislation for protecting Indigenous rights. "This is part of the sociocultural heritage of the community," he'd written. (Nine months later, he'd received no reply.) The *palapa* had an upstairs section, where a wooden flute began to play. A little later, a shirtless, barefoot man in baggy cotton pants descended the stairs and, ignoring the meeting, wandered off into the sunlight. Suárez wrapped things up after Enrique Robles, from the Seri council of elders, arrived to issue a brief statement for the Facebook feed. "The medicine is from *here,*" Robles stressed on camera; he left immediately afterward. When I asked Suárez how the meeting had gone, he seemed crestfallen but philosophical. "The thing is, because I am not from here, I feel like they are just watching me like, 'This crazy guy is writing more papers.' It's a bit difficult to make them support me. Because they don't really believe in the system."

. . .

The transcendent effects of psychedelics can make it easy to overlook that many traditions have histories of violent suppression, followed centuries later by appropriation—an arc that has become especially pronounced during the psychedelic boom of the past decade. In North America, peyote ceremonies were outlawed and driven underground for most of the twentieth century, even as white researchers documented and extracted knowledge from Indigenous practitioners. In the Amazon, ayahuasca has been exported as a wellness product, often with little benefit to the communities that preserved it. In Mexico, the Mazatec psilocybin healer María Sabina was canonized by Western seekers while being ostracized by her community and having her chants and rituals commodified. Advocates for Indigenous traditions have pointed out the injustice of being sidelined by modern psychedelic research, of having their intellectual property rights infringed by psychedelic patents, of their historically sacred medicines being stripped of cultural and spiritual context, and of being largely excluded from the profits of the burgeoning industry. In Denver, during the closing address of Psychedelic Science, a group of Indigenous activists took the stage to protest their lack of agency in determining the future of psychedelics. "This is not a revolutionary movement if you are leaving people out of the conversation," one of the activists shouted, to uneven support from the room.

As 5-MeO-DMT has been propelled toward the center of the psychedelic renaissance—the retreats, the investors, the clinical trials—these tensions are reaching the Seri tribe, whose involvement with the origin mythology of toad smoking was instrumental in popularizing the practice. But this familiar dynamic has a wrinkle, in that relatively few Seri participate in the psychedelic toad economy or use the substance themselves. A few days after New Year's, I was introduced to a young man from the Barnett clan, Aaron, who told me that at gatherings of the extended family "nobody talks about toad smoking." This was surprising to me, given that several Barnetts had publicly embraced the practice for more than a decade. Three generations of the family were involved: the elders Chapo and Pancho, a few of their children, and now a few of their grandchildren, who were in their early twenties. "When they're not doing ceremonies, it isn't a big part of their lives," Aaron continued. Most of the Barnetts, himself included, had never experienced the medicine. "Most people in the community have probably never even *seen* it," he added.

When I asked how many Seri had become toad shamans, he counted on his fingers and consulted a friend, putting the total at fewer than ten, with another two in Desemboque. "It's expanding slowly," he said. "People are coming from all over the world for this experience, so the provider says, 'Yes, of course this is traditional.' And so it replicates." His tally matched what others in the community had told me, meaning that less than one in a hundred Seri were serving toad medicine. Aaron said that a few others had attempted to become toad shamans but given up. "The established ones already have a client base," he explained. "They've got the market cornered."

An exception, he told me with some amusement, was the young man I'd spoken with over the snails—a former apprentice to Raymundo Barnett who had recently struck out on his own. During his ceremonies, he was known for chanting "random Seri songs," Aaron said, "like about birds and lizards." Traditional healers in the past had used specific *hacáatol cöicóos,* the power songs, for spiritual connection and healing. "Now people can just sing whatever they want—nobody can tell," Aaron said. He emphasized that there were traditional songs "for everything in the Seri universe"—weddings, wars, winds, hundreds of plants and animals—"but not toads," which he viewed as further evidence of the insignificant role toads had played in Seri culture. Elders in the community had advised the young man that he wasn't using the songs correctly, but he shrugged them off. "People here find it funny," Aaron told me. "The situation is kind of absurd."

But there were also worries among the Seri, he continued, that their cultural heritage was being cheapened. "Becoming a shaman used to mean undertaking a vision quest and dedicating your life to learning Indigenous knowledge. Now you can just light the venom and put it in someone's mouth."

A few days later, I had a conversation with Manvir Singh, an anthropology professor at the University of California, Davis, whose interests include shamanism and psychedelics. When I described what I'd observed in Seri territory, he recognized recurring themes of psychedelic tourism more broadly. "People arrive with certain expectations," he said, "and have that projected back at them." He pointed me to the work of an Austrian researcher named Bernd Brabec de Mori, who lived in the Amazon for several years in the early '00s. An ethnomusicologist by training, Brabec de Mori became interested in the *ikaro* songs performed during ayahuasca ceremonies. Unlike other traditional songs, which varied widely across the region, these *ikaros* were uniform in structure and often sung in non-Amazonian languages like Spanish and Quechua. Similarly, linguistic terms for the use of ayahuasca were nearly identical in different communities, even though Amazonian peoples speak a vast array of languages. This suggested that ayahuasca was a comparatively recent introduction in many places, an idea that was supported by historical and ethnographic evidence. If anything, it appeared that some Indigenous groups had adopted the practice only within the past few decades.

But the "globalization of ayahuasca," Brabec de Mori argued, rested on a contradictory belief: that Amazon shamans had been using the substance ceremonially for millennia. This created incentives for Indigenous practitioners to embellish their traditions to fulfill the expectations of tourists. "A simplistic view is imposed on the indigenous people, as if they all have been traditional ayahuasca shamans since ancient times," Brabec de Mori wrote. "Age-old indigenous knowledge is used as an item of advertisement."

He raised two ethical concerns: first, that money from ayahuasca tourism was deepening economic inequality in many Amazonian communities; second, that traditional healers were shifting from treating their own people to curating psychedelic experiences for visitors, resulting in a "vacuum of medical care." The economy had become especially appealing for younger self-styled shamans, Brabec de Mori observed: "They are trying to bring to perfection the visionary experience of ayahuasca but no longer study the whole system of Amazonian medicine."

He might as well have been speaking with Aaron Barnett, who articulated a growing worry among some Seri people that older healing practices were "being put on the back burner" as a consequence of toad smoking. "It's like there are fewer service providers in the community for traditional practices," Aaron told me. The Barnett clan had long been regarded as custodians of spiritual knowledge; now they were known primarily as the *sapo* family. Even so, people respected their choices, Aaron said. That was the Seri way.

• • •

Brabec de Mori described what he had observed in Amazonian communities as a "double discourse," with separate narratives internally and for outsiders. He once explained in an interview how locals would tell tourists "the stories they think are interesting for *them,* and not what they really live with."

I got a sense of how divergent these stories were among the Seri, but also how accommodating the tribe was of dissonance, when I spoke with Pastor Kelly, the head of the Apostolic Church in Punta Chueca.

Kelly grew up in the village and is a fisherman; a rattling fridge on his stoop was stocked with crabs and shucked mollusks. His mother, an ancient and jovial woman named Lidia, was sitting beside him with some sage bundles and necklaces, sizing me up as a potential customer. Lidia had been born on Tiburón Island in the 1940s, when many Seri were still hunter-gatherers, and was renowned as a traditional singer and craftswoman; people knew her as *la Artesana Mayor,* "the Great Artisan." Kelly mimed picking up a toad and handing it to her. "If I did this," he said, "she would be afraid of it." Lidia theatrically gasped. Kelly continued, "It isn't part of our culture. If you see a deer or turtle, that's part of us. But this is something new." As Aaron had done, Kelly and his mother then enumerated the many animals that appeared in Seri songs: coyotes, tortoises, sea turtles, dolphins, many birds, but not toads.

"Foreigners think it's a Seri tradition," Kelly said, "so this was adopted. Some people here work with it. They mix *sapo* with Seri songs, and so on." He conceded that this had brought some economic benefits: "One of the toad shamans told me, 'Before, I was afraid of the toad, but it's making me money.' Now they live very well—a good car, good food, good clothes. You can see the change." Then Kelly paused and corrected himself. "They're not shamans. They're charlatans. They're taking advantage of our traditions."

His own relationship with traditional Seri culture was complicated by his position at the church, where many ritual songs remained forbidden. "We don't approve of them," he said. "But singing is also very important in this community, and we need to respect that." Gesturing toward his mother, he said, "She knows how and when to use them. But the charlatans don't respect the limits."

It had been the same church, beginning in the early 1950s, that had suppressed Indigenous Seri practices, a process accelerated by modernity and acculturation—until Octavio, set on finding an ancestral tradition of toad smoking, had reawakened interest in the chants, channeling them in an entirely new direction. (Or a bygone and forgotten one, in his telling.) Had Octavio preserved Seri culture or harmed it? Or was the answer both?

"He exchanged the toad for our traditions," Kelly said. "He took more than he gave, and he made a lot of money." Yet whenever tourists came by, inquiring about toad medicine, Kelly directed them to the right people. One of his own nephews had become a toad shaman, and Kelly sometimes rented one of his fishing boats to him for taking clients to Tiburón Island, a popular location for ceremonies. "It's a practical arrangement," Kelly said. "I don't want to judge." But he was also perturbed by the spiritual consequences of the toad phenomenon. "When they sing, they invoke powerful spirits," he said. "And if it's not God, who else can it be?"

On one occasion, his nephew had served toad to two women who had "been possessed by demon spirits," Kelly said. Unable to end their torment, his nephew brought them to the church, a bare building with an uninsulated metal roof near the middle of Punta Chueca, where Kelly's predecessor performed an exorcism, casting demons from the women's bodies. "My nephew realized the power of God that day," Kelly told me. Afterward, he continued working as a toad shaman.

More alarming, Kelly felt, was the flow of visitors arriving in Punta Chueca to "train with the Seri" and learn to administer toad "the Indigenous way." This had accelerated within the past few years, he said. "They're wearing our clothes, singing our songs," Kelly told me. "They're stealing our identity and customs." He spoke as someone who both understood the spiritual chants and feared them; the idea of foreigners using them seemed to cause him dread. "Hippies coming here brings an economy—that's okay," he said. "I'm not against *sapo* but how it's used." He warned of "legions of demons" being unleashed.

And so it was a surprise to me when he mentioned that one of his own sons had smoked toad three years ago, as a treatment for crystal meth addiction.

"Nothing changed," Kelly said. His son had remained an addict.

. . .

By the water's edge nearby, outside a house strung with dream catchers, some bare-chested young men were rolling joints and charging their phones. They wore linen and had their long hair tied up in loose buns. One was strumming a ukulele; another had a Mayan wooden flute. When I introduced myself, the flutist told me that he identified as Toltec—a Mesoamerican culture that predated the Aztecs. He was handsome and fair-skinned. His Instagram handle identified him, among other things, as a bufo facilitator and practitioner of "sacred intimacy artistry" (accentuated with a leopard emoji). My driver kept a straight face in his presence, then burst out laughing afterward. "*Tolteca*? More like *fresa*"—a strawberry, pejorative slang for someone superficial and wealthy.

I recognized the man who had traipsed through the Fair Trade Toad meeting and said hello to him. He had a full beard and shaved head with the wisp of a ponytail. To my amazement, he greeted me in a South African accent: "Howzit?" His name was Johan, and he'd been traveling around the Americas for more than a year, apprenticing in various psychedelic traditions. "I got connected with the Matzes in Peru to learn about kambo," he said, "then I went to Chile, drank ayahuasca there." He'd done peyote, DMT, "a lot of mushrooms, even a bit of *iboga*." He'd taken peyote with members of the Lakota tribe but chafed at the strict protocols of the ceremony. "It was very 'speak when you're spoken to,'" he told me. "I like to be freer with the medicine, more creative." He was working with some Brazilian tribes to smuggle *rapé*, by way of his mother's house, to South Africa. "There's a legal way of doing it, but that costs money," he reasoned.

He'd grown up in an Afrikaans neighborhood outside Cape Town, my home city. His father had been conscripted into the army during apartheid and used racial slurs when talking about the Black people he'd killed. Johan described him as "very emotionally scarred," adding, "He never showed emotion unless it was anger. He also drank until he cried." At seventeen, Johan was sent to rehab for smoking pot; he later started using meth and heroin. He was kicked out of a notorious Christian rehab center for "being untreatable," but later found healing through plant medicine. He had smoked toad once before in South

Africa with a traveling Mexican practitioner (not Octavio). "You die," he told me. "It's very shamanic, very sacred."

He had come to Punta Chueca to find a bufo mentor, traveling thirty-six hours by bus from southern Mexico. On Instagram he had seen other people posting about training with the Seri, sharing selfies with shamans. There was, for example, a Utah-based aesthetician who specialized in body sculpting; she had rebranded herself as a toad practitioner, been featured in a Fox News segment about toad smoking ("What the medicine showed me was that I was the truth in everyone and everything. . . . I experienced myself as a god, absolutely"), and claimed in promotional material to have "extensively studied and trained with the Seri," using "ethically clean sourced Bufo 5-MeO-DMT." She happened to be holding a retreat that Seri New Year, attended by bankers, attorneys, and oil industry executives; when we spoke briefly, she said her goals were "predominantly humanitarian-based," adding, "We help others go directly to the source." Or there was the psychedelic church founded by a man from Texas who had been molested as a child, used cocaine from a young age, and quit cold turkey after his first toad experience. He had also appeared on Fox (the host of both segments, Jesse Watters, had developed something of a fascination with toad smoking) and now organized tours to Seri territory for people to "learn about shamanism and using *otac* as a sacrament." In 2023, his ex-fiancée alleged on Facebook that he had sexually assaulted her after serving her a "whiteout" dose of toad. He initially solicited positive testimonials from female clients and posted, "My own self-worth and love for who I am has never been greater." He later claimed that their sexual encounter had been consensual and shared footage of them being intimate on other occasions. A judge served him with an injunction for stalking, and he reportedly negotiated a plea deal to avoid being criminally charged for sexual assault, although details do not appear to be publicly available.

Johan told me that he was looking for "someone from the original people to give me the blessing" to work with bufo. "Otherwise I can just become another facilitator," he said. "It's not authentic. I want that integrity." But he'd been underwhelmed by what he'd discovered in Punta Chueca. "A few of the *abuelos* over here, they smoke crack and crystal," he said. "That's not a good energy for serving." He'd met some toad shamans and spoken with them in broken Spanish, coming to the realization that they expected payment, which didn't sit well with him. "I don't want to pay someone to teach me how to work with nature. It should be very authentic and passed along," Johan said. "I want to trade my wisdom and my knowledge for theirs."

He had proposed teaching them "tapping," a form of alternative therapy for processing emotion and trauma, but nothing had come of it. (He seemed unembarrassed about trying to barter for shamanic status in a village grappling with poverty.) In the meantime, he linked up with a Mexican woman who had married into the Seri tribe. She was offering toad sessions with a man from Tucson; they were open to doing an exchange. "I resonated the most with them," Johan told me.

"I know that part of your intention coming here was to learn an Indigenous bufo practice," I said, choosing my words carefully, "so I guess I'm curious if you feel you're getting that with an American and a Mexican woman."

"Dude, they're very authentic."

When I asked if they were providing ceremonies in a traditional Seri way, he assured me that they were: "white clothes, drums, speaking the language." Would they be chanting? The American had informed him that the Seri didn't do that. In a critical tone, Johan described the tribe's approach to toad medicine as "quite hardcore, quite masculine, quite warrior." He added, "I prefer the softness, the gentleness. It's like dying, so I want to be held."

When we spoke a few days later, he was still processing two ceremonies he'd done with the non-Seri practitioners: one that morning, one the evening before. Both experiences had been ecstatic, but he confessed to me that he was feeling lonely. During his travels he had married a woman in southern Mexico who was subsequently diagnosed with terminal cancer. She had stopped chemotherapy and was doing "chakra healing and Osho treatments" with a healer in Tulum. She and Johan had fallen out over her treatment and were no longer speaking. There was pain in his blue eyes. "I miss my wife," he said.

Johan had initially struck me as something of a comic figure—the misguided psychedelic tourist, wandering around in search of meaning—but in that moment I felt the weight of what he, like so many others, was looking for: an escape from the self into something like freedom. In my role as a reporter I could tend toward a detachment that sometimes collapsed, leaving me momentarily disorientated, as if a trapdoor had swung open into my own inner world.

Johan took me to see the woman he'd smoked toad with. Her name was Melissa. She was from Hermosillo, in her thirties, a former beautician. Her father had formed a relationship with one of the Barnett toad shamans after being diagnosed with a terminal illness, attending around a dozen toad ceremonies in quick succession. A few days before he died, he had arranged for Melissa to be "adopted" by the tribe. Though I asked a few times, I was unable to clarify what she meant by this—she was smoking a joint while rolling another, visitors were coming in and out of the yard; Johan had produced a mouth harp from his voluminous cotton pants and was playing it for Melissa's small daughter, who was carrying around an inflatable tube and wanted to go swimming—but Alberto Mellado, a Seri community representative I spoke with later, dismissed the idea of someone being adopted in such a way as "craziness." "I am part of the Seri community," Melissa repeatedly told me. She had been serving bufo for five years.

Her husband, a thin and reserved Seri man named Charlie, sometimes assisted during ceremonies but wasn't regarded as a toad shaman. In summer, his role was to help collect toads. The previous night, a few of them had gone toading on a farm in the irrigated zone between Hermosillo and Kino Bay, where groundwater depletion was contaminating the soil with salt. Even though it hadn't rained yet, there was pumped water in the troughs and ditches, and the toads were out mating and feasting beneath the floodlights, singing to one another. Melissa's group had caught about forty toads, but instead of milking them there, where they were more likely to encounter *sicarios,* they brought them back to Punta Chueca. As part of Johan's tutelage, they had taught him to milk the toads that morning—streams of ego-dissolving exudate, now drying on panes of glass around the yard.

They had intended to take the toads back and release them in the evening, Melissa said, but the window for that had passed. They would return them the next day instead, more than forty-eight hours after catching them. The toads were heaped in a plastic blue drum in the yard, some fat like grapefruits, some scrawnier juveniles. They were wrestling fitfully with each other to reach the top, pooled in brown water and the muck of their own excrement; occasionally one of them softly clucked. Johan eagerly grabbed a toad to show me what he'd learned, squeezing its glands beside a pane smeared with secretions. They had already been milked twice that day; almost nothing came out. "*Poquito,*" Johan said, laughing, "just a little bit," and reached for another one.

. . .

People had told me about a U.S. military veteran hanging around Punta Chueca, smoking toad and organizing ceremonies for other veterans. At the New Year's party, while feeling the effects of *ololiuqui,* I ran into him. His name was Michael Manion, and as people danced around us and the light show whirled, he struck me as grounded, strong, clear-eyed, and alert. When I explained what I was working on, Manion looked me in the eye and said, "This place is an absolute circus."

We met the next morning at a hotel in Kino Bay. Manion is of Louisiana Creole descent and grew up in South Central L.A. He enlisted at nineteen and quit in his early forties, suffering from depression and PTSD. "It started rubbing against my soul," he told me. He gained more than a hundred pounds and joined a biker gang. In 2019, he smoked toad for the first time, an experience he described as life-changing. He shed the weight in four months and, in early 2020, decided to go to Punta Chueca and train with a toad shaman. "I was like, 'Let me go find me a Seri,'" he said. "My intention was to come and *learn* this medicine, then go back to the U.S. and hold circles for veterans."

He found an American bufo church online that offered "initiations" with the Seri for $5,000. (The pitch was that, afterward, you would "be a shaman" yourself, Manion said.) Someone at the church put him in touch with a medicine man in Punta Chueca. Manion went down for a ceremony with him—a "beautiful, very deep bufo experience, more ancestral than my previous journeys," he recalled. "But it only took me about twenty minutes to figure out the rest."

The destitution of the village was irreconcilable with the fees he'd been quoted. "If anybody was paying $5,000 to come here," he said, "then where the hell's it at, and who's getting it?" His ceremony had been on Tiburón Island, and on the way back to the mainland the outboard motor cut out, leaving them stranded in the channel for hours. "I started thinking, 'I can probably hustle up a few bucks and get these guys a new engine,'" Manion said. He raised $3,000 on GoFundMe and found a suitable engine in the United States, but the shaman urged him, "Just send the money. I'll get one here." Manion was soon back in Punta Chueca, and they headed out to the island. "We're getting ready to come back, and the damn propellor falls off the engine we just bought"—Manion hooted at the memory—"which they probably just pulled off another boat! Now, I *know* what the street looks like. I *know* game. And I was like, 'Okay, whatever else happens here has to happen with a real clear presence of mind, and very slow.'"

What he observed, as he spent more time in the village, was a discordant split screen. To one side was a predominantly Christian community who "wanted nothing to do with bufo" but recognized the economic opportunities it brought in. "The majority of them exist in survival mode," Manion said, "and when they see tourists rolling through, it's like, 'How do I get involved in that?'"

Manion also perceived the reality that Punta Chueca lies in one of the world's most violent territories, and that nearly every household owned one or more powerful guns. He began offering trainings for the Seri traditional guard, thinking this would help them resist the influence of cartels, but stopped when rumors reached him that he was "training a gang." Gradually, he became aware of the tribe's fraught internal politics. The governorship confers almost unfettered control of Seri funds, including lucrative permits auctioned each year to trophy hunters for shooting bighorn sheep on Tiburón Island. A single permit can fetch upward of $90,000; fifteen or more are sold each year. Minus brokerage fees, this money, around $1 million annually, is paid out to the Seri tribe via the governor's private account. There are no formal records of its expenditure, and much of it seemingly vanishes. Amid the cramped, bare houses of Punta Chueca are a few larger homes—imposing gates, tiled entrances, upper floors—belonging to former governors. A few months earlier, brawls had broken out among rival factions in the village over accusations of corruption. Assault rifles were fired into the air, several people were stabbed, and "a buddy of mine was smashed over the head with a two-by-four," Manion told me.

A community leader in Punta Chueca later explained the conflict to me in more detail. The previous governor—yet another member of the Barnett clan—had refused to relinquish his position when challenged by the council of elders. In theory, the council had the power to appoint and remove governors; at the New Year's celebration, it was their duty to hand over the ceremonial staff. But at that time, the council had dwindled to only one member—Enrique Robles, whose father had welcomed Octavio into the community. For years, the Robles family had treated leadership of the council as hereditary, essentially a monarchy. Yet this entire system of governance was only a few decades old, and disputes over legitimacy were ubiquitous, sometimes resolved through the Mexican court system and sometimes through violence. After a protracted standoff, the Barnett governor eventually stood down, but fought to retain control of the Seri fishing cooperative, which had recently received a fleet of eighty new boats from the Mexican government, worth around $3 million—another source of political power. Months later, in the dead of night, Enrique Robles was abducted from his home by a group of armed men, purportedly cartel members, and held for ten hours before being rescued by the Mexican authorities.

"They are pocketing as much as they can," the community leader said, of the governors. Their money went into second homes in Hermosillo; into purchasing cars to operate as Uber vehicles; into paying off patronage networks ("vultures") that helped get them elected. Some developed drug and alcohol problems. An aging former governor with the surname Casanova once spent several months in jail for brandishing an AK-47 while protesting an election he'd lost, only to be arrested soon after his release when he crashed his truck into a street pole. He was drunk and had been using cocaine, with another AK-47 in his possession, and was accompanied by a Mexican sex worker.

Meanwhile, around a third of the tribe, including some of the eldest members of the community, was "in extreme need," unable to afford food or basic medical care, the community leader continued. Diabetes, virtually unheard of before the 1970s, was endemic. The Seri, who once had strict protocols for sharing resources, had come to resemble the wider society they were being absorbed into, organized around the uneven distribution of wealth.

This was one side of the split screen: a divided community in an unforgiving landscape. On the other was the putative ancestral home of toad smoking. In a typical week, Manion would see around a hundred *sapo* tourists arrive, looking for toad ceremonies. "You watch a van pull up on the reservation, and all of them jump out wearing those hats and the feathers, complete with crystals in their pockets and a little medicine pouch—I call it the spiritual uniform," Manion said. "They think, *This is it.* They fall for it hook, line, and sinker."

In the 1960s, the ethnobotanist Richard Felger, who exhaustively documented traditional ecological knowledge among the Seri, took to hiding the fact that he was working with Indigenous people to "avoid having to bring along enthusiastic followers," he wrote toward the end of his career. "Native values were being 'rediscovered.' Sometimes there was an unrealistic utopian worship of anything native American."

Felger added, "I grew weary of armchair idealists interpreting other people's cultures and even deciding what was good for someone else. The Seris were just like anyone else but with a different background: some were wonderful and fun to be with, others jerks and obnoxious, some were brilliant and creative, and others dullards."

Reading this, I thought of Johan and Naytxe and all the other seekers I had spoken to, all on pilgrimages of healing or self-discovery, and how this layered over the social geography of Sonora. "They move in different spheres," the community leader told me. Nevertheless, these worlds were connected, each feeding into the other—an ecosystem.

Manion also described a more pernicious side to the flow of tourists into Seri territory. Where many visitors were on personal quests, others appeared to have nakedly economic motives. "Some folks are coming down with the intention of making a connection with the Seri," he told me, "then going back into the U.S. and telling everybody that they've trained with them." One practitioner in Texas had leveraged this into an entire training program of her own; she had recently brought around two dozen participants to Punta Chueca for a workshop costing $5,000 per head. Another American woman, after her first toad experience in Punta Chueca, immediately began bringing down clients for ceremonies, booking out some of the most expensive rentals on the Kino beachfront. Some of this money reached people in the Seri community, and there were sometimes good-faith efforts to provide resources for the tribe. "But the pennies you're dropping off here have got nothing on the thousands you're making up there," Manion said.

"Morally and ethically," he went on, "you can't show up here with an intention of leaving with a certificate. You should do the work, put in the time, fix yourself before you try to fix somebody else. But here you have the opportunity to bypass all that. You can just come on down and pay somebody. That's the sentiment. You can attach your name to the Seri and leave." There were no certificates, although selfies in Punta Chueca arguably served the same purpose.

. . .

Just as outsiders were seeking to capitalize on Seri traditions, there were Seri people seeking to capitalize on the influx of outsiders. And why not? It was sometimes difficult to tell who was taking advantage of whom, though the balance of power and payouts was highly uneven. The situation was mutually opportunistic. If people needed an Indigenous tradition of toad smoking, a number of Seri would oblige.

Manion recounted a comical interaction he'd had with one toad shaman he worked with, a rakish and enterprising man named Luis Miguel López. "I asked how old he was the very first time he'd smoked bufo," Manion said, "and he said he was twelve." The two men had already discussed the coincidence of being born days apart in 1971. "So the math wasn't mathin'," Manion said. "And I told him, 'Bro, when we were twelve, it was 1983, and toad smoking didn't get here until 2011.'" López laughed. "Okay," he replied, "maybe I wasn't twelve. Maybe it was just a few years back."

Prior to his career as a medicine man, López had been a preacher in Kino Bay. Prior to that, he was governor of the tribe for a spell, dressing in expensive cowboy boots and tearing around in a giant SUV "like he was being chased by *sicarios*," an associate of his recalled. And prior to that he was an impoverished young fisherman who once told a Mexican anthropologist, prophetically, "Being Seri can mean many things."

"It's mind-blowing," the anthropologist Rodrigo Rentería-Valencia said when I called him. "The Seri have this chameleonic capacity to reinvent themselves and perform the role perfectly." He described Seri culture as "an open-source society," adding, "They can always get new software, like in *The Matrix*."

Now an associate professor at Central Washington University, Rentería-Valencia began his ethnographic research with the Seri in 2001 and continued, off and on, for fourteen years. He saw the arrival of toad smoking and recalls rolling his eyes. "But I knew it would have some Velcro," he said—some cultural traction. Ever since the Castaneda era, in the late 1960s, he explained, "educated Mexicans with hippie tendencies" had romanticized the idea of Indigenous psychedelic traditions. Chapo Barnett, whose sons Octavio later treated for meth addiction, had been the first Seri to embrace this role, entertaining "poets, artists, and philosophers" from Hermosillo in a cave south of Punta Chueca, where they smoked marijuana and took acid together. Among this crowd were Odily Fuentes and Xixi, who would later introduce Octavio to the community. "This was the seed of toad use later on," Rentería-Valencia told me.

Though he saw toad smoking as a new phenomenon, he understood it as part of a deeper history. Since precolonial times, surviving in the desert had required the Seri to not only tolerate but encourage "a wild individualism," he said. The ephemeral rains and scarcity of resources had selected for opportunism culturally, just as it had ecologically. His graduate supervisor, Tom Sheridan, the University of Arizona academic who compiled detailed historical accounts of the Seri, told me something similar when we spoke. "The Seri had to be mobile and responsive," he said, "and developed a cultural trait of being quick to take advantage of different situations." This was amplified during the colonial era—livestock raiding, guerrilla wars—and continued through to the present, "whether fishing in the gulf, cartel activity, or gringos coming down who want to lick toads," Sheridan said. "Toad may be a new thing, but adopting to new things in Seri society goes back many thousands of years."

Sheridan was agnostic on the question of whether the Seri had historically made use of toads. "We have to hold in tension that maybe they did," he told me. "There's no way of knowing." More interesting, to him, was what the toad-smoking phenomenon revealed about modern culture. "It says more about the people who go there wanting spiritual experiences than it does about the Seri," he said.

And what *does* it say? That people are lonely, polarized, sick, distracted, medicating with alcohol and drugs, spiritually undernourished, disenchanted with religion? That we feel powerless about the state of the world, insufficiently loved, numbed by algorithmic feeds? That we collectively yearn for ways of being that have been irrevocably lost? A part of me wished deeply to believe in the narrative of traditional use, to smoke toad on the shores of Tiburón Island and feel myself connected to something ancient and pure. But I would have been faking it.

"If toad smoking is completely new among the Seri, it doesn't mean it's illegitimate," Sheridan told me. "People are adopting new practices all the time." But this particular practice, ensnared in the commodification of psychedelics, was creating a vicious cycle for Seri culture. A homogenizing influence was at play—the dream catchers, the sweat lodges, the cacao ceremonies now on offer. Punta Chueca increasingly felt like a caricature of what psychedelic tourists expected to see.

At the back of the village one day, on the site of an old garbage dump, I came across a white house surrounded by giant cardon cactuses—upturned limbs, pulpy red fruits—that had likely stood for more than a century, since the end of the Seri genocide. Tents on the stony ground flapped in the wind. One wall of the house had a mural of a Seri elder; another featured a crudely rendered toad with a tobacco pipe in its mouth. Around the back was a sun-bleached altar with toad figurines, a Buddhist statue, a dream catcher, a sage bundle, some shells, a yellow rubber Minion, and various other trinkets. Inside, the walls were decorated with a painted turtle shell and dozens of mandalas. A bleary group of tourists lounged around a table, picking at tortilla chips. When I greeted them, a pallid man in a floral shirt inquired in a Russian accent whether I was "there with a local person." Before I could answer, he scolded me: "Yeah, that's going to be a problem."

The rules of the Seri tribe, he informed me, were that I needed permission to be on their lands. It was his first visit to the area—and his last, he declared. He had smoked toad with three different shamans in three days, most recently that morning, in a cave with one of the Barnetts. I asked how his experiences had been. "Uhh," he began. He had watery blue eyes and a frayed expression. "You can be honest," a Mexican man at the table encouraged him. The Russian hesitated. "It's extremely . . . *hard* conditions for me. Like, everything." He had been tormented by the heat. He had been bitten ragged by sand fleas. "I want to leave today; I want to leave right now, by the way!" he cried out suddenly. "I want a hotel, nice food, bed, air-conditioning. But when I leave, that's dependent on God." He had been waiting hours for a taxi. He had no faith it would arrive. "If I'm not going to get this today, it's fine," he told me. "I will sleep in the tent." Noticing an edge of desperation in his voice, I offered him a ride back to Kino Bay that evening. "I'm really okay, man," he said. "I'm chill. I'm good."

. . .

In spite of his growing cynicism about *sapo-turismo,* Manion continued returning to Punta Chueca. He had brought down a total of around sixty people for ceremonies and filed papers to establish a nonprofit, in some ways replicating what he had criticized others for doing. "If I can get the results I know I can get with these veterans," he said, "the circus matters not."

In his view, smoking toad with the Seri was richer and more powerful than consuming the molecule in other ways, even if he questioned the origin mythology. The first time he heard the chants during a ceremony, he recalled, "it felt like my soul knew." It was as if the songs were cradling him throughout the trip. "And it allowed me to fall back into it and go someplace else," he said.

But he also understood that, for most people, the appeal of visiting the tribe depended on toad smoking being a deep-rooted tradition. If the Seri were to announce that psychedelic toads were a recent introduction to their community, their share of the bufo economy—already meager—would undoubtedly shrink. Manion recognized the life-changing potential of the experience, its importance to the Seri, and the ways in which it stirred local tensions. The more we spoke, the more conflicted he seemed.

"The Seri have more game than anyone," he told me. "As long as it's beneficial to them, they're going to capitulate."

"Like a race to the bottom?" I asked.

"Exactly."

Competition among toad shamans had already driven down the price of a typical ceremony to less than 2,000 pesos, or around $100. Conflicts were rising among rival providers. Psychedelic tourists, like the toads, had become a competitive resource. While driving through the village one day, I saw a tattered cardboard sign ("Ceremonia de sapo medicina ancestral") outside the run-down home of one of the newest toad shamans, who was said to be charging less than anybody else.

If anything, I found it strange that even more Seri people hadn't entered the trade, until Manion reminded me what serving toad involved. There were stories in the village of tourists vomiting, becoming aggressive, or tearing off their clothes during ceremonies, behaviors Pastor Kelly had described to me as "demonic." Over the past decade, untold thousands of people had smoked toad with Seri practitioners, who had developed an approach based on the tribe's traditions, however loosely. "They embody love and acceptance, unconditionally," Manion said of the toad shamans he'd worked with—another instance, in his view, of the Seri adapting skillfully to a new opportunity.

Other shamans in the community were known for a looser approach, serving toad at parties or while inebriated. "There'll be people dancing, having a drum circle, and everything else," Manion said, "and you'll look over your shoulder and someone will be doing bufo right there." One of Octavio's first Seri patients, a former meth addict, was nicknamed Tecate, a Mexican beer he routinely drank while holding ceremonies. "In a week, he can make 60,000 pesos with toad," a neighbor of his told me, or around $3,000, "and in a week that money is gone. He likes to party."

What most concerned Manion, as seekers flocked to Punta Chueca to smoke one of the world's most powerful psychedelics, was the possibility of something going wrong in a ceremony. "If you're desperate to make money serving medicine, you're going to take on all comers," he said. I thought of the young woman in black I'd seen yelling during the inauguration. The idea of her smoking toad with an inexperienced young shaman was chilling. "You don't know what they're bringing with them," Manion said. "There's not enough safety."

. . .

Alberto Mellado, the Seri community representative and historian, lives in a modest home next door to one of the elder Barnett toad shamans. The properties are separated by a thin fence of ocotillo cactus poles. You can look from one dusty yard directly into the other. Mellado has an outhouse on his side of the fence and, while going to use the toilet, sometimes passes within ten meters of a toad ceremony. "It was funny in the beginning," he recalled. "They were making chants toward the sunset very solemnly, and I'm just going about my business. But then it became very annoying."

Now in his early forties, with a boyish face and contemplative manner, Mellado is a councillor in Hermosillo, serving as a liaison between the municipality and the tribe. Before being elected to this position, he worked as a conservationist for many years and authored a series of books based on the history of the Seri. His initial reaction to toad smoking, he told me, was that it was alien to the community, and he regarded the arrival of psychedelic tourists as "disgusting in many aspects." They smoked pot in the streets or got drunk with locals. People urinated against his fence. "We have many conservative families here," Mellado said, "but these hippies ignored our rules. They were everywhere in town. They had no respect for our customs."

But as time went on, he came to reconsider these judgments. Many of the tourists, he realized, were "broken people—widows, divorcées, people with cancer or AIDS. They come from a world where there are many religions: They have yoga, therapists, psychologists, excellent physicians, hospitals, medicines. If they don't find something *there* to cure them or alleviate their suffering, and if toad medicine helps them? Good for them. We as a community have a lot of respect for that." He felt proud, he told me, of the role his tribe had played in the global spread of toad medicine.

He was also clear-eyed about its economic necessity in what he described as "one of the most vulnerable communities in northern Mexico." People who came to smoke toad often stayed for a few days. They rented accommodations, purchased artworks, took boat trips to the island. "At some point they receive the toad medicine," Mellado said. "And by the time they leave, they've touched the economy of the village in many ways. The cost of the toad experience is a small fraction of the benefits they deliver."

At the same time, it concerned him to see outsiders profiting off Seri identity, bringing in tourists for toad ceremonies or posing as custodians of Indigenous traditions. "Someone wearing a traditional shirt, using face paint, selling *sapo,* and singing our songs wrong? That's upsetting to people in this community," he said. "It's a distortion of who we are." This had been a pattern ever since Octavio arrived in Punta Chueca: "He used us to advertise his business. And many others have copied him." It would be an injustice, Mellado went on, "if the business model is that outsiders always make 90 percent of the money."

Earlier in our conversation, I had asked him if he saw toad smoking as a Seri tradition. "The community is very clear on what our culture is and what it is not," he said. But he later expressed openness to the idea that his ancestors had smoked toad in the past. "I can't imagine that we were here for thousands of years with the toad at our feet, ignoring the power of the substance," he said. "Maybe that knowledge was accidentally reintroduced to the tribe in modern times. It can never be proved. And for the future it doesn't matter. The answer to this question has not discouraged people from coming. They do, and they will continue to do so."

People of the Desert and Sea, the ethnobotanical tome authored by Felger and Mary Beck Moser, was published in 1985. It included the statement that amphibians were "inconsequential in Seri culture," with all species lumped together under the generic name of *otac.* But in 2000, Felger wrote in an autobiographical essay that he harbored one regret about the project. The book's preface had originally included a carefully worded paragraph stating that it covered "only a fragment" of Seri traditional knowledge. "We knew we had only scratched the surface," Felger explained. But the publishers had conceived of the book as a definitive work and insisted on removing the paragraph. What might have been missed or kept secret? The possibility remains that the Seri once knew about the toad's psychoactive properties, only for that knowledge to be revived, improbably, by Octavio. But the alternate story—where Octavio introduced the practice and sparked a psychedelic movement, drawing on people's expectations of indigeneity while pulling the Seri into a complex new age—is no less remarkable and strange. Both stories culminate with 5-MeO-DMT entering the brain and inducing a kind of whiteout, which could be framed as a collapse of meaning but often feels like the opposite: a blinding, wordless revelation of truth.

In July 2021, without any preparation whatsoever, Mellado ended up having his own experience with toad medicine. Luis Miguel López, the shaman who worked with Michael Manion, had been conducting ceremonies on a beach belonging to Mellado's in-laws. Mellado ran into him there one day, lazing in a hammock after serving toad to some tourists.

"How was it?" he asked.

"Perfect," López replied. "You're next."

Moments later, Mellado—who had never used cannabis before, let alone psychedelics—was inhaling from a pipe. He felt physical vibrations so strong, he said, that "my body and my consciousness separated by force." For a while he was terrified, believing he was dying. Then brilliant white light poured down from the sky like a waterfall; he tried to shield his face with his hands, but his hands, along with the rest of his body, had vanished. The sound of López's rattle encircled him like a meshwork that reconfigured with every shake. "I could see the sound," Mellado said. "There was a different physics." The light faded and he perceived a mountain of sand in front of him. Every grain signified something beautiful in his life—his wife and children, his health, his job. "Every day," he thought, "I wake up on this mountain of good things." The peak of the trip lasted four minutes but felt like four hours; when it was over, Mellado sobbed with gratitude. He experienced an afterglow that lasted for days.

Ever since, he had viewed the world a little differently, he said. But the blissful sense of perspective had faded. Mellado had seen Octavio promise to heal meth addicts in the community, only for most of them to relapse. Transformation, he knew, could be fleeting, even illusory. A seductive deception brought on by flashes of insight is that whatever preceded them can be effortlessly left behind, that a new way of being not only is possible but will endure into the future. Octavio himself had expressed this view on a podcast in 2017: "Once you see the light and feel the light, then all the darkness is just vanished, because it doesn't exist anymore. That's the toad medicine."

Mellado was more philosophical about what he'd experienced. Epiphanies can obscure as much as they reveal, which is perhaps why we refer to them as "blinding." After moments of transcendence, ordinary life reasserts itself. "Eventually, you move back to where you were before," Mellado said. "Life will make you *you* again."

Epilogue

That summer, I caught a bus to Tucson before flying home. It was mid-July and the rains were delayed. People kept glancing uneasily at the sky. Each sweltering day, clouds built up without releasing; sometimes rain fell but evaporated before reaching the ground, hanging in mirage-like streaks called virga. "Might be a failed monsoon," one ecologist said to me. Tucson was enduring a record-breaking heat wave—temperatures above 100 degrees for forty-five days straight, with highs reaching 115. That month, Pima County recorded an average of three heat-related deaths every day, half of them undocumented border crossers or people without shelter. I kept thinking of the toads in their multitudes, hidden in the parched landscape, ready to erupt to the surface. Their presence gave the desert a charged quality, like a loaded spring.

Then, one afternoon, the clouds gathered more thickly than before, rolling upward in billowing columns. Their upper surfaces were blinding white, their undersides dark and heavy. They continued to grow, climbing higher and spreading wider, even as the sun burned them off at the edges. Robert Villa, the toad conservationist, texted me a screenshot from his weather app. "It's happening!" he wrote. The monsoon had begun.

I was outside the city, visiting another toad contact, and as I drove back the western horizon was curtained by black sheets of rainfall, broken in places to expose a burning red sunset. Villa was waiting for me at his home, a tiny row house with no AC, stacked to the ceiling with rare books, the yard a tangle of potted succulents. I had spent the past few days with him there, sheltering from the heat and discussing the psychedelic toad world. "It's really fucking dystopian," Villa said at one point, "like a Philip K. Dick novel"—blurred realities, opaque systems of control, a creeping sense of paranoia. He kept reminding me that beneath this sprawling human saga was an ecological one. "You need to see more toads," he declared.

With the arrival of the rains, he had assembled some friends for a toad mission. There was an artist who made sculptures out of old books, a biologist turned poet wearing a kerchief and suspenders, and a young man whose work involved preserving indigenous Sonoran seeds. Someone joked that we needed a flashing green light for the roof: "Toad Squad." We piled into Villa's beat-up old SUV, a case of beer in the back, and set off on a highway toward the southern border. He put on a CD of West Coast jazz and explained that this route, back then a gravel road, had become famous among reptile collectors in the 1950s. Now there were fewer reptiles and more fences. "So it goes," Villa said.

As we approached the Tohono O'odham reservation, which is bisected by the border, we passed through a Border Patrol checkpoint: a fluorescent-lit tunnel with sniffer dogs and cameras. This was not a crossing but a surveillance post, forming part of an immigration enforcement apparatus that extends deep into southern Arizona. The agents waved us through, but on our return asked to see my passport, which I had not thought to bring with me. They ordered us out of the car and positioned spikes beneath the wheels. I gave my details to one of the agents, who went to look me up on a database. While we were waiting, Villa asked another of the uniformed men if the bright lights attracted reptiles at night. "Yeah," came the puzzled reply. "Lot of rattlesnakes."

It was past two in the morning by the time we were allowed to leave. Our boots and clothes were muddy. We had spent hours hunting for toads. "You have to keep your ears open," Villa had said at the outset, turning onto an unlit road. "I drive with the windows down and listen for a wall of sound." But at our first few stops the ground looked concerningly dry, and when he switched off the engine, the desert silence was like a vacuum. "If all else fails, we'll go to this cattle tank where they're all floating around and making love," Villa promised. We made our way there, but it was empty.

The scholar Robert DeGraaff has described the songs of toads as "earth's primeval music." For more than four billion years, until the first amphibians dragged themselves ashore, there were no voices in the world, and nothing listening for them. Any sounds on land arose without being perceived—the fall of rain, wind in a desert, rustling leaves. This stillness endured for 95 percent of earth's history. Then the ancestors of toads developed vocal cords, along with the ability to hear one another. They filled their lungs with air and cried out to attract mates, giving rise to a wondrous cacophony. One North American field guide describes the calls of various toads as "a shipload of seasick landlubbers," "a sheep with a cold," and "an idling diesel engine." Another book, authored by a herpetologist who lost a thumb to a snakebite, offers even more vivid descriptions: "a fingernail along the stiff teeth of a large comb," "an irate policeman's whistle," "the exhaust noise of a distant tractor."

These songs are gradually fading, silenced by the relentless advance of humanity. We have entered an era of mass extinction, of life's diversity being thinned. Scientists warn of impending "biological annihilation," involving not only individual species but the intricate networks they form part of—a sweeping and irreversible ecological diminishment. Every living organism is connected to a larger whole and, via an unbroken chain of ancestors, to the origins of life itself. Steadily, often invisibly, these connections are being severed. Octavio brought attention to an ecological marvel with profound implications for humanity, but perhaps the greatest insight would prove too difficult to integrate: that we focus inward too much, absorbed and diverted by ego, instead of on all that surrounds us.

"Most of the feeling we call religious," John Steinbeck once wrote, "is really the understanding and the attempt to say that man is related to the whole thing, related inextricably to all reality." He reached this insight on a 1940 voyage through the Sea of Cortez while collecting specimens with his friend Ed Ricketts, a marine biologist who inspired the character of Doc in *Cannery Row.* At one point, they anchored off Tiburón and scanned the shoreline for Seri. Unknown to them, Miguel Barnett was sheltering on the island with his young children—including Chapo, whose own sons would become the first Seri to receive toad from Octavio. Steinbeck and Ricketts shared a view of nature that approached the mystical: a wonder at the depth and grandeur of biology, stretching from the earliest unicellular organisms to what Steinbeck called "the tragic miracle of consciousness." Ricketts, for his part, was obsessed with the idea of "breaking through," of experiencing the sublime or sensing life's fundamental unity. "All things are one thing," Steinbeck wrote in his account of their expedition. "One thing is all things—plankton, a shimmering phosphorescence on the sea and the spinning planets and an expanding universe, all bound together by the elastic string of time."

Still searching for toads, we passed through a town on the reservation where coyotes scavenged at the roadside and dogs howled from behind fences. The Mexican border was twenty miles away. It had rained patchily: In some places the smell of creosote and petrichor rushed through the open windows; in others the ground was bone-dry. Villa followed a road with few other cars, surrounded by dark vegetation. At one point, lights flashed from the bushes and went dark—a group of migrants, almost certainly, waiting for a pickup. Then we heard toads in the distance. We parked and walked toward a riverbed, passing discarded items from previous travelers: backpacks, water bottles, a threadbare jacket. Rodents skipped across the gravel and dived into their burrows. A coiled rattlesnake lay in wait. The sound led us to a wash with standing puddles of water; previous floods had scoured away the riverbank, exposing the roots of mesquite trees. We found a few muscular Sonoran Desert toads clambering around at the edges, their snouts still dusty from being underground, like children with dirty faces. I picked them up and they clucked like chickens—all males, indignant at being handled. Farther upstream, in a muddy pond, there were dozens of other toads, mostly spadefoots, which bleated at one another like sheep. They fell silent when we approached and peeked at us from the water. A few tentatively called out; we bleated back, and soon the whole pool was in song. Altogether we counted five species, including an enormous *alvarius* that materialized in the shallows. He stood defiantly in front of us before hopping away, as if he had somewhere more important to be. It had rained and the desert was blooming; soon everything would dry up again. Winged ants and termites were swirling in the beams of our flashlights, and bats were tumbling through the air. The toads were in the water, singing new life.

Acknowledgments

This book began as a speculative reporting project in early 2020. It would have been impossible without the patience and generosity of everyone I have spoken to since then. Thank you for sharing your stories with me—sometimes at considerable personal risk—and helping me understand the contexts in which they unfolded. Special thanks to Alan Davis, Jules Evans Josh Hardman, Cathy Moser Marlett, Eva McGarry, Gary Nabhan, Scott Shannon, Robert Villa, Andrew Weil, and the late Bill Atkinson and Flor Bollini for your contributions, both behind the scenes and on the page. And thank you, Octavio, for participating as fully as you did.

I wrote the first drafts of this story as a graduate student at New York University's Arthur L. Carter Journalism Institute. I am indebted to Robert Boynton, director of the literary reportage program, for giving me this extraordinary opportunity, and to Ted Conover for his guidance and encouragement. I also had the immense privilege of being mentored by Patrick Radden Keefe, who helped me in more ways than I can say. Thank you to David Remnick and the editorial staff at *The New Yorker* for giving me a chance to write for the best magazine in the world, and to my editors Daniel Zalewski and Tyler Foggatt for working your magic on the draft. Huge thanks, too, to the tenacious fact-checkers who collaborated with me: Natalie Meade, Fabrice Robinet, and Hélène Werner.

For advice on reporting in Mexico, I am grateful to Murphey Woodhouse, Matthew Bremner, and Frank Smyth. I would have been lost without my driver and interpreter, the groundbreaking artist Miguel Fernández de Castro. Betty Meza helped me conduct crucial interviews in León. For accommodation, anecdotes, and the loan of a van, thank you to Greg Smart and others at the Prescott College Kino Bay Center. To my sources in the Seri community, several of whom asked to remain anonymous: *axatipe.*

I was able to develop a proposal for this book with financial support from the Ferriss–UC Berkeley Psychedelic Journalism Fellowship. I am thankful to Michael Pollan for advice and productive reporting leads, and to my fellow grantees—in particular Rachel Nuwer, Chris Walker, Olivia Goldhill, and Shayla Love—for camaraderie and inspiration. Without my agent, Alex Kane, this book would have remained an inchoate set of ideas: thank you for your insights, savvy, and reassurance throughout the process. Thanks as well to everyone else at WME: Laura Bonner, Fiona Baird, Carolina Beltran, and Alicia Everett.

At Doubleday, I got to work with three incredible editors: Yaniv Soha, who acquired the book and helped me hone its direction, followed by the duo of Edward Kastenmeier and Chris Howard-Woods, who grasped what I was trying to write and steered me closer. Words can't express how grateful I am for your skill and care with this manuscript, and for the wider team at Doubleday for bringing it into reality: Vimi Santokhi, Andrew Dorko, Ingrid Sterner, Oliver Munday, Betty Lew, Julie Ertl, Anne Jaconette, and Bill Thomas. Big thanks are also due to Lee Brackstone and team—Lily McIlwain, Georgia Goodall, Sophie Nevrkla—at White Rabbit in the U.K. My chapter on 5-MeO-DMT drug development was commissioned and edited by Katie Ryder at *New York* magazine, with scrupulous fact-checking by Jack Denton and legal review by Jillian Robbins—thank you all for helping me wrangle this material.

I count myself lucky to have friends who read and commented on drafts or provided various forms of support, especially Sean Christie, Liam Kruger, Shaun Swingler, Brett Petzer, Carla Lamkin, and Meg Bernhard, who also helped out with translation. I am luckier still to have a mother and sister, Aliki and Yanna Romano, who love and encourage me in all that I do. Thank you to Steve Connolly for our conversations about publishing and so much more, and to my in-laws, Sue Willis and Paul Schissler, for so many years of *New Yorker* subscriptions. Matt Schissler, my brother-in-law, helped me think through knotty research problems. Above all, thank you to Jenny, my smart, courageous, and beautiful wife, for being with me every step of the way. This book would not exist without you.

Notes

Prologue

xv This releases a powerful: A 5-MeO-DMT facilitator and podcast host named Martin Ball credits himself with coining the phrase. In a lengthy email to me, he wrote of his first encounter with the molecule, "The only honest description I could give of the experience was that I'd just experienced the infinite reality of God, that God was the ONLY reality, and that THIS is what I actually was, in my non-egoically-identified and individuated form. For the first time in my life, I became comfortable and confident to use the word 'God,' as I could think of nothing better to give a name to what I'd just experienced. I also decided, at that time, that 'The God Molecule' was the most significant psychedelic that existed, and since no one really knew what it was, devoted myself to educating the world about it in whatever way I could, and made it the central focus of my podcast, talks, interviews, and subsequent books."

xv "If most hallucinogens": Davis and Weil, "Identity of a New World Psychoactive Toad."

xv Michael Pollan smoked: Pollan, *How to Change Your Mind.*

xv Hunter Biden credited: Biden, *Beautiful Things.*

xvi Mike Tyson rhapsodized: *The Joe Rogan Experience #1227—Mike Tyson.*

xvi In the 1950s, a pair: Hansen and Vial, "Defensive Behavior and Effects of Toxins in *Bufo alvarius.*"

xvi All toads produce toxins: Kennedy, "*Ecce Bufo.*"

xvi "It is a gaunt land": Van Dyke, *Desert,* 26.

xvii Biologists classify the Sonoran: This description is drawn from conversations with the desert ecologists Mark Dimmitt, Gary Nabhan, and Robert

Villa, as well as from Dimmitt, Comus, and Brewer, *Natural History of the Sonoran Desert,* chapters five and seven.

xvii Some scientists believe: Decades ago, Mark Dimmitt conducted research with spadefoot toads, another species adapted to life in the desert. He placed vibrating electric motors at the surface, and the toads "just came up like popcorn," he told me. Nobody has repeated the study with Sonoran Desert toads. See Dimmitt and Ruibal, "Environmental Correlates of Emergence in Spadefoot Toads."

xvii Males clasp onto females: The toads have also clutched "unsuspecting herpetologists." See Villa, "Toad in the Road."

xviii "How he did protestingly": Wright and Wright, *Handbook of Frogs and Toads,* 138.

xviii As many as four: This estimate was provided by Brian Sullivan, a professor at Arizona State University. There has been no formal research to date on Sonoran Desert toad survival rates.

xviii One of the toads was once: Luccioni and Wyman, "*Incilius alvarius* (Sonoran Desert Toad)."

CHAPTER 1: The Rise of the Toad Doctor

3 "Sooner or later, everyone": Descriptions of Octavio's various talks are drawn from online recordings, many of them available on his personal YouTube account.

4 an antidote to the materialism: Harvey, "La Vie Boheme."

4 Burning Man "*is* Silicon Valley": Willmetts, "Why Burning Man Is Silicon Valley."

5 Scholars had speculated: This mystery is explored further in chapter 2. See Davis and Weil, "Identity of a New World Psychoactive Toad."

5 "It allows you to have a dialogue": Rettig Hinojosa, *Toad of Dawn,* 122.

6 Octavio was born: For details on Octavio's childhood, I drew on his memoir, *Toad of Dawn.*

7 Like Octavio, Sandoval came from: Sandoval's biography is drawn largely from his own memoir, *The God Molecule.*

11 One of the first was Ralph Metzner: Metzner's work with 5-MeO-DMT is described in his landmark 2013 book, *The Toad and the Jaguar.*

14 The psychiatrist Stanislav Grof: Grof's account of using the molecule is from *When the Impossible Happens,* "*Gateway to the Absolute.*"

14 Another prominent voice: Oroc, *Tryptamine Palace.*

15 They carried out an online survey: Davis et al., "Epidemiology of 5-Methoxy-N,N-Dimethyltryptamine (5-MeO-DMT) Use."

15 But after conducting: Davis et al., "Psychedelic Treatment for Trauma-Related Psychological and Cognitive Impairment Among US Special Operations Forces Veterans."

15 The first formal lab study: Barsuglia et al., "Case Report SPECT Study and Theoretical Rationale for the Sequential Administration of Ibogaine and 5-MeO-DMT in the Treatment of Alcohol Use Disorder."

15 Many studies have identified: Reviewed in Barsuglia et al., "Intensity of Mystical Experiences Occasioned by 5-MeO-DMT and Comparison with a Prior Psilocybin Study."

16 It had never occurred: Most, *Bufo alvarius.*

17 A friend from that time: This characterization is by Rak Razam, a self-described "experiential journalist" from Australia, and appears in an introduction to Octavio's memoir. (Presumably Octavio enjoyed the phrase.)

19 Wherever he went: I obtained these from Octavio's Facebook account—he posted there prolifically, even addictively—and private groups for 5-MeO-DMT users.

19 "There couldn't be a better": Razam, introduction to *Toad of Dawn,* by Rettig Hinojosa.

20 Octavio starred: *Bufo Alvarius: The Underground Secret;* "Octavio Rettig & the Sonoran Desert Toad," an episode of *Shamans of the Global Village; The Toad, the Whale, and the Sun.*

21 During his research: Pollan, *How to Change Your Mind.*

CHAPTER 2: Magical Mystery Toads

22 In 1935, two chemists: Their findings were published in German, reflecting the scientific and political ties between the two countries, soon to become allies in World War II. Hoshino and Shimodaira, "Über die Synthese des Bufotenin-Methyl-Äthers (5-Methoxy-N-Dimethyl-Tryptamin) und Bufotenins (Synthesen in der Indol-Gruppe XV)."

22 Such tiny changes: Levi, *Periodic Table,* 60.

23 The new molecule's name: Molecule diagrams courtesy of Marvin JS by Chemaxon.

23 This changed in 1959: A concise history of the molecule is provided in Ermakova et al., "Narrative Synthesis of Research with 5-MeO-DMT."

23 For thousands of years: I drew ethnobiological detail from Torres and Repke, *Anadenanthera.*

23 In the early 1950s: Schultes, "New Narcotic Snuff from the Northwest Amazon"; Schultes, "Fifteen Years of Study of Psychoactive Snuffs of South America."

24 A tall, bespectacled man: For biographical detail on Schultes, I drew on Davis's excellent book, *One River,* and a *New Yorker* profile by Kahn, "Jungle Botanist." I also referred to two obituaries: Plotkin, "Richard Evans Schultes: Brief Life of a Pioneering Ethnobotanist and Conservationist," and Kandell, "Richard E. Schultes, 86, Dies."

24 "Time is running out": Schultes, "Burning the Library of Amazonia."

24 Then, in 1964: Davis and Weil, "Identity of a New World Psychoactive Toad."

25 His lifelong interest: Details on Erspamer are drawn from Whitaker-Azmitia, "Discovery of Serotonin and Its Role in Neuroscience," and Negri, "Vittorio Erspamer (1909–1999)."

25 "Land and sea are populated": Erspamer, Vittorio, and Pietro Melchiorri, "Active Polypeptides: From Amphibian Skin to Gastrointestinal Tract and Brain of Mammals." *Trends in Pharmacological Sciences* 1, no. 2 (1980): 391–95.

25 "an inexhaustible mine": Erspamer, "Peptides, Amphibian (Skin)."

25 Colleagues from around: These details are from the methodology section of Erspamer et al., "5-Methoxy- and 5-Hydroxy-Indolealkylamines in the Skin of *Bufo alvarius.*"

25 a small cohort of psychonauts: The underground history of synthetic 5-MeO-DMT experimentation is covered, patchily, in Davis and Weil, "Identity of a New World Psychoactive Toad," and Oroc, *Tryptamine Palace.* The first formal record of its use dates to 1970, when the psychedelic chemist Sasha Shulgin informed colleagues that he was conducting human trials with the compound. Nine volunteers, "all with considerable experience with drugs that can alter one's state of consciousness," he later wrote, were given five to ten milligrams of 5-MeO-DMT each, rolled into joints with dried tansy leaves. "The onset of action occurs in less than 60 seconds, reaches a plateau in the 2nd to 3rd minute, and is largely dissipated at 20 minutes, although there may be some lingering awareness for the remainder of an hour," Shulgin noted. "Centrally, there is the loss of some reality sense, some eyes-closed imagery and a general feeling of being enclosed and isolated." See de Smet, "Multidisciplinary Overview of Intoxicating Enema Rituals in the Western Hemisphere."

26 In 1956, a psychiatrist: Fabing and Hawkins, "Intravenous Bufotenine Injection in the Human Being."

26 Accounts like these: This description of Fabing's research is drawn from an essay he wrote for *Harper's Magazine,* "Toads, Mushrooms, and Schizophrenia."

27 Intriguingly, many of them shared: Molecule diagrams courtesy of Marvin JS by Chemaxon.

28 Across Mesoamerica, archaeologists: For a concise overview, see Davis and Weil, "Identity of a New World Psychoactive Toad."

28 Of the psychoactive plants: Weil and Davis, "*Bufo alvarius.*"

28 *Bufo marinus:* This chapter is indebted to Wade Davis, who wrote extensively about the mystery of psychedelic toads, including in "*Bufo marinus*" and, more fully, in *The Clouded Leopard,* 171.

28 "The Olmecs had a predisposition": Weaver, cited in Lyttle, Goldstein, and Gartz, "Bufo Toads and Bufotenine."

29 In the early 1970s: Knab's experiment is recounted in Kennedy, "*Ecce Bufo,*" and Davis and Weil, "Identity of a New World Psychoactive Toad."

30 Alison Kennedy was the heiress: Boulware, "Mondo 1995."

30 But Kennedy concluded: Kennedy, "*Ecce Bufo.*" This marvelously strange paper is worth a read.

32 In the early 1980s: Morgan, *Toads and Toadstools,* xiii.

32 While Morgan was pursuing: Stephanie Lewis, *Cane Toads,* 70.

34 But in 1988: Davis recounts the moral panic in "Smoking Toad." See also Lyttle, Goldstein, and Gartz, "Bufo Toads and Bufotenine."

34 Later that year, a doctor: Horgan, "Bufo Abuse."

34 At a conference on crack: Lyttle, Goldstein, and Gartz, "Bufo Toads and Bufotenine."

35 The DEA official later: Horgan, "Bufo Abuse."

36 Wade Davis stumbled: Davis wrote a book about this research: *The Serpent and the Rainbow.* In 2013, at the start of my journalism career, a writer friend lent me a copy, which he had found on a nonfiction reading list for sci-fi and fantasy authors. The contention of the list was that imaginary worlds ought to be at least as complex and strange (to Western readers) as those that had evolved in reality.

36 "At any one time": Davis, *One River,* 20.

36 "a macabre assortment": Davis, *The Clouded Leopard,* 180.

38 provided inmates for scientific experiments: Staff Writer, "Ohio Inmates, Soldiers Were Subjects of Risky Postwar Medical Testing," and Hirschmann, "From Squirrels to Biological Weapons."

38 Upon being injected: Fabing and Hawkins, "Intravenous Bufotenine Injection in the Human Being." The full quotation, published in a respected scientific journal, now reads as breathtakingly casual: "If the color of an eggplant were diluted, it would approximate the unique purple hue of the faces of these subjects."

38 In the 1950s, a pharmacologist: My description of the drug farm is from Campbell, Olsen, and Walden, *Narcotic Farm.*

38 "If you wanted it": Details on the MKUltra program are from Marks, *Search for the "Manchurian Candidate,"* 64.

39 Yet Isbell could find: This letter is quoted in Turner and Merlis, "Effect of Some Indolealkylamines on Man." Isbell also described his bufotenine experiments in Wassén and Holmstedt, "Use of Paricá."

39 There would be just one: Opacity, "Central Islip State Hospital."

39 In this study, schizophrenic: Turner and Merlis, "Effect of Some Indolealkylamines on Man."

40 Perhaps because of their appalling: An abstruse debate continues today about the psychoactivity of bufotenine. After conducting an array of self-experiments in the 1990s, which he termed "psychonautic bioassays," the ethnobotanist Jonathan Ott reported that the substance imparted a shimmering "magical varnish" over reality and "occasionally a sudden and dramatic dimming of the visual field, as though the starting of a heavy motor had dropped line-voltage and dimmed the lights." He concluded that bufotenine was psychoactive via multiple routes of administration and dismissed counterarguments as "wrong-headed" and "embarrassing." For a review of these and other studies, see Torres and Repke, *Anadenanthera,* chapter five.

40 after reviewing this perplexing literature: Davis, "*Bufo marinus.*"

40 Weil had a polarizing: Pollan, *How to Change Your Mind,* and Lattin, *Harvard Psychedelic Club.*

41 He once testified: Weil, "Saturn Return."

42 people typically smoked small pinches: Erowid, "5-MeO-DMT Timeline."

42 "I and most other Church": Lyttle, "Drug Based Religions and Contemporary Drug Taking."

42 "It will be necessary": This advice appeared in Gottlieb, *Legal Highs.*

43 The first person in modern times: Information on Nelson is drawn from *Hamilton's Pharmacopeia,* season 3, episode 1, "Synthetic Toad Venom Machine," aired Jan. 4, 2021; Rodrigue, "Story Behind a 1984 Hallucinogenic Pamphlet from Denton Is Just as Trippy as Its Subject"; and Villa, "Toad in the Road."

44 His identity would remain: *Hamilton's Pharmacopeia,* season 2, episode 1, "The Psychedelic Toad," aired Nov. 28, 2017.

45 One of them was a fixture: In addition to my own interviews, this portrait

of White Dog is drawn from Gallagher, "Smoking Toad," and Davis, "Smoking Toad." (Are the titles a coincidence?)

46 An academic reviewer: Davis, *The Clouded Leopard,* 196.

46 More publicity in this vein: "Missionary for Toad Venom Is Facing Charges," *New York Times.*

47 During their research: Furst, "Symbolism and Psychopharmacology."

CHAPTER 3: People of the Desert and Sea

50 He was also, as one: For descriptions of the Barnetts and other prominent Seri clans, I am indebted to Yetman, *Where the Desert Meets the Sea,* and Burckhalter, *Among Turtle Hunters and Basket Makers.*

50 Miguel was known: Further details on Miguel Barnett appear in Ogarrio Huitrón's thesis, "Icóos," and Harrington, "Seri Dreams."

51 In 2017, he was awarded: Gobierno de México, "Entregan los Premios Nacionales de Ciencias, Artes y Literatura 2017."

51 "Their predilections lie": Yetman, *Where the Desert Meets the Sea.*

52 "Seri towns probably": Bourillón-Moreno, "Exclusive Fishing Zone as a Strategy for Managing Fishery Resources by the Seri Indians."

52 "His face was full": Rettig Hinojosa, *Toad of Dawn,* 140.

53 The village was undeniably: My description of Punta Chueca in 2011 is from interviews with Octavio and researchers who were working there at the time.

55 Long before Spanish settlers: This account of precolonial Seri life, and their subsequent encounters with Spanish settlers, is drawn largely from Sheridan, *Empire of Sand,* and Spicer, *Cycles of Conquest.* Another key text is Felger and Moser, *People of the Desert and Sea.*

56 "There is no people": Moser and Marlett, "Seri Kinship Terminology."

56 "Such behavior undoubtedly": Felger and Moser, *People of the Desert and Sea,* 6.

56 Sometimes they stumbled: Felger, "Seris and the Guy Who Cuts the Tops off Plants."

57 "It breasts gales": Further ethnographic details are from McGee, *Seri Indians.* This monograph, written in the late nineteenth century, is fraught with racial prejudice yet offers a detailed portrait of certain Seri customs.

57 While riding these vessels: Burckhalter, "William Neil Smith and the Seri Indians."

57 "The tribe abounds": McGee, *Seri Indians.*

57 "Sometimes a man": Felger and Moser, *People of the Desert and Sea.*

58 The site became known: Nabhan, *Desert Terroir,* chapter 8.

62 As he lay dying: McGee, *Seri Indians,* 75.

63 That decade, the development: Bourillón-Moreno, "Exclusive Fishing Zone as a Strategy for Managing Fishery Resources by the Seri Indians."

63 There is a photograph: The photograph, plus a description of the totoaba fishery, is in Bahre, Bourillón, and Torre, "Seri and Commercial Totoaba Fishing."

63 "The North Americans amused themselves": See Spicer, *Cycles of Conquest,* chapter 4.

64 Both episodes are true: The Sinaloa cartel boss was Héctor Salazar; in retaliation for his wife's death, he had his rival's three children executed. The drug trafficker who underwent plastic surgery was Amado Carrillo Fuentes; his surgeons were tortured and encased in concrete-filled steel drums.

65 The event had been promoted: The stream was broadcast on the official Facebook page of Mexico Tourism: www.facebook.com/share/v/1FfGbD9zxH/.

65 Accompanying him in the truck: The footage aired alongside an accompanying article by the reporter Norma Ponce: "De Francia, EU y Alemania viajan a México para probar 'la medicina del sapo.'"

66 "He gives the impression": Ball, "Psychedelic Bromance."

68 "Before, nobody": The tarred road was completed in 2013, less than two years after Octavio first visited Punta Chueca, so the timing was likely coincidental. See Marlett, "'Trooqui Treen.'"

68 Alcoholism ran rampant: My description of Punta Chueca in the 1930s is based largely on Coolidge and Coolidge, "Last of the Seris," and Burckhalter, "William Neil Smith and the Seri Indians."

69 Within just two years: William Neil Smith, quoted in Marlett, *Shells on a Desert Shore.*

69 "The news spread": Felger, "Seris and the Guy Who Cuts the Tops off Plants."

69 This shift formed part: Bourillón-Moreno, "Exclusive Fishing Zone as a Strategy for Managing Fishery Resources by the Seri Indians."

70 They knew it as: Marlett, *Shells on a Desert Shore,* vxii.

70 In one fight between: The gunfight was described by the anthropologist William Neil Smith in a 1946 letter to his mother. See Burckhalter, "William Neil Smith and the Seri Indians."

70 The mule hobbled ashore: McGee, *Seri Indians,* 112.

70 But the market promptly: Bourillón-Moreno, "Exclusive Fishing Zone as a Strategy for Managing Fishery Resources by the Seri Indians."

70 "The process of acculturation": Carmony and Brown, *Tales from Tiburon,* viii.

71 One Desemboque man had both: This anecdote is related in Burdick, "They Wouldn't Be Civilized."

71 In 1940, John Steinbeck: Steinbeck, *Log from the Sea of Cortez,* 295.

71 Yet even as economic: My descriptions of Seri traditional culture are drawn largely from Felger and Moser, *People of the Desert and Sea.* Other details are from Ogarrio Huitrón's thesis.

72 Yurchenco had to wait: Goren, "Henrietta Yurchenco."

72 "Seri culture, once concerned": A colorful biography of Smith appears in Burckhalter, "William Neil Smith and the Seri Indians."

73 One of their early visitors: Felger, "Seris and the Guy Who Cuts the Tops off Plants."

CHAPTER 4: Backlash

78 As a subsequent investigation: I obtained hundreds of pages of legal documents from Villalpando, who trained as a lawyer himself.

84 In the 1960s, Coe: Cyphers, Zuñiga, and Di Castro, "Another Look at *Bufo marinus* and the San Lorenzo Olmec," and Davis and Weil, "Identity of a New World Psychoactive Toad."

85 A former beauty queen: In 2004, at nineteen years old, Arredondo appeared in a photo shoot for Nuestra Belleza Coahuila, a state beauty pageant.

85 On December 26: Olivares, "Rescatan cuerpo de ahogada en Cenote."

86 But during a conference: Octavio gave this talk at "Beyond Psychedelics," a conference in Prague. It was recorded: slideslive.com/38908636/light-and-shadows-of-current-use-of-toad-medicine.

86 "It is astonishing": This was in a public letter, published at the URL 5-meo-dmt-malpractice.org, that has subsequently been taken off-line.

87 "It is not necessary": Peluso et al., "Reflections on Crafting an Ayahuasca Community Guide for the Awareness of Sexual Abuse."

87 In the 1980s, before: Passie, "Early Use of MDMA ('Ecstasy') in Psychotherapy."

87 But in 2018: Busby, "MDMA Trials Under Review in Canada over Alleged Abuse of Study Participants."

87 In a civil claim brought to court: Lindsay, "As Psychedelic Therapy Goes Mainstream, Former Patient Warns of Danger of Sexual Abuse."
88 "In the wake of two decades": Evans et al., "Extended Difficulties Following the Use of Psychedelic Drugs."
90 During one impromptu group: These details from the trip are from Ball, "Psychedelic Bromance."
92 "One of the biggest fears": Octavio said this in May 2018 at "Exploring Psychedelics," a conference in Oregon. An online recording has since been deleted.
94 After Octavio starred: The title of Octavio's VICE documentary was "Getting High with a Hallucinogenic Toad Prophet." Gerry appeared in *Hamilton's Pharmacopeia,* season 2, episode 1, "The Psychedelic Toad," aired Nov. 28, 2017.
97 "What I've learned": This was said by Mario Garnier, the founder of the World Bufo Alvarius Congress, at "Exploring Psychedelics" in 2018.
98 A psychotherapist who smoked: This account is documented in Oroc, *Tryptamine Palace,* appendix 6, "Heaven and Hell."
98 "I thought I was really": These trip reports are from the long-running psychedelic database Erowid. See Cavebaby, "Knocked Me on My Ass"; Scala, "Road to Hell and Back"; and vokest, "I Ended Up Praying to Jesus Christ."
98 found dead on a camping trip: Sklerov et al., "Fatal Intoxication Following the Ingestion of 5-Methoxy-N,N-Dimethyltryptamine in an Ayahuasca Preparation."
98 an artist from Wyoming: "Coroner's Inquest Rules Death of Birkholz Accidental but Possibly Preventable," *Buckrail.*
98 Spanish porn star: Fitz-Gibbon, "Spanish Porn Actor Charged with Murder in Toad-Venom Death."
99 In a grim foreshadowing: Metzner, *The Toad and the Jaguar,* 65.
99 "And when I see": Octavio said this on a panel at "Beyond Psychedelics," a 2018 conference in Prague: slideslive.com/38909130/challenges-and-shadows-of-current-psychedelic-movement-panel-discussion.
99 an alcoholic in his forties: This admission occurred at the International Transpersonal Conference, also in Prague, in 2017: slideslive.com/38903120/otac-toad-medicine-and-its-role-in-modern-world.
102 He had made a "star entrance": Shewey, "Romancing the Toad." The author also shared his private notes from the congress with me.
103 breezily described some of his methods: Psymposia, "After a Year of Con-

troversy, MAPS Canada Executive Director Mark Haden Announces Resignation."

103 A month after the uproar: The panel discussion was titled, fittingly, "Challenges and Shadows of the Current Psychedelic Movement": slideslive.com/38909130/challenges-and-shadows-of-current-psychedelic-movement-panel-discussion?ref=speaker-5282-latest.

105 Signaling a shift: The WBAC website no longer exists, but a copy of the letter was posted on a web forum called DMT Nexus: www.dmt-nexus.me.

105 Four deaths were documented: The original letter is no longer available online but was covered by various psychedelics blogs: Lorna Liana, "Bufo Deaths & Fraud Involving Toad 'Shamans' Octavio Rettig & Gerry Sandoval," *EntheoNation,* accessed Sept. 10, 2020, entheonation.com/blog/death-fraud-octavio-rettig-gerry-sandoval/.

106 Following the publication: Gerry posted this to a Facebook account he administered: The Bufo Alvarius Foundation's Post, Facebook, May 13, 2019, www.facebook.com/BUFOFOUNDATION/posts/pfbid0Zo77Ui5EZCFKEj8ft5YgBSXzan1mtBDaDP1CydAMB8MnhLojdV88jD2B5SMUJDLAl.

106 In a 2023 documentary: Channel 4, "The Psychedelic Toad Revolution," www.youtube.com/watch?v=DzApbkgu89k&t=1291s.

CHAPTER 5: The Sonoran Toad Rush

113 In the summer of 1952: Waldron, "Carnival of Frogs."

114 During the Great Depression: For this material on Broel, I am indebted to Sarah Laskow, author of the fantastic *Atlas Obscura* piece "The Giant Frog Farms of the 1930s Were a Giant Failure."

114 The European Union: Auliya et al., "Numerous Uncertainties in the Multifaceted Global Trade in Frogs' Legs with the EU as the Major Consumer."

115 Only the most inventive creatures: The weasels anecdote is from Morgan, *Toads and Toadstools,* 53. Smaller species of toad are more vulnerable to predation. In an unusual trophic backflip, baby spadefoot toads, also native to the Sonoran Desert, are sucked into the mud and devoured by the larvae of horseflies, which bury themselves beside ephemeral ponds. "Adult spadefoot toads might on occasion gulp down the very fly that as a larva digested one of the toad's childhood companions," notes one study, cited in DeGraaff, *The Book of the Toad,* 58. Raccoons have learned to flip

Sonoran Desert toads and tear into their soft bellies, avoiding their poison glands altogether.

115 tasted like smoked chicken: Davis, *The Clouded Leopard,* 179.

115 In another experiment: Wassersug, "On the Comparative Palatability of Some Dry-Season Tadpoles from Costa Rica."

116 The toads kept on coming: Groffen and Porter, *Kimberley Toad Busters.*

116 The dog was soon dead: Musgrave and Cochran, "*Bufo alvarius,* a Poisonous Toad."

117 Mexico was on its way: Lopez, "Mexico Named Deadliest Country for Environmental Activists."

118 The Yaqui would decorate: Villa, "Toad in the Road."

118 a VICE documentary about the toads: *Hamilton's Pharmacopeia,* season 2, episode 1, "The Psychedelic Toad," aired Nov. 28, 2017.

119 Villa saw the flood: Villa, "Toad in the Road."

119 Amphibians are the most: Luedke et al., "Ongoing Declines for the World's Amphibians in the Face of Emerging Threats."

119 "an ethically dubious trip": deKorne, "Network Feedback," 14.

120 Fossils of their skeletons: These geological details are from Van Devender and Brusca, "Deep History of the Sonoran Desert," p. 67.

120 Nearly fifteen hundred years ago: Sheridan, "Human Ecology of the Sonoran Desert," 102.

120 In the nineteenth century, settlers: Moreno, "Never-Ending Source of Water."

121 "With a few exceptions": Wright and Wright, *Handbook of Frogs and Toads,* 135.

121 "Octavio is simply unstoppable": Ball, "Psychedelic Bromance."

121 deployed military troops: Sotomayor, "Militarization in Mexico and Its Implications."

121 Mexico's drug wars intensified: According to the UN Office on Drugs and Crime, Mexico's homicide rate in 2007, per 100,000 people, was 8; by 2011 this had risen to 24.

125 there was a feeling: My reconstruction of the WBAC conference is drawn from videos of the sessions and eyewitness descriptions by attendees.

125 He was living in poverty: I obtained a criminal complaint from the U.S. District Court in Arizona describing Amistron's deportation history.

129 more than 100,000 such victims: Amnesty International, *Disappearing Again.*

131 "When held in the hand": Wright and Wright, *Handbook of Frogs and Toads,* 137.

131 Global production of cocaine: According to the UN Office on Drugs and Crime, global cocaine production in 2023 exceeded 3,700 tons. United Nations Office on Drugs and Crime, *World Drug Report 2025.*

132 Researchers have documented: Stringham et al., "Dark Web Trades Wildlife, but Mostly for Use as Drugs."

132 The dealer later appeared: A German documentary crew released an entertaining and disturbing documentary about toad smoking in 2023. See STRG_F, *Krötengift gegen Depressionen* (Toad Venom for Depression: Does It Really Work?).

132 "I don't think there is a good": This talk was at the World Bufo Alvarius Congress. The footage appeared in *Hamilton's Pharmacopeia,* season 3, episode 1, "Synthetic Toad Venom Machine," aired Jan. 4, 2021.

134 Vendors abandoned their market stalls: This description is drawn from a video report by *Milenio,* "Tras enfrentamiento, 'sitian' Magdalena de Kino en Sonora," available on YouTube: www.youtube.com/watch?v=JV8EJqoJtS0. Further details were obtained from Mexican newspaper coverage.

134 Toad poachers have snuck: Victor, "National Park Service Asks Visitors to Please Stop Licking Toads."

134 Border agents have intercepted: "Jeff Moore, a senior wildlife inspector with the U.S. Fish and Wildlife Service, said that people have been caught attempting to bring the toad or its secretions into the United States." See Kutz, "Hallucinogenic Toad in Peril."

135 Afterward, a scientific expedition: Emory, *Report on the United States and Mexican Boundary Survey.*

135 These were shipped: Fouquette, "Remarks on the Type Specimen of *Bufo alvarius* Girard." Charles Frédéric Girard seldom ventured into the field, working mainly with museum specimens. Shortly after identifying the toad, he took a trip to Paris, where he remained until the American Civil War broke out in 1861. In a departure from taxonomy, he then became a leading French supporter of the Confederacy, supplying its army with medical equipment and weapons. He slipped through a naval blockade and visited the South, writing propagandistic accounts of the war in an unsuccessful effort to convince Emperor Napoleon III to intervene. After a stint as a medical doctor, Girard spent his final years writing technical papers about fishes and flatworms.

135 One of the toad specimens: The catalog number for this specimen at the Smithsonian (viewable online) is USNM 2572.

136 Illegal border crossings: Putzel-Kavanaugh and Soto, "Shifting Patterns

and Policies Reshape Migration to U.S.-Mexico Border in Major Ways in 2023."

136 Its construction had involved: A fuller description of the peak, which is named Cerro del Fresnal: "Construction material and rubbish, like rebar and steel mesh are present here. There is no protective fencing to keep people, vehicles, wildlife or livestock out of the area. There is no signage or warning devices to alert people to the extreme danger present here. A commercial generator from the site had slid down slope and slammed into the border wall." See Traphagen, *Border Wall Restoration Site Reports.*

136 Yet the wall remained: Perez, "2 Arizona Border Wall Gaps Closed, 50 Remain near Sasabe as Construction Continues."

136 Mexican cartels, as the historian: Nolan, "On the Iron River."

136 Controlling migrant corridors: Verza, "How Mexican Cartels Manage the Flow of Migrants on Their Way to the US Border."

136 Not long after I passed: This description is drawn from press coverage, for example, Loew, "War Between Drug Cartels Forcing Residents of Mexican Border Town to Flee into Arizona," and Asmann, "Sonora, Mexico, Under Siege amid Sinaloa Cartel Battle over Migrant Smuggling."

136 hundreds dead since 2020: For an overview of the conflict, see Mendoza, "Depoliticizing Conflict in Sonora, Mexico." Further details from press coverage, for example, Luna, "Hallan 10 cuerpos en carretera de Sonora."

136 Signs everywhere advertised: Some details on the migrant smuggling economy are drawn from Asmann and Dudley, "Desperation in the Desert."

138 "Evidently he was in the wrong": Melendez, "U.S. Grad Student Brutally Killed on Mexican Field Trip."

138 People familiar with his operation: At \$150 per gram, a kilogram of toad secretion would be worth \$150,000. Five kilograms would be worth \$750,000.

138 They are among the poorest: Ortega et al., "Agribusiness, Corporate Social Responsibility, and Health of Agricultural Migrant Workers."

138 Child labor is pervasive: see Range, "Settled and Migrant Child Farm Labor in Sonora."

139 A woman from Canada: This account is drawn from detailed Facebook and TikTok posts by Amistron's accuser, whom I am not identifying here. She emphasized in public comments that she would not be taking legal action against Amistron.

140 A biochemical engineer: See, for example, Barraza-Guardado, "Effluents

of Shrimp Farms and Its Influence on the Coastal Ecosystems of Bahía de Kino, Mexico."

140 "I felt as if my eyes": Cantú, "What 120 Degrees Looks Like in One of Mexico's Hottest Cities."

143 Ortiz and Santos-Barrera, meanwhile: Their research was featured in *New York Times:* Nuwer, "These Toads Have Psychedelic Powers, but They'd Prefer to Keep It Quiet."

144 "opens up access to the subconscious": Bill Atkinson published detailed instructions for manufacturing and using his pens, which he called Light Wands. See Grace Within, "Jaguar (5-MeO-DMT) Vape Pens."

145 A single gram: In the United States, at the time of this reporting, the cost of a ceremony varied widely but was seldom below $100, so this figure is a conservative estimate.

147 In narco culture, spiritual beliefs: See, for example, Flanagin, "Rise of the Narco-Saints," and Vincent, "Santa Muerte and the 'Religious' Saints Drug Cartels Worship."

CHAPTER 6: Wild, Wild Country

150 They protect themselves: Thomson, *Attenborough's Fabulous Frogs.*

150 "The evil force exits the body": Tastevin, "Le fleuve Murú." A translation of the paper is available on the psychedelic database Erowid.

150 In one paper, he and his colleagues: Erspamer et al., "Pharmacological Studies of 'Sapo' from the Frog *Phyllomedusa bicolor* Skin."

150 Despite scant clinical evidence: Sacco et al., "Kambo."

151 "It kind of looks like a celebrity": Williams, "Can You Poison Your Way to Good Health?"

151 Many frog collectors live: See Crawford, "Is Kambo Ethical?," and Williams, "Illegal, Occasionally Deadly, and Not Much Fun."

156 "Watch out, Brian!": I filmed the entire encounter on my phone, and it is the wildest video I have ever recorded.

159 On the winter solstice: My description of this episode is drawn from eyewitness accounts. It is also widely spoken about in the Seri community, although not always to outsiders.

165 In 1961, a Seri man: Johnston provides a history of this trade in "Seri Ironwood Carving."

166 Even by the nonconformist: This portrait of Astorga is drawn from multiple sources, including Yetman, *Where the Desert Meets the Sea,* 25, and Burckhalter, *Among Turtle Hunters and Basket Makers,* 29. The coral snake detail is from Burdick, "They Wouldn't Be Civilized."

166 Astorga was a master: Yetman, "Miguel's Last Santo."
166 Astorga's wife had peculiarities: Yetman, *Sonora,* 165.
166 "Their transition": In Carmony and Brown, *Tales from Tiburon,* 6.
166 "They are tested, studied": Johnston, *Seri Indians of Sonora, Mexico.*
166 The Seri had become renowned: Ryerson, "Seri Ironwood Carving."
167 Dense stands along the floodplains: Felger and Moser, *People of the Desert and Sea,* 176.
167 In one version, Astorga: These accounts are sourced, variously, from Yetman, *Where the Desert Meets the Sea,* Narchi, "One Knowledge, Two Conduits," and conversations with the ethnobiologist Gary Nabhan.
167 There are also more prosaic: Felger and Moser, *People of the Desert and Sea,* 174; Johnston, "Seri Ironwood Carving."
169 The book was later unmasked: A thorough debunking of Castaneda's story is provided in de Mille, *Castaneda's Journey.*
169 Gordon Wasson, a banker: Vidriales and Ovies, "Psychedelic Tourism in Mexico, a Thriving Trend."
170 An editor of Castaneda's: Marshall, "Dark Legacy of Carlos Castaneda."
170 "They are mostly a slinking": Yetman, *Where the Desert Meets the Sea,* 106.
172 no longstanding tradition of sweat lodges: Nabhan burst out laughing when I told him about the sweat lodge theory and confirmed that these were a recent introduction to Seriland.
172 "The Seris hated authority": Felger, "Seris and the Guy Who Cuts the Tops off Plants."
174 "Sometimes we milk": Kilham, "On the Toad Road."
175 "The buzz of power tools": St. Antoine, "Ironwood."
178 "An unusual number of those": Evans, "Sowilo."
178 "The ability to induce": Novak, "LSD Before Leary."
179 As the journalist Jules Evans: In around 2020, after a Miami court ruled that Cluzel owed an investor $115,000, he fled to Mexico and never paid the sum. "He's on the run," Evans told me, noting that Cluzel had not responded to his reporting, either before or after publication. At the time, Cluzel was also a defendant in an ongoing trial in Miami for fraudulent inducement, breach of fiduciary duty, civil conspiracy, unfair trade practices, and negligent misrepresentation. See Evans, "Sowilo."
179 "This is the medicine of the ego": Evans, "Victoria Wueschner on Harm Reduction."
180 He warned about the dangers: Welwood, "On Spiritual Bypassing and Relationship."

CHAPTER 7: Rocket Ship into the Void

182 It was built: The National Heritage List for England has a detailed entry for Beckley Park: historicengland.org.uk/listing/the-list/list-entry/1001087.

182 "the look of a fairy-tale castle": Foster, "Fairytale Garden Surrounding a 16th-Century Hunting Lodge."

182 appeared in a Harry Potter film: Milligan, "Countess of Cannabis Has a Hole in Her Head and a Job with Canopy."

182 In 1970, she was filmed: An engaging overview of Feilding's trepanation history appears in Turner, "Like a Hole in the Head."

183 Her grandmother was a trailblazing: Fitzmaurice, "Clotilde Brewster."

184 a British spy-catcher: Cardiff, "Sketch of the Life of Ñanamoli Thera (Osbert Moore)."

184 "The flat was a centre": Mellen, *Bore Hole.*

184 "one of the original microdosers": Feilding gave many interviews. This remark is from one of them: www.youtube.com/watch?v=f_9-k_mFkBU.

184 She had recently married: James Donald Charteris, 13th Earl of Wemyss and 9th Earl of March, also known as James Charteris, was a page of honor to the queen mother. See "Lord Neidpath," SourceWatch. His uncle, Baron Charteris of Amisfield, served as private secretary to Queen Elizabeth II.

185 New research—some of it supported: For example, Carhart-Harris et al., "Psilocybin with Psychological Support for Treatment-Resistant Depression."

185 A host of biotech start-ups: Rivlin, "Exploring the Psychedelics Landscape."

186 A facility in the United States: The facility is run by the Usona Foundation, a psychedelic nonprofit.

187 Recent surveys have indicated: Substance Abuse and Mental Health Services Administration, *Key Substance Use and Mental Health Indicators in the United States.*

187 Critics have coined a term: See www.psymposia.com/corporadelic/.

187 Major early investors in psychedelics: O'Brien, "Business Gets Ready to Trip."

187 In 2021, one industry publication: Psychedelic Times Staff, "There's a Land Grab for Psychedelic Patents."

188 Numerous clinical trials: See Fuentes et al., "Therapeutic Use of LSD in Psychiatry."

188 He shares his second name: King, "Mind-Altering Trip of Acid Countess Amanda Feilding."

188 Cosmo has joked: This was during a panel discussion at Psychedelic Science 2023, which I attended.

189 his first documentary: *Breaking the Taboo* (2011).

189 a streak of business acumen: Cremades, "Cosmo Feilding Mellen on Selling His First Company for $80 Million."

189 "There was this burst": This was also at Psychedelic Science 2023.

189 He has described Beckley: Cosmo has said this on multiple occasions. See Cremades, "Cosmo Feilding Mellen on Selling His First Company for $80 Million."

189 They appointed some: The scientific advisory board, chaired by Amanda Feilding, included such luminaries as Robin Carhart-Harris, Matthew W. Johnson, and Frederick Reinholdt. Janssen hires included Steve Wooding, former head of global commercial strategy and market access; Fiona Dunbar, former vice president of global medical affairs and patient engagement; and Frank Wiegand, an esteemed neuroscientist.

190 Numerous studies with psychedelics: Reckweg et al., "Evaluation of the Peak Experience Scale as a Rapid Assessment Tool."

190 slip through the blood-brain barrier: Reckweg et al., "Clinical Pharmacology and Potential Therapeutic Applications of 5-Methoxy-N,N-Dimethyltryptamine (5-MeO-DMT)."

190 A 2025 brain-imaging study: Timmermann et al., "Exploring 5-MeO-DMT as a Pharmacological Model for Deconstructed Consciousness."

191 the dogs stiffened their muscles: These details were disclosed in a patent filing: "Pharmaceutical Composition Comprising 5-Methoxy-N, N-Dimethyltryptamine."

192 Schönharting's family owned: Many of these biographical details are sourced from the Danish press, for example, Kailay, "'Snedig' dansk biotekinvestor satsede og blev forgyldt."

192 "I was second-class": Ostrynski, "Han skulle vise dem."

192 "one of the best stock pickers in the world": Stamm, "Interview with Lars Hellerung Christiansen."

192 Schönharting described this approach: Tüchsen, "Major Investor and Secret Team Behind Outstanding Return on Biotech."

193 Schönharting was tersely efficient: Tüchsen, "He Bites His Tongue for No One."

193 "When he smells blood": Tüchsen, "En enmandshær går i krig."

193 He stocked his Copenhagen apartment: I was told this by a Danish reporter who interviewed Schönharting at home.

193 The first scientific survey: Davis et al., "Epidemiology of 5-Methoxy-N,N-Dimethyltryptamine (5-MeO-DMT) Use."

194 "miracle drug": Harbonic_Older, "Journey to the Center of the Onion."

194 Her research showed: Uthaug et al., "Single Inhalation of Vapor from Dried Toad Secretion Containing 5-Methoxy-N,N-Dimethyltryptamine (5-MeO-DMT) in a Naturalistic Setting Is Related to Sustained Enhancement of Satisfaction with Life, Mindfulness-Related Capacities, and a Decrement of Psychopathological Symptoms."

195 disclosed in subsequent patent filings: Terwey, "Treatment of Mental Disorders."

196 would not mandate any therapy: These statements were made in corporate filings with the SEC and in public presentations of GH's research.

197 In March 2019, two years: Reckweg et al., "Phase 1, Dose-Ranging Study to Assess Safety and Psychoactive Effects of a Vaporized 5-Methoxy-N,N-Dimethyltryptamine Formulation (GH001) in Healthy Volunteers."

198 people could be dosed multiple times in a day: Reckweg et al., "Evaluation of the Peak Experience Scale as a Rapid Assessment Tool."

198 Those who made it: Reckweg et al., "Phase 1/2 Trial to Assess Safety and Efficacy of a Vaporized 5-Methoxy-N,N-Dimethyltryptamine Formulation."

200 On the final morning: "From Observational Research to Therapeutic Applications: 5-MeO-DMT," virtualtrip.maps.org/video/from-observational-research-to-therapeutic-applications-5-meo-dmt/.

201 Before him, on the same stage: "5-MeO-DMT as a Mental Health Tool," virtualtrip.maps.org/video/5-meo-dmt-as-a-mental-health-tool-exploring-possible-mechanisms-of-action-the-reactivation-phenomenon-and-some-ethical-considerations-regarding-the-sonoran-desert-toad/.

201 During its phase 1 trials: Rucker et al., "Phase 1, Placebo-Controlled, Single Ascending Dose Trial." I obtained further details about the trial from Beckley staffers who spoke with me anonymously.

202 This was dramatically underscored: Kupferschmidt, "What's Next for Psychedelics After MDMA Rejection?"

203 "The treatment is the human": Rowland, "Thanks to This Man, MDMA Could Soon Be Legal for Therapy."

204 According to Beckley's published findings: Rucker et al., "Phase 1, Placebo-Controlled, Single Ascending Dose Trial."

206 complaints to a British health-care agency: Evans, "Psychedelic Treatments for Depressed Mums."

207 open-access method for synthesizing: Sherwood et al., "Synthesis and Characterization of 5-MeO-DMT Succinate for Clinical Use."

210 The title of her talk: virtualtrip.maps.org/video/a-life-of-science-and-dreams-the-dawn-of-the-psychedelic-age/.

210 Feilding was joined onstage: virtualtrip.maps.org/video/a-family-legacy-from-a-mother-to-her-sons/.

210 He once joked on a podcast: Rock made this comment on episode 77 of *Trip on This with Kat Walsh,* "Psilocybin Mushroom Therapy After Traumatic Events." Rock also described his mother as loving and warm. "A lot of children feel a bit embarrassed by their parents," he added. "It was definitely not the easiest mom to have . . . I definitely bristled."

210 After graduating from Oxford: Rock founded a development company called Socially Conscious Capital, "a strategic land promotion company with a difference." One of their projects, in a woodland area near Norwich, drew fierce local resistance and was ultimately turned down by planning officials. "The issue is not about housing supply," said the local mayor, who was opposed to the development. "It is about making a profit from land which has been used by generations for public recreation."

211 an earl twice over: "Publishers and Knights Bankrolling UKIP," Channel 4.

211 entered conservative politics: For a detailed account of Rock's political career and involvement with Grenfell, see O'Hagan, "Tower."

211 "They're not some panacea": This was also at Psychedelic Science, during a panel discussion about psychedelic-assisted therapy, although the video has since been taken down from the event archive.

211 Emails revealed afterward: At a subsequent inquiry, Rock said that he had only "skimmed" an email about the safety of the cladding. He had, however, given aesthetic feedback on the design. "I'd personally prefer the battleship grey," he wrote. "I am less convinced by the champagne colour." See Symonds, "Grenfell Councillor Queried Colour of Cladding but Not Safety." Also see Booth, "Grenfell: Councillor Was Told About Cheaper Cladding Plan Before Fire."

211 tone-deaf piece in *Newsweek:* Feilding-Mellen, "I Was Attacked as a Politician."

212 She was enthralled: Feilding gave many interviews about this notion, for example, Adams, "Amanda Feilding: 'LSD Can Get Deep Down and Reset the Brain.'"

212 a formative trauma: Miller, "Amanda Feilding—Countess and Pioneering Psychonaut."

212 notorious early figure in the counterculture: Penner, "Psychedelic Pioneer and Confidence Man."

213 "an absurd fiction": "Our English Hapsburgs," in Round, *Studies in Peerage and Family History.*

213 acquired a third of Beckley Psytech: "Atai Life Sciences Makes $50M Investment in Beckley Psytech," Psychedelic Alpha.

213 sweeping European patent: Psychedelic Alpha covered the brewing IP war between Beckley and GH in detail: Smith, "Pα+ Psychedelic Patent Analysis."

214 further toxicology studies: GH has developed a proprietary device for vaporizing its 5-MeO-DMT formulation, seeking to replace the commercially available Volcano. In corporate presentations, the company has described this as part of its wider patent strategy. The clinical hold was first revealed in September 2023, with the FDA demanding further toxicology studies and device information. As of August 2025, the hold has not been lifted, causing GH's share price to fall sharply. For deeper analysis, see "Pα+ Psychedelic Bulletin #204," Psychedelic Alpha.

214 In an additional blow: Porta Sophia, "All Pending Claims Rejected for GH Research Ireland Ltd. U.S. Patent."

214 Feilding died of cancer: Rosenwald, "Amanda Feilding, Eccentric Countess Who Backed Psychedelic Meds, Dies at 82."

214 deal valued at $370 million: Hardman, "Breaking: Atai Moves to Acquire Beckley."

CHAPTER 8: All the Darkness Is Vanished

226 peyote ceremonies were outlawed: Copes et al., "'Plants Don't Have a Culture to Appropriate.'"

226 María Sabina: Nolan, "The Healer, the Journalist, and the Murder That Brought Them Together."

226 Advocates for Indigenous traditions: For a review, see Celidwen et al., "Ethical Principles of Traditional Indigenous Medicine to Guide Western Psychedelic Research and Practice."

226 "This is not a revolutionary movement": Lekhtman, "Why Indigenous Protesters Stopped a Global Psychedelic Conference."

228 an Austrian researcher: Singh has written vividly about Brabec de Mori. See Singh, "Psychedelics Weren't as Common in Ancient Cultures as We Think." A frequent contributor to *The New Yorker,* Singh is also the author of *Shamanism: The Timeless Religion,* which came out in 2025, just as I was completing this book.

229 "Age-old indigenous knowledge": These quotations are drawn from Brabec de Mori, "Tracing Hallucinations."

229 "the stories they think are interesting": Singh, "Psychedelics Weren't as Common in Ancient Cultures as We Think."

233 featured in a Fox News segment: "Here's How Some People Are Finding God by Smoking Toads," Fox News.

233 the host of both segments: Watters included a chapter on toad smoking in his book *Get It Together.*

233 his ex-fiancée: The woman claimed that she was penetrated without consent while incapacitated from a large dose of toad. When she pushed him off, she wrote, "he stood in front of me and said, 'finish me babe.'" She ended their relationship soon afterward, but he stalked and harassed her, including by breaking into her home when she was out and video calling from her bed while naked. He posted nude pictures of her online and, in an especially farcical claim, accused her of holding ceremonies despite having "no formal training as a bufo facilitator."

238 A single permit: For an overview of the hunting program, see Wilder et al., "Local Extinction and Unintentional Rewilding of Bighorn Sheep." I also discussed this dynamic with several Seri community members and researchers working with the tribe.

238 Minus brokerage fees: These figures were provided to me by a Seri community leader (he had not run for the governorship himself, in part due to concerns about corruption) and verified with researchers who work with the tribe.

238 After a protracted standoff: This was reported on in the local press, for example, "Entrega CONAPESCA y Gobierno del Estado de Sonora dos unidades básicas de infraestructura pesquera," Radio Sonora.

238 Months later, in the dead of night: I was told about this incident by researchers who work with the Seri; it was also reported on locally, for example, Frescas, "Comando armado retuvo varias horas a presidente de Consejo de Ancianos de comunidad seri."

239 An aging former governor: Bourillón-Moreno, "Exclusive Fishing Zone as a Strategy for Managing Fishery Resources by the Seri Indians."

239 Diabetes, virtually unheard of: Burckhalter, "Seri Indians Today."

240 "utopian worship": Felger, "Seris and the Guy Who Cuts the Tops off Plants."

243 At the back of the village: Cardon cacti can live two hundred years or longer; the Seri genocide ended less than 150 years ago. This means that that some of the largest individuals have likely stood since the war was ongoing.

247 he harbored one regret: Felger, "Seris and the Guy Who Cuts the Tops off Plants."

Epilogue

250 That month, Pima County: Data from Smith, Goff, and Kaufman, "Why Has Arizona's Heat-Related Death Rate Increased Tenfold in Twenty Years?," and the Pima County Office of the Medical Examiner.

252 The scholar Robert DeGraaff: DeGraaff, *Book of the Toad,* 31.

252 One North American field guide: These examples are quoted in DeGraaff, *Book of the Toad,* 32.

252 Scientists warn of impending: Ceballos, Ehrlich, and Dirzo, "Biological Annihilation via the Ongoing Sixth Mass Extinction."

252 "Most of the feeling": Steinbeck, *Log from the Sea of Cortez,* 267.

253 Unknown to them: The anthropologist who recorded Miguel Barnett's dreams interviewed him on the island in 1941, meaning his family had not yet resettled on the mainland.

253 Ricketts, for his part: Ricketts, *Breaking Through,* 89.

Bibliography

Adams, Tim. "Amanda Feilding: 'LSD Can Get Deep Down and Reset the Brain—Like Shaking Up a Snow Globe.'" *Guardian,* Feb. 10, 2019.

Amnesty International. *Disappearing Again: Violence and Impacts Experienced by Women Searchers in Mexico.* Amnesty International, 2025.

Asmann, Parker. "Sonora, Mexico, Under Siege amid Sinaloa Cartel Battle over Migrant Smuggling." InSight Crime, Nov. 22, 2023. insightcrime.org.

Asmann, Parker, and Steven Dudley. "Desperation in the Desert: The Industrialization of Migrant Smuggling on the US-Mexico Border." InSight Crime, Oct. 5, 2022. insightcrime.org.

Auliya, Mark, Sandra Altherr, Charlotte Nithart, Alice Hughes, and David Bickford. "Numerous Uncertainties in the Multifaceted Global Trade in Frogs' Legs with the EU as the Major Consumer." *Nature Conservation* 51 (Feb. 2023): 71–135.

Bahre, Conrad J., Luis Bourillón, and Jorge Torre. "The Seri and Commercial Totoaba Fishing (1930–1965)." *Journal of the Southwest* 42, no. 3 (2000): 559–75.

Ball, Martin W. "A Psychedelic Bromance, Some Toads, an Irishman, and a Lady of Wisdom." *Dragibus Magazine* 3, no. 3 (2015).

Barraza-Guardado, Ramón H., José A. Arreola-Lizárraga, Marco A. López-Torres, et al. "Effluents of Shrimp Farms and Its Influence on the Coastal Ecosystems of Bahía de Kino, Mexico." *Scientific World Journal* 2013 (June 2013): 306370.

Barsuglia, Joseph, Alan K. Davis, Robert Palmer, et al. "Intensity of Mystical Experiences Occasioned by 5-MeO-DMT and Comparison with a Prior Psilocybin Study." *Frontiers in Psychology* 9 (2018): 2459.

Barsuglia, Joseph P., Martin Polanco, Robert Palmer, Benjamin J. Malcolm, Benjamin Kelmendi, and Tanya Calvey. "A Case Report SPECT Study and Theoretical Rationale for the Sequential Administration of Ibogaine and 5-MeO-DMT in the Treatment of Alcohol Use Disorder." *Progress in Brain Research* 242 (2018): 121–58.

Basu, Sukanya, and Sarah Pearlman. "Violence and Migration: Evidence from Mexico's Drug War." *IZA Journal of Development and Migration* 7, no. 1 (2017): 18.

Biden, Hunter. *Beautiful Things: A Memoir.* Gallery Books, 2021.

Bitrán Goren, Yael. "Henrietta Yurchenco: Ethnomusicology Pioneer in Mexico and Guatemala." In *Oxford Research Encyclopedia of Latin American History.* Oxford University Press, 2018.

Bogenschutz, Michael P., and Matthew W. Johnson. "Classic Hallucinogens in the Treatment of Addictions." *Progress in Neuro-Psychopharmacology and Biological Psychiatry* 64 (Jan. 2016): 250–58.

Booth, Robert. "Grenfell: Councillor Was Told About Cheaper Cladding Plan Before Fire." *Guardian,* May 28, 2021.

Boulware, Jack. "Mondo 1995: Up and Down with the Next Millennium's First Magazine." *San Francisco Weekly,* Oct. 11, 1995.

Bourillón-Moreno, Luis. "Exclusive Fishing Zone as a Strategy for Managing Fishery Resources by the Seri Indians, Gulf of California, Mexico." PhD diss., University of Arizona, 2002.

Brabec de Mori, Bernd. "Tracing Hallucinations: Contributing to a Critical Ethnohistory of Ayahuasca Usage in the Peruvian Amazon." In *The Internationalization of Ayahuasca,* edited by Beatriz Caiuby Labate and Henrik Jungaberle. LIT, 2011.

Buckrail. "Coroner's Inquest Rules Death of Birkholz Accidental but Possibly Preventable." May 18, 2017. buckrail.com.

Burckhalter, David. *Among Turtle Hunters and Basket Makers: Adventures with the Seri Indians.* Treasure Chest Books, 1999.

Burckhalter, David. "The Seri Indians Today." *Journal of the Southwest* 42, no. 3 (2000): 384–402.

Burckhalter, David. "William Neil Smith and the Seri Indians: Photographs, Letters, and Field Notes." *Journal of the Southwest* 55, no. 1 (2013): 1–118.

Burdick, Clifford L. "They Wouldn't Be Civilized." *Desert Magazine* 17, no. 6 (1954).

Busby, Mattha. "MDMA Trials Under Review in Canada over Alleged Abuse of Study Participants." *Guardian,* June 20, 2022.

Campbell, Nancy D. "'A New Deal for the Drug Addict': The Addiction Research Center, Lexington, Kentucky." *Journal of the History of the Behavioral Sciences* 42, no. 2 (2006): 135–57.

Campbell, Nancy D., J. P. Olsen, and Luke Walden. *The Narcotic Farm: The Rise and Fall of America's First Prison for Drug Addicts.* University Press of Kentucky, 2021.

Cantú, Elda. "What 120 Degrees Looks Like in One of Mexico's Hottest Cities." *New York Times,* July 6, 2023.

Cardiff, Maurice. "A Sketch of the Life of Ñanamoli Thera (Osbert Moore)." Path Press. Accessed Aug. 14, 2025. pathpress.org.

Carhart-Harris, Robin L., Mark Bolstridge, James Rucker, et al. "Psilocybin with Psychological Support for Treatment-Resistant Depression: An Open-Label Feasibility Study." *Lancet Psychiatry* 3, no. 7 (2016): 619–27.

Carmony, Neil B., and David E. Brown, eds. *Tales from Tiburon: An Anthology of Adventures in Seriland.* The Southwest Natural History Association, 1983.

Cavebaby. "Knocked Me on My Ass! An Experience with 5-MeO-DMT (Exp3147)." Erowid, Oct. 7, 2000. www.erowid.org.

Ceballos, Gerardo, Paul R. Ehrlich, and Rodolfo Dirzo. "Biological Annihilation via the Ongoing Sixth Mass Extinction Signaled by Vertebrate Population Losses and Declines." *Proceedings of the National Academy of Sciences* 114, no. 30 (2017).

Celidwen, Yuria, Nicole Redvers, Cicilia Githaiga, et al. "Ethical Principles of Traditional Indigenous Medicine to Guide Western Psychedelic Research and Practice." *Lancet Regional Health—Americas* 18 (Feb. 2023): 100410.

"Challenges and Shadows of Current Psychedelic Movement—Panel Discussion." June 21, 2018. Accessed Aug. 5, 2025. slideslive.com/38909130/challenges-and-shadows-of-current-psychedelic-movement-panel-discussion?ref=og-meta-tags.

Channel 4 News. "The Publishers and Knights Bankrolling UKIP." Aug. 8, 2013.

Columbia University Mailman School of Public Health. "New Study Estimates over 5.5 Million U.S. Adults Use Hallucinogens." Aug. 18, 2022. www.publichealth.columbia.edu.

Coolidge, Dane, and Mary Anne Coolidge. *The Last of the Seris.* E. P. Dutton, 1939.

Copes, Heith, Haley Copeland, Lynne Vieraitis, Michael Cherbonneau, and Peter Hendricks. "'Plants Don't Have a Culture to Appropriate': Accounting for Accusations of Cultural Appropriation of Peyote Ceremonies." *Sociology Compass* 19, no. 3 (2025): e70048.

Crawford. "Is Kambo Ethical?" Reality Sandwich, Sept. 8, 2021. realitysandwich.com.

Cremades, Alejandro. "Cosmo Feilding Mellen on Selling His First Company for $80 Million and Now Raising $100 Million to Fuel Psychedelics." Alejandro Cremades. Accessed Aug. 14, 2025. alejandrocremades.com.

Cyphers, Ann, Belem Zuñiga, and Anna Di Castro. "Another Look at *Bufo marinus* and the San Lorenzo Olmec." *Current Anthropology* 46, no. S5 (2005).

Davis, Alan K., Joseph P. Barsuglia, Rafael Lancelotta, Robert M. Grant, and Elise Renn. "The Epidemiology of 5-Methoxy-N,N-Dimethyltryptamine (5-MeO-DMT) Use: Benefits, Consequences, Patterns of Use, Subjective Effects, and Reasons for Consumption." *Journal of Psychopharmacology* 32, no. 7 (2018): 779–92.

Davis, Alan K., Lynnette A. Averill, Nathan D. Sepeda, Joseph P. Barsuglia, and Timothy Amoroso. "Psychedelic Treatment for Trauma-Related Psychological and Cognitive Impairment Among US Special Operations Forces Veterans." *Chronic Stress* 4 (Jan. 2020): 2470547020939564.

Davis, Wade. "*Bufo marinus:* New Perspectives on an Old Enigma." *Revista de la Academia Colombiana de Ciencias Exactas, Fisicas y Naturales* 16, no. 63 (1988): 151–57.

Davis, Wade. *One River: Science, Adventure, and Hallucinogenics in the Amazon Basin.* Touchstone Books, 1998.

Davis, Wade. *The Clouded Leopard: Travels to Landscapes of Spirit and Desire.* Douglas & McIntyre, 1998.

Davis, Wade. *The Serpent and the Rainbow.* Simon & Schuster, 1985.

Davis, Wade, and Andrew T. Weil. "Identity of a New World Psychoactive Toad." *Ancient Mesoamerica* 3, no. 1 (1992): 51–59.

DeGraaff, Robert M. *The Book of the Toad: A Natural and Magical History of Toad-Human Relations.* Park Street Press, 1991.

De Hoyos, Rafael, Carlos Gutierrez Fierros, M. Vargas, and J. Vicente. *Idle Youth in Mexico: Trapped Between the War on Drugs and Economic Crisis.* World Bank, 2016.

DeKorne, Jim. "Network Feedback." *The Entheogen Review* 2, no. 4 Winter Solstice (1993): 14.

de Mille, Richard. *Castaneda's Journey: The Power and the Allegory.* Capra Press, 1976.

De Smet, Peter A.G.M. "A Multidisciplinary Overview of Intoxicating Enema Rituals in the Western Hemisphere." *Journal of Ethnopharmacology* 9, no. 2–3 (1983): 129–66.

Dimmitt, Mark A., Patricia Wentworth Comus, and Linda M. Brewer, eds. *A Natural History of the Sonoran Desert.* 2nd ed. Arizona-Sonora Desert Museum Press, 2015.

Dimmitt, Mark A., and Rodolfo Ruibal. "Environmental Correlates of Emergence in Spadefoot Toads (*Scaphiopus*)." *Journal of Herpetology* 14, no. 1 (1980): 21–29.

Easteal, S., and R. B. Floyd. "The Cane Toad—an Amphibian Weed." In *The Ecology of Exotic Animals and Plants: Some Australian Case Histories,* edited by Roger Laurence Kitching. J. Wiley, 1986.

Emory, William H. *Report on the United States and Mexican Boundary Survey.* Texas State Historical Association, 1987.

Ermakova, Anna O., Fiona Dunbar, James Rucker, and Matthew W. Johnson. "A Narrative Synthesis of Research with 5-MeO-DMT." *Journal of Psychopharmacology* 36, no. 3 (2022): 273–94.

Erowid. "5-MeO-DMT Vault: Timeline." Dec. 28, 1999. erowid.org.

Erspamer, V., T. Vitali, M. Roseghini, and J. M. Cei. "5-Methoxy- and 5-Hydroxyindoles in the Skin of *Bufo alvarius.*" *Biochemical Pharmacology* 16, no. 7 (1967): 1149–64.

Erspamer, Vittorio. "Peptides, Amphibian (Skin)." In *Comparative Neuroscience and Neurobiology,* edited by Louis N. Irwin. Birkhäuser, 1988.

Erspamer, Vittorio, Giuliana Falconieri Erspamer, Cinzia Severini, et al. "Pharmacological Studies of 'Sapo' from the Frog *Phyllomedusa bicolor* Skin: A Drug Used by the Peruvian Matses Indians in Shamanic Hunting Practices." *Toxicon* 31, no. 9 (1993): 1099–111.

Evans, Jules. "Psychedelic Treatments for Depressed Mums." Ecstatic Integration. Accessed Aug. 14, 2025. www.ecstaticintegration.org.

Evans, Jules. "Sowilo: The Psychedelic Retreat from Hell." *DoubleBlind Magazine,* May 1, 2024.

Evans, Jules. "Victoria Wueschner on Harm Reduction in the 5-MeO-DMT Community." Ecstatic Integration. Accessed Aug. 14, 2025. www.ecstatic integration.org.

Evans, Jules, Oliver C. Robinson, Eirini Ketzitzidou Argyri, et al. "Extended Difficulties Following the Use of Psychedelic Drugs: A Mixed Methods Study." *PLoS ONE* 18, no. 10 (2023): e0293349.

Fabing, Howard D. "Toads, Mushrooms, and Schizophrenia." *Harper's Magazine,* May 1957.

Fabing, Howard D., and J. Robert Hawkins. "Intravenous Bufotenine Injection in the Human Being." *Science* 123, no. 3203 (1956): 886–87.

Feilding-Mellen, Cosmo, and Timothy Mason. Pharmaceutical Composition Comprising 5-Methoxy-N,N-Dimethyltryptamine. U.S. Patent US20230382858A1, filed May 2, 2023, and issued Nov. 30, 2023. patents.google.com/patent/US20230382858A1/en.

Feilding-Mellen, Rock. "I Was Attacked as a Politician. Then I Did Psychedelic Therapy." *Newsweek,* Aug. 19, 2023.

Felger, Richard Stephen. "The Seris and the Guy Who Cuts the Tops off Plants." *Journal of the Southwest* 42, no. 3 (2000): 521–43.

Felger, Richard Stephen, and Mary Beck Moser. *People of the Desert and Sea: Ethnobotany of the Seri Indians.* University of Arizona Press, 1985.

Fitz-Gibbon, Jorge. "Spanish Porn Actor Charged with Murder in Toad-Venom Death." *New York Post,* March 19, 2021.

Fitzmaurice, Laura. "Clotilde Brewster: American Expatriate Architect." *Nineteenth Century* 34, no. 2 (2014): 17–27.

Flanagin, Jake. "The Rise of the Narco-Saints." *Atlantic,* Aug. 14, 2014.

Foster, Clare. "A Fairytale Garden Surrounding a 16th-Century Hunting Lodge." *House & Garden,* Nov. 3, 2021.

Fouquette, M.J.J. "Remarks on the Type Specimen of *Bufo alvarius* Girard." *Great Basin Naturalist* 28 (1968): 70–71.

Fox News. "Here's How Some People Are Finding God by Smoking Toads." April 13, 2022.

Frescas, Guillermo. "Comando armado retuvo varias horas a presidente de Consejo de Ancianos de comunidad seri." *El financiero,* Sept. 3, 2023.

Fuentes, Juan José, Francina Fonseca, Matilde Elices, Magí Farré, and Marta Torrens. "Therapeutic Use of LSD in Psychiatry: A Systematic Review of Randomized-Controlled Clinical Trials." *Frontiers in Psychiatry* 10 (Jan. 2020): 943.

Furst, Peter T. "Symbolism and Psychopharmacology: The Toad as Earth Mother in Indian America." In *Religión en Mesoamerica: XII mesa redonda, Sociedad Méxicana de Antropología,* edited by Jaime Litvak King and Noemí Castillo Tejero. La Sociedad, 1972.

Gallagher, Larry. "Smoking Toad." *Esquire,* Sept. 1994.

Gottlieb, Adam. *Legal Highs: A Concise Encyclopedia of Legal Herbs and Chemicals with Psychoactive Properties.* 20th Century Alchemist, 1978.

Grace Within. "Jaguar (5-MeO-DMT) Vape Pens." Erowid, Feb. 16, 2021. erowid.org.

Grof, Stanislav. *When the Impossible Happens: Adventures in Non-Ordinary Realities.* Sounds True, 2006.

Groffen, Jordy, and Stacey Porter, eds. *Kimberley Toad Busters: 10 Years of Com-*

munity Effort Fighting an Alien Invasion. Kimberley Specialists in Research, 2015.

Hammerson, Geoffrey, and Georgina Santos-Barrera. "Sonoran Desert Toad: *Incilius alvarius.*" IUCN Red List of Threatened Species 2004. 2004. dx.doi.org/10.2305/IUCN.UK.2004.RLTS.T54567A11152901.en.

Hanson, Joe A., and James L. Vial. "Defensive Behavior and Effects of Toxins in *Bufo alvarius.*" *Herpetologica* 12, no. 2 (1956): 141–49.

Harbonic_Older. "Journey to the Center of the Onion: An Experience with 5-MeO-DMT (exp34918)." Erowid, Nov 1, 2004. erowid.org/exp/34918.

Hardman, Josh. "Breaking: Atai Moves to Acquire Beckley, if Phase 2b 5-MeO-DMT Data Delivers." Psychedelic Alpha, June 2, 2025. psychedelicalpha.com.

Harrington, Gwyneth. "Seri Dreams." *Journal of the Southwest* 30, no. 4 (1988): 502–21.

Harvey, Larry. "La Vie Boheme: A History of Burning Man, 2000." Lecture. Walker Art Center, Minneapolis, Feb. 20, 2000. burningman.org.

Hirschmann, J. V. "From Squirrels to Biological Weapons: The Early History of Tularemia." *American Journal of the Medical Sciences* 356, no. 4 (2018): 319–28.

Horgan, John. "Bufo Abuse: A Toxic Toad Gets Licked, Boiled, Teed Up, and Tanned." *Scientific American* 263, no. 2 (1990): 26–27.

Hoshino, Toshio, and Kenya Shimodaira. "Über die Synthese des Bufotenin-Methyl-Äthers (5-Methoxy-N-Dimethyl-Tryptamin) und Bufotenins (Synthesen in der Indol-Gruppe. XV)." *Bulletin of the Chemical Society of Japan* 11, no. 3 (1936): 221–24.

Johnston, Bernice. "Seri Ironwood Carving." *KIVA* 33, no. 3 (1968): 155–66.

Johnston, Bernice. *The Seri Indians of Sonora, Mexico.* Revised reprint. University of Arizona Press, 1980.

Kahn, E. K. "Jungle Botanist." *New Yorker,* June 1, 1992.

Kailay, Stefan Singh. "'Snedig' dansk biotekinvestor satsede og blev forgyldt." MedWatch, Jan. 23, 2017. medwatch.dk.

Kandell, Jonathan. "Richard E. Schultes, 86, Dies; Trailblazing Authority on Hallucinogenic Plants." *New York Times,* April 13, 2001.

Kennedy, Alison Bailey. "*Ecce Bufo:* The Toad in Nature and in Olmec Iconography." *Current Anthropology* 23, no. 3 (1982): 273–90.

Keshavan, Meghana. "The Psychedelics Evangelist: A German Financier Wants to Turn Magic Mushrooms into Modern Medicine." STAT, July 1, 2019.

Khmara, Danyelle. "Group Finds Damage, Dangers from Border Wall Work, Urges Action." *Arizona Daily Star,* July 28, 2022.

Kilham, Chris. "On the Toad Road." *Lucid News,* Dec. 1, 2023.

King, Alex. "The Mind-Altering Trip of Acid Countess Amanda Feilding." *Huck,* April 26, 2017.

Kirsch, Tom. "Central Islip State Hospital." Opacity, March 12, 2007. opacity.us.

Kupferschmidt, Kai. "What's Next for Psychedelics After MDMA Rejection?" *Science* 385, no. 6710 (2024).

Kutz, Jessica. "A Hallucinogenic Toad in Peril." *High Country News,* June 7, 2021.

Lancelotta, Rafael, and Alan K. Davis. "Therapeutic Potential of Fast-Acting Synthetic Tryptamines." In *Handbook of Medical Hallucinogens,* edited by Charles S. Grob and Jim Grigsby. Guilford Press, 2021.

Laskow, Sarah. "The Giant Frog Farms of the 1930s Were a Giant Failure." *Gastro Obscura,* Oct. 25, 2017.

Lattin, Don. *The Harvard Psychedelic Club: How Timothy Leary, Ram Dass, Huston Smith, and Andrew Weil Killed the Fifties and Ushered in a New Age for America.* HarperCollins, 2011.

Lekhtman, Alexander. "Why Indigenous Protesters Stopped a Global Psychedelic Conference." *Filter,* Aug. 17, 2023.

Levi, Primo. *The Periodic Table.* Translated by Raymond Rosenthal. Abacus, 1986.

Lewis, Mark, dir. *Cane Toads: An Unnatural History.* Film Australia, 1988.

Lewis, Stephanie. *Cane Toads: An Unnatural History.* Doubleday, 1989.

Lindsay, Bethany. "As Psychedelic Therapy Goes Mainstream, Former Patient Warns of Danger of Sexual Abuse." CBC News, March 18, 2021.

Livne, Ofir, Dvora Shmulewitz, Claire Walsh, and Deborah S. Hasin. "Adolescent and Adult Time Trends in US Hallucinogen Use, 2002–19: Any Use, and Use of Ecstasy, LSD, and PCP." *Addiction* 117, no. 12 (2022): 3099–109.

Llana, Sara Miller. "Ownership Fight Erupts over Maya Ruins." *Christian Science Monitor,* Oct. 17, 2007.

Loew, Morgan. "War Between Drug Cartels Forcing Residents of Mexican Border Town to Flee into Arizona." Arizona's Family, Dec. 5, 2023. www.azfamily.com.

Lopez, Oscar. "Mexico Named Deadliest Country for Environmental Activists." *New York Times,* Sept. 29, 2022.

Luccioni, Marina, and Jules Wyman. "*Incilius alvarius* (Sonoran Desert Toad): Ingestion of Bullet Casing." *Herpetological Review* 52 (Dec. 2021): 827.

Luedtke, Jennifer A., Janice Chanson, Kelsey Neam, et al. "Ongoing Declines for the World's Amphibians in the Face of Emerging Threats." *Nature* 622, no. 7982 (2023): 308–14.

Luna, Óscar. "Hallan 10 cuerpos en carretera de Sonora." *Reforma* (Mexico City), June 20, 2020.

Lyttle, Thomas. "Drug Based Religions and Contemporary Drug Taking." *Journal of Drug Issues* 18, no. 2 (1988): 271–84.

Lyttle, Thomas, David Goldstein, and Jochen Gartz. "Bufo Toads and Bufotenine: Fact and Fiction Surrounding an Alleged Psychedelic." *Journal of Psychoactive Drugs* 28, no. 3 (1996): 267–90.

Marks, John. *The Search for the "Manchurian Candidate": The CIA and Mind Control.* Times Books, 1979.

Marlett, Cathy Moser. *Shells on a Desert Shore: Mollusks in the Seri World.* University of Arizona Press, 2014.

Marlett, Cathy Moser. "The 'Trooqui Treen': A Seri Truck." *Journal of the Southwest* 57, no. 2/3 (2015): 199–212.

Marshall, Robert. "The Dark Legacy of Carlos Castaneda." *Salon,* April 12, 2007.

Martin, Douglas. "Henrietta Yurchenco, Pioneer Folklorist, Dies at 91." *New York Times,* Dec. 14, 2007.

McGee, W. J. "The Seri Indians." In *Seventeenth Annual Report of the Bureau of American Ethnology to the Secretary of the Smithsonian Institution.* Government Printing Office, 1898.

Melendez, Pilar. "U.S. Grad Student Brutally Killed on Mexican Field Trip." *Daily Beast,* June 30, 2023.

Mellen, Joe. *Bore Hole.* Strange Attractor Press, 2015.

Mendoza, Natalia. "Depoliticizing Conflict in Sonora, Mexico: (Il)Legality, Territory, and the Continuum of Violence." *European Review of Latin American and Caribbean Studies,* no. 112 (Dec. 2021): 117–36.

Metzner, Ralph. *The Toad and the Jaguar: A Field Report of Underground Research on a Visionary Medicine.* Regent Press, 2013.

Miller, Richard L. "Amanda Feilding—Countess and Pioneering Psychonaut (78 Years Old)." Confessions of the Psychedelic Elders, July 6, 2021. www.youtube.com/watch?v=f_9-k_mFkBU.

Milligan, Ellen. "The Countess of Cannabis Has a Hole in Her Head and a Job with Canopy." Bloomberg.com, April 1, 2019.

Moreno, José Luis. "'A Never-Ending Source of Water': Agriculture, Society, and Aquifer Depletion on the Coast of Hermosillo, Sonora." *Journal of the Southwest* 54, no. 4 (2012): 545–68.

Morgan, Adrian. *Toads and Toadstools: The Natural History, Folklore, and Cultural Oddities of a Strange Association.* Celestial Arts, 1995.

Moser, Mary B., and Stephen Marlett. "Seri Kinship Terminology." *Work Papers of the Summer Institute of Linguistics, University of North Dakota Session* 37, no. 1 (1993).

Most, Albert. *Bufo alvarius: The Psychedelic Toad of the Sonoran Desert.* Venom Press, 1984.

Mulford, Robert D. "Experimentation on Human Beings." *Stanford Law Review* 20, no. 1 (1967): 99–117.

Musgrave, M. E., and Doris M. Cochran. "*Bufo alvarius,* a Poisonous Toad." *Copeia,* no. 173 (Oct. 1929): 96.

Nabhan, Gary Paul. *Desert Terroir: Exploring the Unique Flavors and Sundry Places of the Borderlands.* University of Texas Press, 2014.

Nabhan, Gary Paul. *Singing the Turtles to Sea: The Comcáac (Seri) Art and Science of Reptiles.* University of California Press, 2003.

Nabhan, Gary Paul, and John Lee Carr, eds. *Ironwood: An Ecological and Cultural Keystone of the Sonoran Desert.* Conservation International, 1994.

Narchi, Nemer Eduardo. "One Knowledge, Two Conduits: The Social, Demographic, and Toxicological Factors That Govern Seri Ethnomedicine." PhD diss., University of Georgia, 2011. openscholar.uga.edu/record/19315.

Narchi, Nemer Eduardo, Luis Ernesto Aguilar-Rosas, José Jesús Sánchez-Escalante, and Dora Ofelia Waumann-Rojas. "An Ethnomedicinal Study of the Seri People, a Group of Hunter-Gatherers and Fishers Native to the Sonoran Desert." *Journal of Ethnobiology and Ethnomedicine* 11, no. 1 (2015): 62.

Negri, Lucia. "Vittorio Erspamer (1909–1999)." *Medicina nei secoli* 18, no. 1 (2006): 97–113.

New York Times. "Missionary for Toad Venom Is Facing Charges." Feb. 20, 1994.

Nolan, Rachel. "On the Iron River." Review of *Exit Wounds: How America's Guns Fuel Violence Across the Border,* by Ieva Jusionyte and Jason de León. *London Review of Books,* Nov. 21, 2024.

Nolan, Rachel. "The Healer, the Journalist, and the Murder That Brought Them Together." *New York Times,* Aug. 16, 2022.

Novak, Steven J. "LSD Before Leary: Sidney Cohen's Critique of 1950s Psychedelic Drug Research." *Isis* 88, no. 1 (1997): 87–110.

Nuwer, Rachel. "These Toads Have Psychedelic Powers, but They'd Prefer to Keep It Quiet." *New York Times,* July 10, 2025.

O'Brien, Jeffrey M. "Business Gets Ready to Trip: How Psychedelic Drugs May Revolutionize Mental Health Care." *Fortune,* March 2020.

Ogarrio Huitrón, Jesús Ernesto. "Icóos: Territorio, memoria y resistencia: El

Hant Comcaac en la palabra de un pueblo cantor." Master's thesis, Universidad Autónoma Metropolitana, 2016.

O'Hagan, Andrew. "The Tower." *London Review of Books,* June 7, 2018.

Olivares, Edgar. "Rescatan cuerpo de ahogada en Cenote." *Diario respuesta,* Dec. 26, 2022.

Oroc, James. *Tryptamine Palace: 5-MeO-DMT and the Sonoran Desert Toad.* Inner Traditions International, 2009.

Ortega, María Isabel, Samantha Sabo, Patricia Aranda Gallegos, et al. "Agribusiness, Corporate Social Responsibility, and Health of Agricultural Migrant Workers." *Frontiers in Public Health* 4 (March 2016).

Ostrynski, Nathalie. "Han Skulle Vise Dem." *Berlingske,* April 6, 2008.

Passie, Torsten. "The Early Use of MDMA ('Ecstasy') in Psychotherapy (1977–1985)." *Drug Science, Policy, and Law* 4 (Jan. 2018): 2050324518767442.

Peluso, Daniela, Emily Sinclair, Beatriz Labate, and Clancy Cavnar. "Reflections on Crafting an Ayahuasca Community Guide for the Awareness of Sexual Abuse." *Journal of Psychedelic Studies* 4, no. 1 (2020): 24–33.

Penner, James. "Psychedelic Pioneer and Confidence Man." *Los Angeles Review of Books,* Feb. 19, 2020.

Perez, José Ignacio Castañeda. "2 Arizona Border Wall Gaps Closed, 50 Remain near Sasabe as Construction Continues." *Arizona Republic,* Nov. 28, 2023.

Plotkin, Mark J. "Richard Evans Schultes: Brief Life of a Pioneering Ethnobotanist and Conservationist, 1915–2001." *Harvard Magazine,* July–Aug. 2022.

Pollan, Michael. *How to Change Your Mind: What the New Science of Psychedelics Teaches Us About Consciousness, Dying, Addiction, Depression, and Transcendence.* Penguin Press, 2018.

Ponce, Norma. "De Francia, EU y Alemania viajan a México para probar 'la medicina del sapo,'" *Milenio,* July 18, 2021.

Porta Sophia. "All Pending Claims Rejected for GH Research Ireland Ltd. U.S. Patent Application Describing 5-MeO-DMT to Treat Depression." May 5, 2025. www.portasophia.org.

Psychedelic Alpha. "Atai Life Sciences Makes $50M Investment in Beckley Psytech." Jan. 4, 2024. psychedelicalpha.com.

Psychedelic Alpha. "Pα+ Psychedelic Bulletin #204." July 25, 2025. psychedelicalpha.com.

Psychedelic Times Staff. "There's a Land Grab for Psychedelic Patents: Here's What We Can Do About It." *Psychedelic Times,* April 19, 2021.

Psymposia. "After a Year of Controversy, MAPS Canada Executive Director Mark Haden Announces Resignation." Feb. 19, 2021. www.psymposia.com.

Psymposia. *Plus Three.* Episode 32, "It's All Red Flags: 5-MeO-DMT with Dr. Martin Ball." Aired March 18, 2021. www.psymposia.com.

Putzel-Kavanaugh, Colleen, and Ariel G. Ruiz Soto. "Shifting Patterns and Policies Reshape Migration to U.S.-Mexico Border in Major Ways in 2023." Migration Policy Institute, Oct. 24, 2023. www.migrationpolicy.org.

Radio Sonora. "Entrega CONAPESCA y Gobierno del Estado de Sonora dos unidades básicas de infraestructura pesquera." Sept. 12, 2023. radiosonora.com.mx.

Range, Teresa Rojas. "Settled and Migrant Child Farm Labor in Sonora." *Textual,* no. 74 (2019): 461–91.

Reckweg, Johannes T., Cees J. Van Leeuwen, Cécile Henquet, et al. "A Phase 1/2 Trial to Assess Safety and Efficacy of a Vaporized 5-Methoxy-N, N-Dimethyltryptamine Formulation (GH001) in Patients with Treatment-Resistant Depression." *Frontiers in Psychiatry* 14 (June 2023): 1133414.

Reckweg, Johannes T., Malin V. Uthaug, Attila Szabo, et al. "The Clinical Pharmacology and Potential Therapeutic Applications of 5-Methoxy-N, N-Dimethyltryptamine (5-Meo-DMT)." *Journal of Neurochemistry* 162, no. 1 (2022): 128–46.

Reckweg, Johannes T., Natasha L. Mason, Cees Van Leeuwen, Stefan W. Toennes, Theis H. Terwey, and Johannes G. Ramaekers. "A Phase 1, Dose-Ranging Study to Assess Safety and Psychoactive Effects of a Vaporized 5-Methoxy-N, N-Dimethyltryptamine Formulation (GH001) in Healthy Volunteers." *Frontiers in Pharmacology* 12 (Nov. 2021): 760671.

Reckweg, Johannes T., Natasha L. Mason, Eef L. Theunissen, Claus B. Svendssen, Theis H. Terwey, and Johannes G. Ramaekers. "Evaluation of the Peak Experience Scale as a Rapid Assessment Tool for the Strength of a Psychoactive Experience with 5-MeO-DMT." *Frontiers in Psychology* 16 (June 2025): 1543640.

Rettig Hinojosa, Octavio. "Antonia Troiano y OTAC en Venezuela, Eglee Martinez, Testimonial." YouTube video, 2014. www.youtube.com/watch?v=vYVGxkFjQvY.

Rettig Hinojosa, Octavio. *The Toad of Dawn: 5-MeO-DMT and the Rising of Cosmic Consciousness.* Divine Arts, 2016.

Ricketts, Edward Flanders. *Breaking Through: Essays, Journals, and Travelogues of Edward F. Ricketts.* University of California Press, 2006.

Rivlin, Adrienne. "Exploring the Psychedelics Landscape: Looking Ahead to Funding in 2024." L.E.K. Consulting, 2024.

Rodrigue, Daniel. "The Story Behind a 1984 Hallucinogenic Pamphlet from Denton Is Just as Trippy as Its Subject." *Dallas Observer,* April 13, 2021.

Rosenwald, Michael S. "Amanda Feilding, Eccentric Countess Who Backed Psychedelic Meds, Dies at 82." *New York Times,* June 12, 2025.

Round, John Horace. *Studies in Peerage and Family History.* Longmans, Green, 1901.

Rowland, Katherine. "Thanks to This Man, MDMA Could Soon Be Legal for Therapy." *Guardian,* Feb. 29, 2024.

Rucker, James Jonathan, Claire Roberts, Mathieu Seynaeve, et al. "Phase 1, Placebo-Controlled, Single Ascending Dose Trial to Evaluate the Safety, Pharmacokinetics, and Effect on Altered States of Consciousness of Intranasal BPL-003 (5-Methoxy-*N, N*-Dimethyltryptamine Benzoate) in Healthy Participants." *Journal of Psychopharmacology* 38, no. 8 (2024): 712–23.

Ryerson, Scott H. "Seri Ironwood Carving: An Economic View." In *Ethnic and Tourist Arts,* edited by Nelson H. H. Graburn. University of California Press, 1976.

Sacco, M. A., A. Zibetti, C. F. Bonetta, et al. "Kambo: Natural Drug or Potential Toxic Agent? A Literature Review of Acute Poisoning Cases." *Toxicology Reports* 9 (2022): 905–13.

Sandoval Isaac, Gerardo Ruben. *The God Molecule: 5-MeO-DMT and the Spiritual Path to the Divine Light.* Divine Arts, 2016.

Scala. "The Road to Hell and Back: An Experience with 5-MeO-DMT (Exp2236)." Erowid, June 27, 2000. www.erowid.org.

Schultes, Richard Evans. "Fifteen Years of Study of Psychoactive Snuffs of South America: 1967–1982—a Review." *Journal of Ethnopharmacology* 11, no. 1 (1984): 17–32.

Schultes, Richard Evans. "Burning the Library of Amazonia." *Sciences* 34, no. 2 (1994).

Schultes, Richard Evans. "A New Narcotic Snuff from the Northwest Amazon." *Botanical Museum Leaflets, Harvard University* 16, no. 9 (1954): 241–60.

Secretaría de Cultura. "Entregan los Premios Nacionales de Ciencias, Artes y Literatura 2017." Secretaría de Cultura, Gobierno de México, April 2, 2018. www.gob.mx.

Sheridan, Thomas E., ed. *Empire of Sand: The Seri Indians and the Struggle for Spanish Sonora, 1645–1803.* University of Arizona Press, 2021.

Sheridan, Thomas E. "Human Ecology of the Sonoran Desert." In *A Natural History of the Sonoran Desert.* 2nd ed. Arizona-Sonora Desert Museum Press, 2015.

Sherwood, Alexander M., Romain Claveau, Rafael Lancelotta, Kristi W. Kaylo, and Kelsey Lenoch. "Synthesis and Characterization of 5-MeO-DMT Succinate for Clinical Use." *ACS Omega* 5, no. 49 (2020): 32067–75.

Shewey, Don. "Romancing the Toad." Reality Sandwich, Sept. 10, 2018. reality sandwich.com.

Singh, Manvir. "Psychedelics Weren't as Common in Ancient Cultures as We Think." *VICE,* Dec. 10, 2020.

Sklerov, Jason, Barry Levine, Karla A. Moore, Theodore King, and David Fowler. "A Fatal Intoxication Following the Ingestion of 5-Methoxy-N, N-Dimethyltryptamine in an Ayahuasca Preparation." *Journal of Analytical Toxicology* 29, no. 8 (2005): 838–41.

Smith, Noah. "Pα+ Psychedelic Patent Analysis: A Mebufotenin Melee (Dec '23 & Jan '24)." Psychedelic Alpha, Feb. 22, 2024. psychedelicalpha.com.

Smith, Slade, Kirin Goff, and Sonia Kaufman. "Why Has Arizona's Heat-Related Death Rate Increased Tenfold in Twenty Years?" White Paper No. 22. Making Action Possible for Southern Arizona (MAP Dashboard), Aug. 2024. mapazdashboard.arizona.edu.

Sotomayor, Arturo C. "Militarization in Mexico and Its Implications." In *The State and Security in Mexico: Transformation and Crisis in Regional Perspective,* edited by Brian Bow and Arturo Santa Cruz. Routledge, 2013.

SourceWatch. "Lord Neidpath." March 1, 2015. www.sourcewatch.org.

Spicer, Edward Holland. *Cycles of Conquest: The Impact of Spain, Mexico, and the United States on the Indians of the Southwest, 1533–1960.* University of Arizona Press, 2006.

Staff Writer. "Ohio Inmates, Soldiers Were Subjects of Risky Postwar Medical Testing." *Columbus Dispatch,* March 5, 2011.

Stamm, Eugen. "Interview with Lars Hellerung Christiansen." Verve Ventures, Dec. 13, 2019. www.verve.vc.

St. Antoine, Sara. "Ironwood: Carving New Life from Ancient Trees." *Pacific Discovery* 47, no. 3 (1994). researcharchive.calacademy.org.

Steinbeck, John. *The Log from the Sea of Cortez.* Viking Press, 1951.

STRG_F, dir. *Krötengift gegen Depressionen: Geht das Wirklich?* 2023. www.you tube.com/watch?v=ddCR0pTv35s.

Stringham, Oliver C., Jacob Maher, Charlotte R. Lassaline, et al. "The Dark Web Trades Wildlife, but Mostly for Use as Drugs." *People and Nature* 5, no. 3 (2023): 999–1009.

Substance Abuse and Mental Health Services Administration. *Key Substance Use and Mental Health Indicators in the United States: Results from the 2024 National Survey on Drug Use and Health.* HHS Publication No. PEP25-07-007. NSDUH Series H-60. Center for Behavioral Health Statistics and Quality, Substance Abuse and Mental Health Services Administration, n.d. www.samhsa.gov.

Symonds, Tom. "Grenfell Councillor Queried Colour of Cladding but Not Safety." BBC, May 20, 2021.

Talayeh, Antonia. "My Healing/Whole-Ing Story." Illuminate Your Truth, June 1, 2023. www.illuminateyourtruth.com.

Tastevin, Constantin. "Le fleuve Murú—ses habitants—croyances et moeurs *kachinaua.*" *La géographie* 43–44 (1925): 403–22 and 14–35.

Terwey, Theis, Conor Burke, and Naoise Gaffney. Treatment of Mental Disorders. U.S. Patent US20240115550A1, filed Sept. 27, 2023, and issued April 11, 2024. patents.google.com/patent/US20240115550A1/en.

Thomson, Sally, dir. *Attenborough's Fabulous Frogs.* PBS, 2014.

Timmermann, Christopher, James W. Sanders, David Reydellet, et al. "Exploring 5-MeO-DMT as a Pharmacological Model for Deconstructed Consciousness." *Neuroscience of Consciousness* 2025, no. 1 (2025): niaf007.

Torres, Constantino Manuel, and David B. Repke. *Anadenanthera: Visionary Plant of Ancient South America.* Routledge, 2006.

Traphagen, Myles. *Border Wall Restoration Site Reports: November 2021—July 2022.* Wildlands Network, 2022.

Tüchsen, Henrik. "En enmandshær går i krig." MedWatch, Aug. 12, 2014. medwatch.dk.

Tüchsen, Henrik. "He Bites His Tongue for No One." MedWatch, Feb. 1, 2012. medwatch.dk.

Tüchsen, Henrik. "Major Investor and Secret Team Behind Outstanding Return on Biotech." MedWatch, Jan. 26, 2012. medwatch.dk.

Turner, Christopher. "Like a Hole in the Head." *Bones,* no. 28 (Winter 2007–08).

Turner, William J., and Sidney Merlis. "Effect of Some Indolealkylamines on Man." *Archives of Neurology and Psychiatry* 81, no. 1 (1959): 121.

United Nations Office on Drugs and Crime. *World Drug Report 2025 (Set of 3 Booklets).* United Nations Research Institute for Social Development, 2025.

Uthaug, Malin. "The Exploration of Naturalistically Used Ayahuasca and 5-MeO-DMT: An Assessment of Their Respective Sub-Acute and Long-Term Effects on Mental Health Related Variables." PhD diss., Maastricht University, 2020.

Uthaug, M. V., R. Lancelotta, K. Van Oorsouw, et al. "A Single Inhalation of Vapor from Dried Toad Secretion Containing 5-Methoxy-N, N-Dimethyltryptamine (5-MeO-DMT) in a Naturalistic Setting Is Related to Sustained Enhancement of Satisfaction with Life, Mindfulness-Related Capacities, and a Decrement of Psychopathological Symptoms." *Psychopharmacology* 236, no. 9 (2019): 2653–66.

Van Devender, Thomas R., and Richard C. Brusca. "Deep History of the

Sonoran Desert." In *A Natural History of the Sonoran Desert.* 2nd ed. Arizona-Sonora Desert Museum Press, 2015.

Van Dyke, J. C. *The Desert: Further Studies in Natural Appearances.* Charles Scribner's Sons, 1901.

Verza, Maria. "How Mexican Cartels Manage the Flow of Migrants on Their Way to the US Border." *AP News,* Oct. 30, 2024.

Victor, Daniel. "National Park Service Asks Visitors to Please Stop Licking Toads." *New York Times,* Nov. 7, 2022.

Vidriales, Arturo Laure, and Diego Hannon Ovies. "Psychedelic Tourism in Mexico, a Thriving Trend." *PASOS: Revista de turismo y patrimonio cultural* 16, no. 4 (2018): 1037–50.

Villa, Robert A. "Toad in the Road: Biocultural History and Conservation Challenges of the Sonoran Desert Toad." *Journal of Psychedelic Studies* 7, no. S1 (2023): 68–79.

Vincent, Isabel. "Santa Muerte and the 'Religious' Saints Drug Cartels Worship." *New York Post,* Dec. 21, 2021.

vokest. "I Ended Up Praying to Jesus Christ: An Experience with 5-MeO-DMT (Exp105060)." Erowid, Feb. 27, 2016. www.erowid.org.

Waldron, Eli. "A Carnival of Frogs." *New Yorker,* April 11, 1953.

Walsh, Roger. "Mysticism: Contemplative and Chemical." In *Zig Zag Zen: Buddhism and Psychedelics,* edited by Allan Badiner. Chronicle Books, 2002.

Warkentin, Ian G., David Bickford, Navjot S. Sodhi, and Corey J. A. Bradshaw. "Eating Frogs to Extinction." *Conservation Biology* 23, no. 4 (2009): 1056–59.

Wassén, S. Henry, and Bo Holmstedt. "The Use of Paricá, an Ethnological and Pharmacological Review." *Ethnos* 28, no. 1 (1963): 5–45.

Wassersug, Richard. "On the Comparative Palatability of Some Dry-Season Tadpoles from Costa Rica." *American Midland Naturalist* 86, no. 1 (1971): 101.

Watters, Jesse. *Get It Together: Troubling Tales from the Liberal Fringe.* HarperCollins, 2024.

Weil, Andrew. *The Natural Mind: A New Way of Looking at Drugs and the Higher Consciousness.* Houghton Mifflin, 1972.

Weil, Andrew. "Saturn Return: Scenes from the Life of a Psychedelic Pioneer." *Harper's Magazine,* Jan. 2024.

Weil, Andrew T., and Wade Davis. "*Bufo alvarius:* A Potent Hallucinogen of Animal Origin." *Journal of Ethnopharmacology* 41, no. 1–2 (1994): 1–8.

Welwood, John. "On Spiritual Bypassing and Relationship." *Science and Nonduality (SAND),* Feb. 10, 2024.

Whitaker-Azmitia, P. "The Discovery of Serotonin and Its Role in Neuroscience." *Neuropsychopharmacology* 21, no. 2 (1999): 2S–8S.

Wilder, Benjamin T., Julio L. Betancourt, Clinton W. Epps, Rachel S. Crowhurst, Jim I. Mead, and Exequiel Ezcurra. "Local Extinction and Unintentional Rewilding of Bighorn Sheep (*Ovis canadensis*) on a Desert Island." *PLoS ONE* 9, no. 3 (2014): e91358.

Williams, Alex. "Can You Poison Your Way to Good Health?" *New York Times*, Jan. 1, 2021.

Williams, Martin. "Illegal, Occasionally Deadly, and Not Much Fun. What Is the Frog Toxin Kambô and Why Do People Use It?" Conversation, May 16, 2023.

Willmetts, Simon. "Why Burning Man Is Silicon Valley." Conversation, Sept. 1, 2015.

Wilson, Edward O. *The Diversity of Life.* Penguin, 1994.

Wright, Albert Hazen, and Anna Allen Wright. *Handbook of Frogs and Toads of the United States and Canada.* 3rd ed. Cornell University Press, 1995.

Yetman, David. "Miguel's Last Santo." *Journal of the Southwest* 42, no. 3 (2000): 403–10.

Yetman, David. *Sonora: An Intimate Geography.* University of New Mexico Press, 2000.

Yetman, David. *Where the Desert Meets the Sea: A Trader in the Land of the Seri Indians.* Pepper Publishing, 1988.

Yurchenco, Henrietta. *La vuelta al mundo en 80 años: Memorias.* Comisión Nacional para el Desarrollo de los Pueblos Indígenas, 2003.

Index

PAGE NUMBERS IN *ITALICS* REFER TO ILLUSTRATIONS.

Abbreviation: SDT—Sonoran Desert toad

ABOUT THE AUTHOR

Kimon de Greef has written for *The New Yorker*, *New York*, *The New York Times*, *The Guardian*, and other publications. His first book, co-authored with Shuhood Abader, is *Poacher: Confessions from the Abalone Underworld*. He lives in Cape Town.

RAISING READERS

Books Build Bright Futures

Dear Reader,

We'd love your attention for one more page to tell you about the crisis in children's reading, and what we can all do.

Studies have shown that reading for fun is the **single biggest predictor of a child's future life chances** – more than family circumstance, parents' educational background or income. It improves academic results, mental health, wealth, communication skills, ambition and happiness.[1]

The number of children reading for fun is in rapid decline. Young people have a lot of competition for their time. In 2024, 1 in 10 children and young people in the UK aged 5 to 18 did not own a single book at home.[2]

Hachette works extensively with schools, libraries and literacy charities, but here are some ways we can all raise more readers:

- Reading to children for just 10 minutes a day makes a difference
- Don't give up if children aren't regular readers – there will be books for them!
- Visit bookshops and libraries to get recommendations
- Encourage them to listen to audiobooks
- Support school libraries
- Give books as gifts

There's a lot more information about how to encourage children to read on our website: **www.RaisingReaders.co.uk**

Thank you for reading.

hachette UK

[1] OECD, '21st-Century Readers: Developing Literacy Skills in a Digital World', 2021, https://www.oecd.org/en/publications/21st-century-readers_a83d84cb-en.html

[2] National Literacy Trust, 'Book Ownership in 2024', November 2024, https://literacytrust.org.uk/research-services/research-reports/book-ownership-in-2024